Emil Hausknecht

The Romaunce of the Sowdone of Babylone

and of Ferumbras his sone who conquerede Rome

Emil Hausknecht

The Romaunce of the Sowdone of Babylone
and of Ferumbras his sone who conquerede Rome

ISBN/EAN: 9783337246129

Printed in Europe, USA, Canada, Australia, Japan

Cover: Foto ©ninafisch / pixelio.de

More available books at **www.hansebooks.com**

The Sowdone of Babylone.

Early English Text Society.

Extra Series. No. XXXVIII.

1881.

BERLIN: ASHER & CO., 13, UNTER DEN LINDEN.
NEW YORK: C. SCRIBNER & CO.; LEYPOLDT & HOLT.
PHILADELPHIA: J. B. LIPPINCOTT & CO.

THE

ENGLISH CHARLEMAGNE ROMANCES.

PART V.

The Romaunce of

The Sowdone of Babylone

and of

Ferumbras his Sone who conquerede Rome.

RE-EDITED

FROM THE UNIQUE MS. OF THE LATE SIR THOMAS PHILLIPPS,

with Introduction, Notes, and Glossary,

BY

EMIL HAUSKNECHT, PH. D.

LONDON:
PUBLISHED FOR THE EARLY ENGLISH TEXT SOCIETY
BY KEGAN PAUL, TRENCH, TRÜBNER & Co.,
PATERNOSTER HOUSE, CHARING-CROSS ROAD, W.C.
MDCCCLXXXI.
[*Reprinted 1891, 1898.*]

CONTENTS.

	PAGE
INTRODUCTION	v
POPULARITY OF THE CARLOVINGIAN ROMANCES ..	v
POPULARITY OF THE FERUMBRAS POEM	vi
THE PROVENÇAL FERABRAS	ix
THE FIERABRAS POEM AN ENLARGED AND RECAST PORTION OF THE OLD BALAN ROMANCE	xi
THE POEM OF THE DESTRUCTION DE ROME ...	xiii
MSS. OF THE FRENCH FIERABRAS ...	xv
THE ENGLISH SIR FERUMBRAS, ITS SOURCE, ETC. ...	xvi
THE POEM OF THE SOWDAN OF BABYLON, ITS SOURCES, ITS DIFFERENCES FROM THE ORIGINAL BALAN ROMANCE AND FROM THE ASHMOLEAN FERUMBRAS	xxii
DIALECT OF THE SOWDAN	xxxiv
METRE AND RHYMES OF THE SOWDAN	xl
DATE AND AUTHOR OF THE SOWDAN	xlv
MS. OF THE SOWDAN	xlvii
ROXBURGHE CLUB EDITION OF THE SOWDAN	xlviii

PAGE

ADDITIONS xlix

THE HANOVER MS. OF THE FRENCH FIERABRAS COMPARED WITH THE SOWDAN xlix

THE HANOVER VERSION COMPARED WITH SIR FERUMBRAS lii

SKETCH OF THE STORY liv

THE ROMAUNCE OF THE SOWDONE OF BABYLONE AND OF FERUMBRAS HIS SONE WHO CONQUEREDE ROME ... 1

NOTES ... 95

GLOSSARIAL INDEX 133

INDEX OF NAMES 141

INTRODUCTION.

The exploits of Charles the Great, who by his achievements as conqueror and legislator, as reformer of learning and missionary, so deeply changed the face of Western Europe, who during a reign of nearly half a century maintained, by his armies, the authority of his powerful sceptre, from the southern countries of Spain and Italy to the more northern regions of Denmark, Poland, and Hungary, must have made a profound and unalterable impression in the minds of his contemporaries, so that for centuries afterwards they continued to live in the memory of the people. Evidence of this high pitch of popularity is given by the numerous *chansons de geste* or romances, which celebrate the deeds, or are connected with the name, of the great and valiant champion of Christendom.

It is true that the sublime figure of Charlemagne, who with his imaginary twelve peers perpetually warred against all heathenish or Saracen people, in the romances of a later period, has been considerably divested of that nimbus of majestic grandeur, which the composers of the earlier poems take pains to diffuse around him. Whereas, in the latter, the person of the Emperor appears adorned with high corporeal, intellectual, and warlike gifts, and possessed of all royal qualities; the former show us the splendour of Royalty tarnished and debased, and the power of the feodal vassals enlarged to the prejudice of the royal authority. Roland, in speaking of Charlemagne, says, in the *Chanson de Roland*, l. 376 :—

"Jamais n'iert hum qui encuntre lui vaillet,"

and again the same Roland says of the Emperor, in *Guy de Bourgoyne*, l. 1061 :—

"Laissomes ce viellart qui tous est assotez."

This glorification of the great Christian hero took its rise in France, but soon spread into the neighbouring countries, and before long Charlemagne was celebrated in song by almost all European nations. Indeed, there are translations, reproductions, compilations of French Charlemagne romances to be met with in Italy, Spain, and Portugal, as well as in Scandinavia and Iceland. Even in Hungary and Russia these *chansons* of the Charlemagne cycle seem to have been known.[1]

A full account of almost all Charlemagne romances will be found in Gaston Paris's exhaustive work of the *Histoire poétique de Charlemagne* (Paris, 1865), and in Léon Gautier's *Epopées françaises* (Paris, 1867).

Of all the Charlemagne romances, that of Fierabras or Ferumbras has certainly obtained the highest degree of popularity, as is shown by the numerous versions and reproductions of this romance, from the 13th century down to the present day.

When the art of printing first became general, the first romance that was printed was a prose version of *Fierabras;* and when the study of mediæval metrical romances was revived in this century, the *Fierabras* poem was the first to be re-edited.[2]

The balm of Fierabras especially seems to have been celebrated for its immediately curing any wound; we find it referred to and minutely described in Florian's *Don Quichotte*, I. chap. 10. The scene of Fierabras challenging to a combat the twelve peers of France, and of his vaunting offer to fight at once with six (or twelve) of them,[3] must also have been pretty familiar to French readers, as the name of Fierabras is met with in the sense of a simple common noun, signifying "a bragging bully or swaggering hector."[4]

Rabelais[5] also alludes to Fierabras, thinking him renowned enough as to figure in the pedigree of Pantragruel.

In 1833, on a tour made through the Pyrenees, M. Jomard wit-

[1] *Histoire Poét.*, p. 133-4.
[2] Gautier, *Epopées*, ii. 308.
[3] Cf. the French *Fierabras*, l. 84; *Sir Ferumbras*, l. 102; *Sowdone*, l. 1067.
[4] Thus in *Scarron*, Gigant, iii.
[5] Pantagruel, ii. chap. 1.

nessed a kind of historical drama, represented by villagers, in which Fierabras and Balan were the principal characters.[1]

That in our own days, the tradition of Fierabras continues to live, is evident from the fact, that copies of the Fierabras story, in the edition of the *Bibliothèque Bleue*, still circulate amongst the country people of France.[2] There is even an illustrated edition, published in 1861, the pictures of which have been executed by no less an artist than Gustave Doré. And like Oberon, that other mediæval hero of popular celebrity,[3] Fierabras has become the subject of a musical composition. There is an Opera *Fierabras* composed by Franz Schubert (words by Joseph Kupelwieser) in 1823, the overture of which has been arranged for the piano in 1827, by Carl Czerny.[4]

The different versions and the popularity of the present romance in France, Italy, Spain, and Germany, having been treated in the Introduction to *Sir Ferumbras*, we need not repeat it again here.[5] As to the popularity of the *Fierabras* romance in the Netherlands, the following passage from Hoffmann, *Horæ Belgicæ* (Vratislaviæ, 1830), I. 50, may be quoted here[6]:—

"Quam notæ Belgis, sec. xiii. et xiv., variæ variarum nationum fabulæ fuerint, quæ ex Gallia septemtrionali, ubi originem ceperunt, translatæ sunt, pauca hæc testimonia demonstrabunt:— . . . . in exordio Sidraci:—[7]

'Dickent hebbic de gone ghescouden,
die hem an boeken houden
daer si clene oerbare in leren,
also sijn jeesten van heeren,
van Paerthenopeuse, van Amidase,
van Troijen ende van *Fierabrase*,
ende van menighen boeken, die men mint
ende daer men litel oerbaren in vint,

---

[1] See the most interesting account of this piece and its curious manner of representation in *Histoire Littéraire de la France*, xvii. 720-21.

[2] Gautier, *Epopées*, ii. p. 308; and *Histoire Poétique*, p. 99.

[3] See *Huon de Bourdeaux*, edd. Guessard and Grandmaison, p. xxxviii.

[4] See G. Nottebohm, *Thematisches Verzeichniss der im Druck erschienenen Werke von Franz Schubert.* Wien, 1874.—Op. 76.

[5] Cf. besides, *Histoire Poétique*, pp. 97, 143, 155, 214, 251; *Epopées françaises*, ii. pp. 307-9; and the *Préface* of the French edition of *Fierabras.*

[6] See also Mone, *Uebersicht der niederländischen Volksliteratur ältere Zeit.* Tübingen, 1836. p. 56.

[7] Cf. Warton, *Hist. of Eng. Poetry*, 1824, vol. i. pp. 147-8.

ende dat als leghene es ende mere,
ende anders en hebben ghene lere,
danne vechten ende vrowen minnen
ende lant ende steden winnen . . . . . .'—

"Nec rarius tanguntur fabulæ de Carolo Magno, *Speculum Historiale*, IV. 1. xxix (cf. Bilderdijk, *Verscheidenh*, I. D. bl. 161-2):—

'Carel es menichwaerf beloghen
in groten boerden ende in hoghen,
alse boerders doen ende oec dwase,
diene beloghen van *Fierabrase*,
dat nie ghesciede noch en was . . . .
die scone walsce valsce poeten,
die mer rimen dan si weten,
belieghen groten Caerle vele
in sconen worden ende bispele
van *Fierabrase van Alisandre*,
van *Pont Mautrible* ende andre,
dat algader niet en was . . . .'"

That the *Fierabras* romance must have been well known and highly popular in England and Scotland, may be gathered from the numerous references to this poem in various Middle English works.

Thus the whole subject of the *Fierabras* romance is found in the following passage, taken from *Barbour's Bruce*, ed. Skeat, 3, 435 ss., where the King is described as relating to his followers:—

"Romanys off worthi Ferambrace,
That worthily our-commyn was
Throw the rycht douchty Olywer;
And how the duz Peris wer
Assegyt intill Egrymor,
Quhar King Lawyne lay thaim befor
With may thowsandis then I can say,
And bot elewyn within war thai,
And a woman; and wa sa stad,
That thai na mete thar within had,
Bot as thai fra thair fayis wan.
Y heyte, sua contenyt thai thaim than;
That thai the tour held manlily,
Till that Rychard off Normandy,
Magre his fayis, warnyt the king,
That wes joyfull off this tithing:
For he wend, thai had all bene slayne,
Tharfor he turnyt in hy agayne,
And wan Mantrybill and passit Flagot;
And syne Lawyne and all his flot
Dispitusly discumfyt he:
And delieryt his men all fre,
And wan the *naylis*, and the *sper*,
And the *croune* that Ihesu couth ber;

And off the *croice* a gret party
He wan throw his chewalry."[1]

In his poem of *Ware the Hawk*, Skelton (ed. Dyce, I. 162) cites *Syr Pherumbras* as a great tyrant. He also refers to him in one of his poems against Garnesche, whom he addresses with the following apostrophe :—

"Ye fowle, fers and felle, as Syr Ferumbras the ffreke."

The story of the combat between Oliver and Ferumbras is alluded to by Lyndsay, in his *Historie of ane Nobil and Wailȝeand Squyer, William Meldrum*, ed. Hall, ll. 1313-16 :—

"Roland with Brandwell, his bricht brand,
Faucht never better, hand for hand,
Nor Gawin aganis Golibras,
Nor *Olyver* with *Pharambras*."

The tale of the fortified bridge of Mauntrible seems also to have been very well known in England and Scotland. In the *Complaint of Scotland*, ed. Murray, p. 63, we find the *Tail of the Brig of the Mantrible* mentioned among other famous romances. In his lampoon on Garnesche, Skelton describes his adversary as being more deformed and uglier than

"Of Mantryble the bryge Malchus[2] the murryon."

As has already been mentioned, amongst all the Charlemagne romances the (originally French) romance of *Fierabras* is remarkable as being one of the first that was rescued from the dust of libraries; and it is worthy of note, in connection with it, that the first printed version was not a French, but a Provençal one, which was published not in France, the birth-place of the romance, but in Germany.

The manuscript of this Provençal version having been discovered by Lachmann in the Library of Prince Ludwig von Oettingen-

[1] It is worthy of notice that the account of the Fierabras romance as given by Barbour, may be considered, on the whole, as identical with the subject of the French *Fierabras* or the English *Syr Ferumbras*, but not with the *Sowdan*, as there is no mention made of the combat before Rome, nor any trace of what makes up the first part of the *Sowdan*. But the spelling *Lawyn* for *Balan* agrees with the spelling of the same name in the *Sowdan*. As to the relics mentioned in the passage above, they differ from all other versions.

[2] In the *Sowdan* the Bridgeward is called *Alagolofre*; cf. Index of Names.

Wallerstein,[1] somewhere about the year 1820, the poem was published in 1829 by Immanuel Bekker.[2]

Raynouard, who drew attention to this edition of the poem in the *Journal des Savants*, March 1831, supposed this Provençal version to be the original.

Soon after Fauriel discovered at Paris two MSS. of the romance in French, and a third French MS. was found in London,[3] by Fr. Michel, in 1838.

In 1852 Fauriel gave an account of the poem in the *Histoire Littéraire de la France, par les religieux bénédictins de congregation de Saint-Maur . . . . . continuée par des membres de l'Institut*, vol. xxii. p. 196 *et seq.*, where he also investigated the question of the originality of the two versions, without arriving at a final solution; as from the comparison of the French and the Provençal version, no conclusion as to the original could be drawn in favour of either of the two poems.[4]

As early as 1829 Uhland and Diez had expressed their opinion, that in all probability the Provençal poem was to be looked upon as a reproduction of some French source;[5] and in 1839 Edelestand du Méril, in France, had pointed out the French poem as the original of the Provençal version;[6] Guessard in his lectures at the Ecole des Chartes, at Paris, had also defended the same opinion; when in 1860, the editors of the French *Fierabras*[7] finally and irrefutably proved the impossibility of considering the Provençal poem as anything but a translation of a French original.

[1] This MS. consisting of 71 parchment leaves in 4to, with coloured initials at the beginning of each rhyme-strophe, had formerly been in the possession "Majoris Monasterii congregationis Sancti Mauri," at Paris. Having passed through many hands during the French Revolution, it finally came to the Library of Wallerstein.

[2] Der Roman von Ferabras, provenzalisch. Berlin, 1829.

[3] British Museum, MS. Reg. 15. E. vi.

[4] Cf. also the *Préface* of the French *Fierabras*, p. iv.

[5] See *Leben und Werke der Troubadours*, by Friedrich Diez, Zwickau, 1829, p. 613 note, and *Berliner Jahrbücher für wissenschaftliche Kritik*, 1831.

[6] In a footnote to his *Histoire de la Poésie scandinave*, p. 183, where he says:—"Le roman de Ferabras, publié à Berlin par M. Bekker, est . . . évidemment traduit du français, et en a conservé trop de formes et d'expressions pour avoir la moindre valeur grammaticale."

[7] *Fierabras chanson de geste*, edd. Krœber and Servois, in the collection of the *Anciens Poëtes de la France*.

In 1865, Gaston Paris, in his *Poetical History of Charlemagne*, pointed out that what we have now of the *Fierabras* romance must be looked upon as a very different version from the old original *Fierabras* (or *Balan*) romance, the former being indeed only a portion, considerably amplified and in its arrangement modified, of the old poem, the first portion of which has been lost altogether. Gaston Paris had been led to this supposition by the rather abrupt opening of the *Fierabras*, which at once introduces the reader *in medias res*, and by the numerous passages of the *Fierabras*, which contain allusions and references to preceding events; several of which, being obscure and inexplicable from the context of the *Fierabras* itself, can only be explained by assuming the existence of an earlier poem.

The main subject of the old *Balan* or *Fierabras* romance may be given as follows :—"The Saracens having invaded Rome and killed the Pope, Charlemagne sends, from France, Guy of Burgundy and Richard of Normandy to the rescue of the city, and follows himself with his main army. After a fierce combat between Oliver and Ferumbras, the city is delivered from the Saracens, and a new Pope established." [1]

[1] For a more detailed analysis, see *Histoire Poét.*, p. 251, and cf. the account given of the old *Fierabras* or *Balan* romance by Philippe Mousket, ed. Reiffenberg, Bruxelles, vol. I. v. ll. 4664—4716, which runs as follows:—

Puis fu Roume par force prise
et la gent destruite et ocise
et li apostoile ocis
Castiaus-Mireors ars et pris
et toute la cité bruie.
li dus Garins et sa mesnie
entrerent en Castiel-Croisant,
quar Sarrasin, Turc et Persant
amenerent trop grant compagne
et devers Surie et d'Espagne ;
si furent crestien dolant,
et manderent tot maintenant
soucours al bon roi Charlemainne
ki sa fieste en France demainne,
et li rois en cele besogne
lor tramist Guion de Bourgogne,
ki nouviaus chevaliers estoit
et des jovenes enfans avoit
devant çou la couronne prise.
et soucoururent sans faintise

Of all the events related in the old *Balan* romance, there is but one which is contained in the *Fierabras* poem, viz. the combat between Oliver and Ferumbras, and even this has been greatly modified in consequence of the composer's transferring the scene of action from Italy to Spain. All the other events related in the *Fierabras*, the love of Floripas and Guy, the capture of the twelve peers, their being besieged in the castle of Agremor, and their deliverance by Charlemagne, and the ultimate wedding of Floripas and Guy are altogether wanting in the original *Fierabras* [Balan] romance.

Therefore Gaston Paris was right in saying that the *Fierabras* poem contained only the second part of the earlier poem, the first part of which had not come down to us.

Now it seemed as though this view, which had been clearly

lor bon roi en la tiere estrange
u il n'orent ni lin ni lange.
en France estoient revenu
et soujourné et bien péu,
mais à cel soucours le tramist
li rois, ki moult s'entremist,—
et si tramist de Normendie
Ricart à la ciere hardie,
si reprirent li Mireour:
et dus Garins vint à l'estour,
ki tint Pavie en quité
s'ot bien Castil-Croisant gardé,
et Karles ot sa gent mandée,
si vinrent de mainte contrée,
quar il lor faisoit tant de biens,
qu 'à ses amis ne faloit riens.
si trest vers Rome li bons rois
et fist as paiens moult d'anois.
dont se combati Oliviers
a Fierabras ki tant fu fiers;
d'armes l'outra, si reconquist
les .ii. barius qu'à Rome prist,
si les gieta enmi le Toivre
por çou que plus n'en péust boivre;
quar c'est bausmes ki fu remés
dont Ihesu Cris fu embausmés.
puis furent mort tot li paien
et mis en Roume crestiien,
si ot autre apostoile fait
et Karles s'en revint à hait,
si gratia Dieu et St. Piere,
que recouvrée ot sa kaiere,
soujourner vint dont à Parise . . .

demonstrated and generally adopted, would have to undergo a thorough modification on the discovery of a new Fierabras Manuscript in Hanover. Professor Grœber, having been informed of the existence of that MS. by Professor Tobler, published from it, in 1873, the poem of the *Destruction de Rome*,[1] which in that MS. precedes the *Fierabras* romance.[2] In his Address to the Assembly of German Philologists at Leipzig,[3] the same scholar attempted to show that this poem represented the first part of the earlier *Balan* romance.

This supposition, however, can only be accepted with reserve, and needs a great modification, as by no means all the references to previous events contained in the *Fierabras* receive explanation in the *Destruction*, although all such previous events must have been narrated in the original *Balan*. Moreover, one of these allusions in the *Fierabras* is in direct contradiction to the contents of the *Destruction*.

Thus ll. 2237 *et seq.* of the *Fierabras*:[4]—

> " .i. chevalier de France ai lontans enamé:
> Guis a nom de Borgoigne, moult i a bel armé;
> Parens est Karlemaine et Rollant l'aduré.
> Dès que je fui à Romme, m'a tout mon cuer emblé,
> Quant l'amirans mes peres fist gaster la cité,
> *Lucafer de Baudas abati ens ou pré,*
> *Et lui et le ceval, d'un fort espiel quarré,*"

where Floripas declares that she has seen Guy before Rome when defeating Lukafer, widely differ from the account given in ll. 1355 *et seq.* of the *Destruction*, where Guy does not arrive at Rome until *after* the departure of Laban's army to Spain.

In the *Destruction* no clue is given which would enable us to explain why Charles should be constantly applying to Richard in the *Fierabras* (ll. 112 *et seq.*) for information about Fierabras, or why Richard, in particular, should know more about Fierabras than any one else. There is no mention in the *Destruction* of Richard chasing

[1] *Romania*, ii. 1873, pp. 1—48.
[2] Cf. *Jahrbuch für romanische und englische Sprache und Literatur*, edd. Lemcke, vol. xiii. p. 111.
[3] Printed in *Verhandlungen der 28sten Versammlung deutscher Philologen und Schulmänner in Leipzig*. Leipzig, 1873, p. 209 *et seq.*
[4] Corresponding to ll. 1410 *et seq.* of the Ashmole *Ferumbras.*

the Emir before him in the plain of Rome, to which event ll. 3708-9 of the *Fierabras*[1] clearly refer.

> "Richars de Normendie au courage aduré,
> Qui cacha l'amirant devant Romme ens el pré."

The allusion contained in l. 2614,[2]

> .... "Richart de Normendie,
> Cil qui m'ocist Corsuble et mon oncle Mautric,"

where Richard is said to have slain Corsuble and Mautrie, the uncle of Floripas, is not cleared up by the *Destruction*, as in the three passages, where Richard is mentioned there (ll. 246, 288, 541), he does not play an active part at all, whereas from Mousket's analysis of the original *Fierabras* [*Balan*] romance, we know how important a part Guy and Richard played in the old poem.[3] There Richard and Guy being sent off by Charlemagne as a first succour to the oppressed Romans, succeeded in delivering Château-Miroir, which had been seized by the Saracens. The story of the combat around Château-Miroir, as related in the *Destruction*, ll. 593 ss., is thoroughly different,[4] as besides other variations, there is neither Richard nor Guy concerned in it.

Therefore, as the contents of the *Destruction* are not identical with Mousket's analysis of the old *Balan* romance, and as several passages alluding to events previously described are left unexplained in the *Destruction;* and as there is even an instance of the *Destruction* being in contradiction to the *Fierabras*, the poem of the *Destruction de Rome* cannot be said to be identical with the first part of the *Balan* romance.[5]

[1] Cf. *Sir Ferumbras*, ll. 8192-3.
[2] Cf. also l. 2784 and *Sir Ferumbras*, ll. 1860 and 2059.
[3] See above, p. xi, footnote, and *Histoire Poétique*, p. 251.
[4] Cf. Grœber, *Verhandlungen*, pp. 217-18.
[5] The following differences between the *Destruction* and the narration of Philippe Mousket are worthy of note:—

(i) the combat around Château-Miroir is described in a different manner in the two poems.

(ii) the scene of action, which at the end of the *Destruction* is transferred to Spain, remains, according to Philippe Mousket, in the neighbourhood of Rome for the whole time.

(iii) Guy of Burgundy and Richard of Normandy play a most important active part before Rome, according to Ph. Mousket, whereas in the *Destruction* this is not the case.

Now, as to the last two items, they must have been in the original such as

The Provençal version and the *Destruction* are each printed from unique MSS., the latter from the Hanover MS., the former from the Wallerstein MS. Of the French *Fierabras* there are seven MSS. known to exist.

a = the MS. of the Bibliothèque Nationale at Paris, Supplém. franç., No. 180, which has been followed throughout by the editors of the French *Fierabras*, who in cases of evident errors or lacunæ of this MS., consulted the three following MSS.:

b = the MS. of the Biblioth. Nationale, Lancelot, 7566 3.3.

c = the MS. of the British Museum, MS. Reg. 15. E. vi.[1]

d = the MS. of the Vatican Library, Regina 1616.

D = the MS. in possession of M. Ambroise-Firmin Didot, a small fragment of which has been printed by Gautier, *Epopées fr.* ii. 307.

E = the Escorial MS., a description of which, together with the variations, has been given by Knust, in the *Jahrbuch für romanische und englische Sprache und Literatur*, vol. ix. p. 43 *et seq.*

H = the Hanover MS., which also contains the *Destruction de Rome.* It has been described by Professor Grœber in the *Jahrbuch*, xiii. p. 111.

they are related by Ph. Mousket. For only thus some obscure passages of *Fierabras*, of which even the *Destruction* affords no explanation, are cleared up. Thus, *Fierabras*, l. 1049,

"Près fu du far de Rome, ses a dedens jetés"—

which is in contradiction to the *Destruction*, is explained by ll. 4705-6 of Mousket's account (see above). Only Mousket relates that Floripas has seen Guy before Rome (*Fierabras*, l. 2240; Ashmole *Ferumbras*, l. 1413), and that Richard took part at the combat there. Therefore the account as given by Ph. Mousket, agreeing with what must have been the contents of the old original, is based on a version older than the *Destruction*, which exhibits significant differences.

These differences between Mousket and the *Destruction*, as well as the fact that several references to preceding events contained in *Fierabras* remain unexplained by the *Destruction*, were some of the reasons which led me in my *Dissertation*, pp. 41—49, to consider the *Destruction* as a poem written by another author than that of the *Fierabras*. In order to clear up the allusions to preceding events contained in the *Fierabras*, the very beginning of which necessarily requires some explanatory account—a circumstance which also gave rise to the 'episode' of the Provençal version—the *Destruction* was composed as a kind of Introduction to the *Fierabras*, whereby it happened that some allusions remained unexplained.

[1] For a description of this magnificent MS., see *Sir Ferumbras*, p. vi, footnote.

As to the English *Fierabras* romances, there are two versions known to exist:[1] the poem of *Sir Ferumbras* contained in the Ashmole MS. 33[2] and the present poem.

In the following we shall attempt to point out the differences of these two versions, and to examine whether there is any relationship between the English and the French poems, and if possible to identify the original of the former.

A superficial comparison of the English poem of *Sir Ferumbras* with the French romance *Fierabras* (edd. Krœber and Servois) will suffice at once to show the great resemblance between the two versions. In my *Dissertation* on the sources and language of the *Sowdan of Babylone* (Berlin, 1879) I have proved (pp. 30—40) that the Ashmolean *Ferumbras* must be considered as a running poetical translation of a French original. Since Mr. Herrtage, in the Introduction to his edition of the Ashmole MS. 33, has also pointed out the closeness with which the translator generally followed the original, which he believes to belong to the same type as the *Fierabras*, edited by MM. Krœber and Servois. "The author has followed his original closely, so far as relates to the course of events; but at the same time he has translated it freely, introducing several slight incidents and modifications, which help to enliven and improve the poem. That he has not translated his original literally, is shown by the fact that the French version consists of only 6219 lines, or allowing for the missing portion of the Ashmole MS., not much more than one-half the number of lines in the latter, and that too, although he has cut down the account of the duel between Oliver and Ferumbras from 1500 to 800 lines, by leaving out Oliver's attempts at converting the Saracen, Charlemagne's prayers, &c."

Now, in my opinion, we ought not to lay too much stress on the fact that the number of lines in the two versions differs, as all translators of poetical works, who wish to follow their original as closely as possible, will easily be able to render it 'literally' as long as they write in prose. But adopting a poetical form for their translation, and still pursuing their intention of a close rendering of their original,

[1] Cf. Warton, *Hist. of Eng. Poetry*, ii. 197-8.
[2] Edited for the E. E. T. S. in 1879, by S. J. Herrtage, B.A.

they must needs be more diffuse, and the consideration of rhythm and rhyme will compel them sometimes to abandon a quite literal translation, and to be content with a free reproduction. This is also the case with the author of *Syr Ferumbras*, who, notwithstanding the many passages where the French text is not given 'literally,' must be considered as a close rhymed translation of the French poem. The only liberty which we see the English author take sometimes, consists in contracting or amalgamating together those *couplets similaires*,[1] or strophes which contain repetitions.

But not always did the author thus give up his plan of rendering his original closely: occasionally he has such repetitionary lines in the same place as the French poem, as, for instance, in ll. 130 *et seq.* corresponding to *Fierabras*, ll. 125 *et seq.*

The closeness and literalness of his translation is well exemplified by his introduction in an English dress of a great many French words which are unknown, or at least of a most rare occurrence, in English, and which in his translation are found in the same place and context, where the French text has them. This will be best illustrated by juxtaposing the corresponding phrases of the two versions.

	Ashmole *Ferumbras*.		French *Fierabras*.
312	Hit ys *rewarded* ous two betwyne þat Olyuer schal wende and take þe batail	301	'Nous jujon Olivier, si l'avons *esgardé* Qu'il fera la bataille au paien deffaé.'
330	*Mercy*, quaþ he to kyng Charles	333	'As piés le roy se jete, *merchi* li a priié.'
369	þat *paynede* crist	377	'— dont vos Diex fu *penés*.'
388	Er y *remuvie* me of þis place	392	'Ains que je m'en *remue* . . .'
399	y *chalenge* wiþ þe to fiȝt	402	'— je te voel *calengier*'
457	*Parfay*, ansuerde erld O.	449	'*Par foi*, dist Oliviers . . .'
533	þat he ne . . maden ȝelde his body to him *creaunt*	548	'se Roland s'i combat, ne faice *recréant*'
537	wiþ my swerd *trenchaunt*	553	'. . . à m'espée *trencant*'
538	*Sarsyns*, said erld O.	554	*Sarrazins*, dist li quans . . .
551	long man in *fourchure*	579	Il ot *l'enfourcéure* grant
558	a ful *gret pite*, etc.	586	j'ai de toi *grant pité*, etc.

[1] Cf. Gautier, *Epopées Françaises*, i. 221.—"Rien n'est plus fréquent, dans la Chanson de Roland et dans nos poëmes les plus anciens, que la répétition double, triple et même quelquefois quadruple, de certains couplets. Cette répétition n'a pas lieu dans les mêmes termes, ni surtout avec les mêmes rimes. Tout au contraire, la même idée est reproduite en vers différents, munis d'assonances ou de rimes différentes."

751 haue *mercy* of me, *iantail* knyȝt	1494-5 — *merci* li a crió: *Gentix* hom . .
781 to *remurie* þe of þis place	1515 ja par moi n'i seriés . . *remués*
817 he was *encombred* with F.	1552 Mais de F. est . . . *encombrés*
922 þey went forth on a *pendant*	1696 Cil s'entornent fuiant le *pendant* d'un laris
947 wan hure spere gunne to *faile*	1712 Quant les lances lor *falent*
984 At *avalyng* of an hulle	1734 À *l'avaler* d'un tertre
1008, 1012 to *rescourre* þe barons	1757 . . les barons *rescous* . .
1016 wel longe hadde þis *chas* ylest	1764 Moult fu grans cele *chace*
1058 and oþre reliques riche ynow wherof y have *plentee*	1806 Et les dignes reliques dont il i ad *plenté*
1227 for to wyte wat þay *be* and hure *covyne* yknowe	2067 Lor *couvine* et lor *estre* enquerre et demander.
1316 By an old forsake ȝeate of þe *olde antiquyte*	2144 Par une gaste porte de *viel antequité*
1773 sittynge on a grene *erber*	2562 . . siét sous cel *arbre* ramé.
1974 Florippe his doȝtre þe *cortoyse* in *chambre* þar she was In þe *paleys* yhurde *noise* and þyder þan she gas	2712 Floripas la *courtoise* a le *nois* escoute Puis issi de la *cambre*, . . . Entresi c'au *palais* . .
2007 þow ert *asotid*	2733 . . vous voi *assoté*.
2538 a gret *repref* it were	3136 . . il nous est *reprouvé*
3665 brydel and *paytrel* and al þe gere wiþ fyn gold yharneyssed were	4117 Li estrier furent d'or, rices fu li *poitrés*
3672 and þe king him gan *ascrie*	4126 . . . si s'est haut *escriés*.
3791 a gret *dul* þay made þere	4236 . . demainent grant *dolour*
4541 with an hard *crestid serpentis* fel	4832 vestu ot la pel d'un dur *serpent cresté*
5753 on þan ston a *cracchede* and in a spatte in *dispit* of god, etc.	5910 en *despit* de Ihesu ens es fons *escraca*.

Besides these undoubted examples of translation, we must bear in mind that there occur some variations of readings, where, indeed, the author of *Syr Ferumbras* seems to have introduced slight incidents and modifications. But examining them more closely, we shall soon become aware that many of them also point to a French original, which we may sometimes identify by comparing these variations with the readings of those French MSS. that are already printed. Thus, the words "þarto ys stede þan tyeþ he," l. 91, render exactly a line of the Escorial MS.[1]—"son cheval aresna à l'abricel rose"—which is omitted in l. 93 of *F* (*i. e.* the French *Fierabras*, as edited by MM. Krœber and Servois).[2]

[1] The variations of this MS. are printed in the *Jahrbuch der roman. and engl. Sprachen*, vol. ix. pp. 43 ss.

[2] This edition, although printed from the MS. *a*, may be said to represent a group (*w*) of four MSS., called *a b c d* (see above xv). Another group (*z*)

The following is another example of *A* (= the Ashmolean *Ferumbras*) differing from *F*, but agreeing with *E:*

A.	*E.*
175 Ne *lyve* he noȝt þys day til evene	175 ke il puisse tant *vivre* que cis jours soit passés
2131 Adoun þay gunne falle, *knellyng* on þe erthe stille . . . & *kussedem everechone*, etc.	2833 Issi *agenoillierent* par bones volentez . . . *Ils baissent* les reliques . . .

Notwithstanding these resemblances of *A* to *E*, in passages where *A* differs from *F*, *E* cannot have been the source of *A*, as there are many instances where *E* and *F* show the same reading, whereas *A* differs from both versions.

Thus, *A*, l. 340 *et seq.*, it is Duke Reyner who blesses his son, and not Charles, as *E* and *F* (l. 357) have it.

The names of Arrenor, Gwychard, Gayot, and Angwyree, given in l. 814, differ from those which are mentioned in the corresponding passage of *E* and *F* (ll. 1548-49).

There is no mention of Kargys being slain by Oliver (*A* 880) to be found in *E* or *F* (l. 1670-76).

In *A* 1178, *Lamasour* advises the Soudan not to slay the prisoners; in *E* and *F* (l. 1948) the same advice is given by *Brulans*.

The names of *Lambrock* and *Colbrant* (*A* 1616, 1618) are not found in *E* and *F*, 2424.

A, ll. 1347-48, are wanting in *E* and *F* (2174).

is formed by the MSS. *E* and *D*. Both groups belong to the same type *y*. Cf. Grœber, *Die handschriftlichen Gestaltungen der chanson de geste Fierabras*, Leipzig, 1869, p. 27, where we find the following stemma:

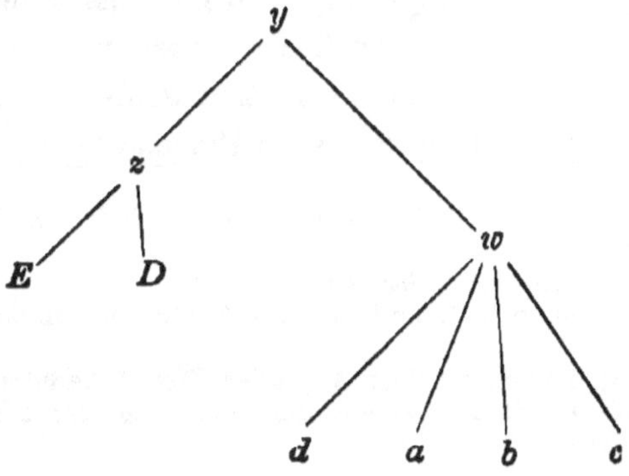

Instead of a giant (*A* 1700) we find a giantess mentioned in *E* and *F* (l. 2483).

Instead of Roland (*A* 1793) it is Naymes who speaks first in *E* and *F*, 2570.

These few instances, the number of which might easily be increased, will certainly suffice to show the impossibility of regarding *E* as the original of *A*.

Only a short passage of the Didot MS. has been hitherto printed;[1] therefore the arguments drawn from a comparison of *A* with that printed passage cannot be considered as altogether irrefutable and final. But as the Didot MS. belongs to the same family of MSS. as *E*, we may at once presume, that as *E* cannot be taken for the original of *A*, the possibility of the Didot MS. being the source of *A*, is not very strong. Besides it may be stated, that no trace of the two additional lines (ll. 19 and 20[2]) which the Didot MS. inserts after l. 63 of *a* (or *F*) is found in *A*, although this version gives, in ll. 52 ss., a pretty close translation of the corresponding passage in *F* (ll. 50 *et seq.*). This may lead us to conclude that the Didot MS. was not the source of *A*.

Comparing now *A* with what is known of the Hanover MS. of *Fierabras*,[3] we find *A* resembling to *H* in the following names: *Lucafer* (only once *Lukefer* in *A* 2204), *Maragounde* (once *Marigounde*, *A* 1364), *Maubyn A* = *Maupyn H.*—*A* 1700 and 2831, which differ from *F*, equally agree with *H*. In the last case *A* agrees also with *E* (although differing from *F*). Now as we know that *H* together with *D* and *E* are derived from the same group *z*,[4] we may perhaps be justified in regarding a MS. of the latter group as the original of *A*. But a more detailed comparison of *A* with *H* being impossible at present, this argumentation wants confirmation.

The impossibility of regarding the Provençal version as the source

[1] *Epopées Françaises*, ii. 307, and *Cat. rais. des livr. de la bibl. d'Ambr. F. Didot*, I, 361.

[2] Grœber, *Handschriftl. Gestaltungen*, p. 6.

[3] *Jahrbuch*, xiii. p. 111, and *Zeitschrift für romanische Philologie*, iv. p. 164.

[4] "Die Vergleichung weniger aus allen Hss. bekannten Versen macht gewiss, dass *H* mit *D* und *E* aus der nämlichen Quelle *z* geflossen ist." *Jahrbuch*, xiii. 113.

of the Ashmolean *Ferumbras*, is proved by the fact that the long additional account, the 'episode' as Professor Grœber calls it,[1] is wanting in *A*. Another proof is given by *A*, ll. 5763 *et seq.*, where *A* agrees with *F*, but widely differs from *P*.[2]

It seems superfluous to point out the inadmissibility of regarding the French prose version as the original of *A*, the first edition of the prose version being of a much later date than the Ashmole *Ferumbras*. But also that version from which the prose romance has been copied or compiled, cannot have been the original of *A*. For although the phrase of *A*, 3888—"A skuntede as a bore"—seems to contain some resemblance of expression with the reading of the prose *Fierabras*—"il commença à escumer come s'il fust ung senglier eschaufé," which Caxton translates—"he began to scumme at the mouthe lyke a bore enchaffed"—the reading of *A*, ll. 1307 ss., which greatly varies from Caxton's version (a translation of the French prose *Fierabras*), renders inadmissible the supposition that the original of the French prose version is the source of *A*.[3]

Having thus compared the Ashmolean *Ferumbras*, as far as can be done at present, with all existing versions of this romance, we arrive at the following conclusions.

The Ashmole *Ferumbras* is a pretty close translation of some French version, which we are at present unable to identify. Its original was neither of the same family (*w*) as the *Fierabras*, edited by MM. Krœber and Servois, nor yet of that of the Escorial version. Nevertheless, the original of *Sir Ferumbras* cannot have differed much from the common original, from which these two groups of MSS. are derived. To this original, called *y* by Grœber, the MS., from which *A* has been copied, appears to have been more closely related than to the Provençal version, from which it certainly is not derived. As the liberties which the author of *Sir Ferumbras* took in translating his original, consist only in very slight modifications, we may con-

NB

[1] *Handschriftl. Gestalt.*, p. 10.

[2] See the note to l. 5763 of *Sir Ferumbras*, and cf. *Fierabras*, 5955.

[3] The number of instances where *A* varies from *C's* version might easily be increased. Thus we find *A* 340 differing from *C* 52/111 and from *F* 357; *A* 814 differing from *C* 79/3 and from *F* 1548; *A* 1616 differing from *C* 102/10 and from *F* 2424; *A* 1238 differing from *C* 92/5 and from *F* 2083; *A* 4652 differing from *C* 171/26 and from *F* 4900, &c.

clude from his closeness of translation in general, that in those passages of *A* which exhibit significant deviations from the known French versions, these variations are not due to the composer of the Ashmolean poem, but were already to be found in its original. Therefore the Ashmole *Ferumbras* may be considered as representing by itself the translation of an independent French MS., which perhaps belonged, or at least was nearly related, to the type *y*.

I now come to the consideration of the *Sowdan of Babylone*, which the simple analysis given by Ellis,[1] shows to be an essentially different work from the Ashmolean *Ferumbras*. Indeed, whilst the *Syr Ferumbras* represents only a portion (viz. the second part) of the original *Fierabras* [or *Balan*, as Gaston Paris has styled it],[2] the *Sowdan* approaches the original more nearly in that it contains the long 'introductory account'.[3] For this first part of the *Sowdan* (as far as l. 970), although it cannot be considered as identical with the first portion of the old *Balan* romance, contains several facts, which, however abridged and modified, show a great resemblance with those which must have been the subject of the lost portion of the old original. Whereas the Ashmolean *Ferumbras* is, on the whole, a mere translation of a French original, the *Sowdan* must be looked upon as a free reproduction of the English redactor, who, though following his original as far as regards the course of events, modelled the matter given there according to his own genius, and thus came to compose an independent work of his own.

This point being fully treated in my *Dissertation*,[4] I need not again enter into discussion of it here. I only mention that the composer of the *Sowdan* has much shortened his original, omitting all episodes and secondary circumstances not necessarily connected with the principal action, so that this poem does not contain half the number of lines which his original had,[5] and that the proportion of the diffuse Ashmolean *Ferumbras* and the *Sowdan* is over five to one.[6]

[1] *Specimens of Early English Metrical Romances*, ed. Halliwell, p. 379 *et seq.*

[2] *Histoire Poétique*, p. 251; cf. also *Revue critique d'Histoire et de Littérature*, ii. 1869, p. 121 *et seq.*

[3] Cf. Mr. Shelley's Paper in Warton, *Hist. of Eng. Poetry*, ii. 197-8.

[4] pp. 17 *et seq.*

[5] *Dissertation*, p. 18.

[6] *Introduction to Sir Ferumbras*, p. xiv.

The subject of the 'introductory account,' or the first part of the *Sowdan*, is nearly the same as that of the *Destruction de Rome*, differing from this poem only in the omission of a few insignificant incidents or minor episodes, and in greater conciseness, which latter circumstances, however, enters into the general plan of the author.

Indeed, the author of the *Sowdan* seems to have known the *Destruction*, as we see from a comparison of the two poems. Thus the following instances show a great resemblance of expression of the two versions:

Sowdan.	*Destruction.*
37 'With kinges xii and admyralles xiv'	420 'Ensemble ou li issirent xv roi corone Et xiv amaceours'
	1154 'Bien i a xxx roi et xiv admiré'
	689 'xxx roi sont ou li et xiv amaceours'
	163 'Et xiv amaceours'
77 'The Romaynes robbed us anone'	115-16 'De cels de Romenie que m'ont fait desrobber. Tiel avoir m'ont robbé'
75 'to presente you'	119 'vous quidai presenter'
76 'a drift of wedir us droffe to Rome'	120 'Uns vens nous fist à Rome parmi le far sigler'
110 'An hundred thousande'	217 'Par C fois M payen'
128 'To manace with the Cristene lore'	228 'pour François menacier'
	332 'Et menace François pour faire les loye'
175-76 'Oure sheldes be not broke nothinge, Hawberkes, spere, ner poleyne, ner pole'	546-47 'Quant encor nen est lance quassée ne brusie, Ne halbers derompus, ne fors targe percie'
224-27 'Lukafere, Kinge of Baldas, The countrey hade serchid and sought, Ten housande maidyns fayre of face Unto the Sowdan hath he broghte'	613-19 'Lucafer de Baldas discent al mestre tre, Devant l'amirail vint, forment l'a encline: Voyant tot ses barnages l'a l'eschec presente, Moignes, prestres et laís, que sont enchence, Hermites et enfants, a tous lor poign lié; As femmes et pucels les os furent bende, Totes vives presentent par devant l'admiré.'
228 ss. 'The Sowdane commaunded hem anone That thai shulde al be slayne . . . He saide "My peple nowe ne shalle With hem noughte defouled be"'	614 'Maintenant soient tot occis et descoupé. Ne voil que mi serjant en soient encombré.'
278 'He clepede his engynour Sir Mavone'	908 'Sortibrans a mande Mabon l'engineor'
289 'Mahoundis benysone thou shalt haue'	627 'Mahon te benoie'
	925 'Mahon te doint honor'

286	'And fille the dikes faste anoone'	934	'Si emplirons les fosses'
292	'Men myght go even to the walle'	918	'K'om poet aler al mure'
		952	'K'om pooit bien au mur et venir et aler'
307	'The hethen withdrowe hem thọ'	979	'Payen se sont retrait'
317	'His baner knowe I ful welle'	997	'Jeo ai bien ses armes conu et avisee'
331	'He entred to the maistre toure'	1011	'Tantost le mestre porte aurons moult bien ferme'
332	'The firste warde thus they wonne'	1057	'Mais tot le premier bail ont Sarasin pople'
346-50	'And Estragot with him he mette With bores hede, blake and donne. For as a bore an hede hadde And a grete mace stronge as stele. He smote Savaryz as he were madde'	1090-94	'Estragot le poursuit, uns geans diffaes, Teste avoit com senglers, si fu rois coronés. El main tient une mace de fin ascier trempé, Un coup a Savariz desur le chef done'
587	'Therfore Gy of Bourgoyne! Myn owen nevewe so trewe'	1179	'Et Guion de Bourgoyne a a lui apelle, Fils est de sa soror et de sa parente: Cosins, vous en irrés . .'
647	'He smote of the traytours hede'	1236	'Le chief al portier trenche'
648	'And saide "Gode gife him care, Shal he never more ete brede, All traitours evel mot thai fare"'	1244	'"Diex" fist il "te maldie et que t'ont engendré, Kar traitour au darain averont mal dehé."'
663	'Ferumbras to Seinte Petris wente'	1260	'Al moustier de saint Piere est Fierenbras ales'
727	'Thre hundred thousande of sowdeours'	1403	'iii C mil chevaliers'
743	'Sir Gye aspied his comynge, He knewe the baner of Fraunce, He wente anoone ayen the Kinge, And tolde him of that myschaunce, Howe that the cursed sowdone, Hath brent Rome and bore the relequis awaye'	1409	'Guis parceut le baniere le roi de saint Dine, Encontre lui chevalche, la novele ont conté Come la fort cité li payen ont gasté; La corone et les clous d'iloec en sont robbé Et les altres reliques . .'
771	'Wynde him blewe ful fayre and gode'	1425	'Li vens en fiert es voilles que les a bien guies'
778	'To londe thai wente iwis'	1427	'il sont en terre entré'
783	'Tithinggis were tolde to Lavan'	1436	'Les noveles en vindrent al soldan diffaié'
787	'With three hundred thousand of bacheleris'	1443	'iii C mile François'

Other instances of resemblance may be found in the following passages:

S 49-50 = *D* 94-99;[1] *S* 103 = *D* 202, 209; *S* 119 = *D* 385; *S* 146 = *D* 445-46; *S* 150 = *D* 503-4; *S* 157 = *D* 509; *S* 300 =

[1] The French text will be found in the *Notes*, which see.

D 967; *S* 303 = *D* 915; *S* 396 = *D* 977; *S* 312 = *D* 989; *S* 340 = *D* 1063; *S* 360 = *D* 1101; *S* 376 = *D* 1119, 1121; *S* 377 = *D* 1133; *S* 380 = *D* 1136; *S* 699 = *D* 1379; *S* 723 = *D* 1384, &c., &c.

Besides, there are some names which occurring in none of the French versions, but in the *Destruction*, point to this poem as to the original of the *Sowdan*. Thus *Savaris*[1] (*S* 171) seems to be taken from *D* 540.

Astragot or *Estragot*, *S* 346, 4902, the name of the giant by whom Savaris is slain, and who is said to be the husband of Barrock, occurs in *D* 1090.

The *Ascopartes*, a people subjected to the Soudan, are mentioned in *D* 98, 426, but not in *F* or *P*.

King *Lowes*, in the context where it occurs (*S* 24) is clearly taken from *D* 9.

Iffrez, *S* 165, is perhaps the same as *Geffroi* in *D* 1139, 1367, 1122.

[*Mounpelers*, *S* 3228, occurs only in *D* 250, 286.]

Persagyn, *S* 1259, seems to be identical with *Persagon*, *D* 162.

The form *Laban* is only met with in the *Destruction*, the French and the Provençal versions, and the Ashmole *Ferumbras* reading *Balan*.[2]

The name of the Soudan's son, *Ferumbras*, is explained by the form *Fierenbras*, which occurs in *D* 57, 66, 71, 91, 343, 1210, 1237, besides the spelling *Fierabras*, which is the only one used in the French, the Provençal and Caxton's versions.

Also the phrase 'sowdan' seems to have been derived from the *Destruction* (l. 1436, 'soldan'), as it does not occur in any other version.

The great number of these resemblances seem evidently to point out the *Destruction* as the original of the first portion of the *Sowdan*; the few points in which the two versions differ not being such as to offer convincing arguments against this supposition.

[1] For these names, the *Index of Names* may be referred to.
[2] In some passages the *Destruction* shows also the spelling *Balan*, but *Laban* is more common.

Indeed if, for instance, we find a lot of nations, the names of which are not in *D*, mentioned by the author of the poem as belonging to the Soudan's empire, this point can be considered as irrelevant, as from many other instances we know how fond many composers of mediæval romances were of citing geographical names, by the great number of which they believed to show their knowledge in that science.[1] Also the three names of Saints (*Qwyntyn*, *Symon*, *Fremond*[2]), and the names of five Saracen gods and of a Saracen bishop,[3] many of which, moreover, seem to be inserted only for the sake of rhyme, cannot be regarded as being of great consequence in establishing the source of the *Sowdan*. Others also, as *Oliborn*, *Focard*, *Hubert*, *Gyndard*, *Tamper* (the last occurring twice as a rhyme-word), being the names of insignificant characters, may be looked upon as mere expletives. Another variation is *Isrez* (ll. 625, 641) for *Tabour* (*D* 1202).

Besides these variations in the names contained in the two poems, we find in the *Sowdan* some slight modifications as to the matter related; none of which, however, is of so significant a character, as necessarily to point to some other original than the *Destruction*, which the very striking points of resemblance above cited show almost decisively to have been the original of the *Sowdan*. The differences in the subject-matter may be explained by the tendency of the poet to follow his original only as far as the principal events are concerned, but to have his own way in the arrangement of the subject-matter, and especially to deal freely with secondary incidents.

Thus he may have thought the combat round Château-Miroir—which, moreover, is related in the *Destruction* in a rather obscure and confused style—to be a rather episodical incident, which he had better leave out in his poem, as not advancing the principal course of events.

A similar explanation may be given of the fact, that the account of Lukafer's desiring the hand of Floripas is given on another occasion in the *Sowdan* than in the *Destruction*. In the *Destruction*, l. 241, Lucafer claims that maiden immediately on arriving in the

[1] See note to l. 1000. [2] See note to l. 2842.
[3] *Dissertation*, p. 20.

Soudan's camp, as a reward for his having travelled such a long way in Laban's service. The poet of the *Sowdan* thinking, perhaps, that this was not a sufficient reason to justify such a claim, mentions this incident at another time, which he may have considered as more properly chosen for demanding a reward. It is on returning from a victorious expedition undertaken by Lukafer that the latter in the *Sowdan*, ll. 224—242, asks for the hand of Floripas.

As to the following or second part of the *Sowdan*, on the whole the same subject is treated of as in the Ashmole *Ferumbras*. But there are many differences between the two poems.

In the *Sowdan*, l. 1411 *et seq.*, Roland is captured by the Saracens at the same time as Oliver, and both on being conducted before Laban at once avow their names. In the Ashmole MS., ll. 909, &c., Oliver is led away to the Soudan together with Gwylmer, Berard, Geoffrey, and Aubray, whereas Roland is among the French peers whom Charlemagne sends on a mission to Laban to demand the surrender of Oliver.[1]

The names of the twelve peers do not agree in both poems. In the *Sowdan* we find the following list (cf. ll. 1653 *et seq.*, and ll. 1730, 880):—Roland, Oliver, Duk Neymes of Bavere, Oger Danoys, Tery Lardeneys, Folk Baliante, Aleroyse of Loreyne, Miron of Braban, Bishop Turpyn, Bernard of Spruwse, Bryer of Mountez,[2] Guy of Bourgoyne.[3]—Richard of Normandye, although a most important personage, is not included amongst the *Douzeperes*. Nor is Guenelyn mentioned as a peer of France. Four of these names, Folk Baliant, Turpyn, Bernard of Spruwse, Aleroyse of Loreyne, do not occur at all in the Ashmolean *Ferumbras*.[4]

The new game which Lucafer wants to teach Neymes, is differently described in the two poems, there being no mention made in the Ashmol. MS. (ll. 2231 *et seq.*) of the thread, needle, and coal, as spoken of in ll. 1998—2000 of the *Sowdan*.

[1] See note to l. 1663. [2] Cf. note to l. 1723.

[3] Mr. Herrtage, in his note to the Ashmol. MS., l. 259, reproduces—from the Roxburghe Club edition, *Introd.* p. vi.—the list of the twelve peers in the French version of the Grenville copy, 10531, which he erroneously takes for that of the *Sowdan*.

[4] But there is one "Alorys þe erld of Brye," mentioned in the Ashm. MS., ll. 935, 2842, 4076, &c.

In the *Sowdan*, l. 2507, Laban, being engaged with his gods, seizes the image of Mahound and smashes it. This incident is omitted in *Syr Ferumbras* (ll. 3345).

In the Ashmole MS., ll. 5760 *et seq.*, Ferumbras tries to persuade his father to become a Christian, whilst Floripas urges Charles not to delay in putting him to death. In the *Sowdan*, l. 3156 *et seq.*, there is no mention of either of them interfering either for or against their father.

Ashm. MS., ll. 130 *et seq.*, differs greatly from the corresponding passage in the *Sowdan* (ll. 1647 *et seq.*). In the latter poem the knights are pulled up from their dungeon with a rope, whilst in the former they have their fetters taken off by means of a sledge-hammer, anvil, and tongs, &c.

In the *Sowdan*, l. 3044, Richard of Normandy is left back as a governor of Mantrible; in the Ashmole version, l. 4881 *et seq.*, Raoul and Howel are ordered to keep that place, whereas Richard accompanies Charlemagne (cf. l. 5499).

In the Ashm. MS., l. 5209, Neymes sees first Charles coming with his host; in the *Sowdan*, l. 3083, it is Floripas who first discovers the banner of France.

The prayer which Charlemagne, seeing Oliver in distress, addressed to Christ, in the *Sowdan*, l. 1304 *et seq.*, is not mentioned in the Ashm. version.

The account of the duel between Oliver and Ferumbras differs considerably in the two versions. In the Ashmolean MS., l. 580, the incident of Oliver assisting Ferumbras to arm (cf. *Sowdan*, 1158) is omitted, and it is not Oliver (as in the *Sowdan*, l. 1270) who is disarmed, but Ferumbras, whom his adversary offers to accept his own sword back (Ashm. MS., l. 680).

In the Ashmolean version, l. 102, Ferumbras offers to fight at once with twelve of Charles's knights; in the corresponding passage of the *Sowdan*, l. 1067, he challenges only six.

In the *Sowdan*, l. 1512 *et seq.*, Floripas advises her father not to slay the captive peers, but to detain them as hostages that might be exchanged for Ferumbras. In the Ashm. MS., l. 1178, it is not Floripas, but Lamasour, who gives that advice to the amirant.

As in many of the variations, mentioned just before, there are many omissions in the Ashmole MS., which are related in the *Sowdan*, it becomes evident that the Ashmolean version cannot have been the original from which the *Sowdan* was copied, which is also proved by several names occurring in the *Sowdan*, but which are not to be found in *Syr Ferumbras.* Thus, for instance, the names of *Espiard, Belmore, Fortibrance, Tamper,*[1] do not occur at all in the Ashmolean version, whereas other names have quite a different form in the latter poem. For *Generyse, S* 1135, 1239, we find *Garin, A* 216, 443; *Barrock, S* 2939, 2943, 3022 = *Amyote, A* 4663; *Alagolofur, S* 2135, 2881 = *Agolafre, A* 3831, 4327; and *Laban* is always spelt *Balan* in the Ashmolean poem, &c.

Now as there are some passages where the *Sowdan*, while it differs from the Ashm. MS., corresponds with the French *Fierabras*, we might be inclined to think that poem to be the original of the *Sowdan.* Thus Charlemagne's prayer and the name of Bishop Turpin, which are omitted in the Ashm. MS., occur in the French *Fierabras.* But there are several differences between the *Sowdan* and the French poem.

In the *Fierabras*, l. 1933, the French prisoners, on being brought before the Soudan, do not avow their true names as they do in the *Sowdan*, l. 1498.

In the French poem, l. 704, Oliver tells his adversary his name before the fight begins; in the *Sowdan*, l. 1249, he does not confess his true name until they had fought for a considerable time.

In the *Fierabras*, l. 1043, Oliver drinks of the bottles of balm, which is not mentioned in the *Sowdan*, l. 1190.

Again, *Fierabras*, ll. 1329 ss., where Ferumbras having disarmed Oliver, tells him to take his sword back again, does not agree with ll. 1279-82 of the *Sowdan.*

Instead of Floripas (*S* 1515), *Brulans* advises the Soudan not to slay the prisoners in *F* 1949.

The French knight slain at the sally of the captives is called *Bryer* in *S* 2604, but *Basin* in *F* 3313.

[1] There is one *Templer* mentioned in the Ashm. MS., l. 2673. But he is not identical with *Tamper* of the *Sowdan*, ll. 2641, 2667.

Concerning the sacred relics there is no mention made of the *cross* (*S* 3236) in the French poem, and the *signe, i. e.* 'the shroud or winding-sheet of the Lord'[1] (*F* 6094), is omitted in the *Sowdan.*

Besides these variations of the two versions there is an incident of Marsedag being killed by Guy, and buried by the Saracens (*S* 2247—2274), which being omitted in the *Fierabras* proves that the author of the *Sowdan* cannot have followed the French poem, or at least not that version which is edited by MM. Krœber and Servois.

Similarly there is no mention made in the French *Fierabras* of Bryer being charged to take care of the relics and of Charles's treasure (*S* 3204).

The game of blowing burning coals is related in *Sowdan,* l. 1996 ss., with several details which are wanting in the French poem, l. 2907.

The names also do not always agree in both versions. Thus we find *Generyse, S* 1139, for *Garin, F* 438; *Mapyn, S* 2325, for *Maubrun, F* 3046; *Alagolofur, S* 2135, for *Agolafre, F* 4290 or *Golafre, F* 4267, 4383; *Bryer, S* 2604, for *Basin, F* 3313; *Maragounde, S* 1563, for *Marabunde, F* 2196; *Boloyne, S* 3238, for *St. Denis, F* 6199; *Barokke, S* 2939, and *Espiard, S* 2145, are not mentioned at all in the French *Fierabras*, nor does *Belmore, S* 3122, occur in the *Fierabras*, either in the corresponding passage, *F* 5867, or elsewhere.

On the fact that the names of the twelve peers (see above, p. xxvii) differ in the *Sowdan* from those mentioned in the *Fierabras*, too much stress need not, I think, be laid, as it might be explained by the simple inadvertence of the composer. The poet in freely reproducing his source, which he generally followed pretty closely as far as relates the course of events, well remembered the names of the principal French knights; but having forgotten those of less important characters, some of whom do not appear again in the poem, and being obliged to fill up their number of twelve, might have placed any names which he remembered having met with somewhere

[1] Greek σινδών. Cf. *Dissertation*, pp. 45-46.

as included in the list of the douzeperes. By an oversight he omitted to mention Richard, whom however we see appear afterwards.[1]

Similarly the names of *Laban* and *Ferumbras* for *Balan* and *Fierabras* afford no convincing proof of the impossibility of the French *Fierabras* being the original of the second part of the *Sowdan*, as the poet, having found those spellings in the *Destruction*, the source of the first portion of his romance, might simply have retained them for the whole poem.

But reviewing all the facts of the case, and taking into account those passages which relate incidents omitted in the *Fierabras*, and which the author of the *Sowdan* therefore cannot have taken from that poem—and further taking into account the several differences between the two versions, which, it may be admitted, generally speaking, are only slight ones—the French *Fierabras*, *i. e.* the version edited by MM. Krœber and Servois, which represents the group *w* (see before, p. xix, footnote), cannot have been the original of the second part of the *Sowdan*.

Proceeding now to a comparison of the *Sowdan* with the Escorial MS.,[2] we have not found any passage where *S* differing from *F* agrees with *E*, as *E* and *F* generally have in those places the same reading. Therefore the Escorial MS. cannot be regarded as the original of the *Sowdan*.

Unfortunately the fragment printed from the Hanover MS. is too short to allow of an exact comparison with that version. We only know[3] that some names, the spelling of which in the *Sowdan* differs from that in the other versions, have the same form in the Hanover MS. as in the *Sowdan*. Thus we find the following names agreeing in both versions: *Lucafer*, *Maragonde*, *Maupyn*. Only instead of *Laban* which is used in the *Sowdan*, we read *Balan*. In the fragment printed by Grœber,[4] we find the name of the Soudan's son

[1] See note to l. 2535.

[2] There being only a small fragment printed of the Didot MS. (*Epopées Fr.* ii. 307), a comparison of the *Sowdan* with this version is impossible at present. But as the Didot MS. belongs to the same group as *E*, what results from a comparison of *S* with *E* may be assumed for the Didot MS.

[3] See *Zeitschrift für romanische Philologie*, iv. pp. 164, 170.

[4] *Jahrbuch für romanische und englische Sprache und Literatur*, xiii. p. 111.

with the same spelling as in the *Destruction*, *Fierenbras*, which is nearer to *Ferumbras* than *Fierabras*.[1]

This resemblance of the names contained in the two versions might lead us to believe the Hanover MS. of *Fierabras* to be the original of the second part of the *Sowdan*, just as the *Destruction*, found in the same MS., is the original of the first part. But as, according to Gaston Paris, the Hanoverian version "is the same as the printed text, differing only in slight variations of readings,"[2] we may suppose it likely that in all passages where the *Sowdan* differs from the printed *Fierabras*, it also differs from the Hanover MS. Nevertheless, as the differences between the *Sowdan* and the printed *Fierabras* are, on the whole, not very significant; for the several instances of omission in the *Sowdan*, being easily accounted for by the general plan of the poet, cannot be regarded as real variations; and as some names, the spelling of which differs in *S* and *F*, are found to be identical in *S* and *H*, we might, perhaps, be entitled to think the second part of the *Sowdan* to be founded on a MS. similar to the Hanover one.

It still remains for us to compare the *Sowdan* with the Provençal version.

In most cases where *S* differs from *F*, it also differs from *P*, therefore *S* cannot have taken those variations of readings from the Provençal poem.

The account of the knights sent on a mission to Laban, in *S* 1663—1738, considerably differs from the corresponding passage in *P* 2211 ss.

In *P* the scene of the whole poem is placed in Spain, there is no mention of the combat before Rome,[3] as in the first part of the *Sowdan*.

The game of blowing a coal, *S* 1996 ss., is not mentioned in the Provençal version.

From these variations, taken at random out of a greater number,

[1] This example is not very striking, as the spelling *Ferumbras* may simply have been retained from the first part of the poem; see above, p. xxxi.

[2] *Syr Ferumbras*, *Introduction*, p. xiv, footnote.

[3] See *Handschriftliche Gestaltungen*, p. 14, and *Dissert.*, p. 29.

it becomes evident that the Provençal poem has not been the original of the *Sowdan.*

If now we compare the *Sowdan* with Caxton's version, which we know to be simply a translation of the French prose romance of *Fierabras;*[1] the few following instances of differences between *C* and *S* will show at once, that also that version from which the prose romance was copied or compiled[2] cannot have been the original of the *Sowdan.*

There are several variations in the names contained in the two versions. Thus we find *Ballant* in *C* for *Laban* in *S; Fyerabras* in *C* for *Ferumbras* in *S; Garin, C* 55/3 = *Generyse, S* 1135; *Amyotte, C* 176/26 = *Barrokk, S* 1135, &c. The game of blowing a coal is told with more details in *S* 1998, and somewhat differently from *C* 118/24; the incident of Laban's seizing the image of Mahound and smashing it, which is related in *S* 2507, is omitted in *C*, &c.

Looking back now to our investigation concerning the original of the *Sowdan*, we sum up what results from it, in the following *resumé:*

Most probably the *Destruction de Rome* is the original of the first part of the *Sowdan.* As to the second part, we are unable to identify it with any of the extant versions. The French *Fierabras,* as edited by MM. Krœber and Servois, is not the original, but the differences between the two poems are not significant; apparently a version similar to the Hanover MS. may be thought to be the original.

The *Sowdan* is no translation, but a free reproduction of its originals; the author of the *Sowdan* following his sources only as far as concerns the course of the principal events, but going his own independent way in arranging the subject-matter as well as in many minor points.

The *Sowdan* differs from the poem of *Syr Ferumbras* in two principal points:

(1) In being an original work, not in the conception, but in the treatment of the subject-matter, whereas the Ashmole *Ferumbras* is little more than a mere translation.

[1] *Histoire Poétique*, p. 157.

[2] And to which only a few very insignificant additions were made by the author; see *Hist. Poét.*, p. 99, bottom.

(2) In representing, in its first portion, the first part of the old *Balan* romance, whereas *Syr Ferumbras* contains only the second. But as that second part of the old *Balan* romance appears to be considerably modified and greatly amplified in the Ashmole *Ferumbras*, so the first part of the *Sowdan* contains a likewise modified, but much shortened, narration of the first part of the old *Balan* poem, so that the *Sowdan* has arrived to become quite a different work from the original *Balan* or *Fierabras* romance, and that a reconstruction of the contents of that old poem would be impossible from the *Sowdan*.

LANGUAGE AND SUMMARY OF GRAMMATICAL FORMS.

As regards the language of the *Sowdan*, the first point is the dialect. Looking at the plurals of the present indicative in *-en* or *-n*, we at once detect the Midland peculiarities of the poem. Thus we find, l. 1331, *gone* rhyming with *one*, l. 1010, *goon : camalyon*, l. 506, *gone : than*, l. 1762, *lyven : gyfen*, l. 1816, *byleven : even*.

The verbal forms of the singular present indicative and of the second person sing. preterite of weak verbs lead us to assign this poem to an East-Midland writer. The 2nd and 3rd person singular present indicative end in *-est*, *-eth*; and the 2nd person sing. preterite of weak verbs exhibits the inflection *-est* : l. 1202, *goist : moost*; 1314, 1715, *knowest*; 1344, *trowest*; 1154, *blowest*; 1153, *saiest*; 2292, *forgetist*; 560, *doist*; 1193, *doistowe*;—1093, *goth : wroth*, 1609 : *loth*, 1620 : *doth*; 1728, *sleith : deth*; 561, *sholdest*; 1244, *shuldist*; 603, *madist*; 563, *hadist*; 2219, *askapedist*, &c.—Twice we find the 2nd person preterite without *-est* (*made*, *wroght*); but see the note to l. 2.

If, now, we examine the phonological and inflectional peculiarities of the *Sowdan*, we find them thoroughly agreeing with those of other East-Midland works,[1] which still further confirms the supposition of the East-Midland origin of the poem.

[1] See Morris's Preface to *Genesis and Exodus*, Skeat's Introduction to *Havelock the Dane*, and Mall's edition of *Harrowing of Hell* (Breslau, 1871).

I or *y*, the descendants of original *u* (which in Old English [Anglo-Saxon] had already become *y* or *i* in consequence of *i*- mutation or *umlaut*)—are found rhyming with original *i* :—ll. 449, 881, *kyn* : *him*, 2060 : *wynne* ; 1657, *fille* : *stille* ; 1973, *fire* : *desire*, &c. It must, however, be noted that the rhyme *king* : *inne* (l. 372) or *king* : *thing* (ll. 173, 236) cannot be regarded as an East-Midland peculiarity, because *king*, *drihten*, *chikken*, the *i* of which is a modification of original *u*, are to be met with in all Middle-English dialects, as has been shown by Professor Zupitza in the *Anzeiger für deutsches Altertum*, vol. vi. p. 6.

Old English short *a*, which is liable to change into *o*, appears in this poem—

(1) always as *o*, before *n*- combinations (*nd*, *nt*, *ng*) :—531, *stronge* : *istonge* ; 3166, *bronte* : *fonte* ; 214, *amonge* : *longe*, &c.

(2) as *a*, before the single consonants *m* and *n* :—1120, *name* : *shame*, 935 : *same*, 1739 : *grame* ; 785, 1773, *man* : *Lavan* ; 3125, *came* : *Lavan* (cf. 2579, *Lavan* : *tane*) ; 2160, *came* : *dame*, &c.—The fact that *com* (ll. 547, 1395, 3095, &c.) is used as well as *cam* as sing. preterite indic. need occasion no difficulty if we remember that the original short *a* (or *o*) of *cam* (or *com*) had already been lengthened into *ó* in the O.E. period.[1] *Came* and *come* as pret. sing. are employed indifferently in *Chaucer* as well as in the *Celestin* (ed. Horstmann, *Anglia*, i. 56), which is known to have been composed in the East-Midland dialect.

O long, from O.E. *â*, in our poem has that broad sound which is peculiar to the East-Midland dialect. We find it rhyming with—

(1) original *ó* :—1025, *wrothe* : *sothe* ; 801, *goo* : *doo* ; 60, *inowe* : *blowe* ; 325, *so* : *ido*, &c.

(2) unchangeable *a* :—257, *Aufricanes* : *stoones* ; 506, *gon* : *than* ; 2049, *agoon* : *Lavan*, &c.

As many East-Midland works[2] the *Sowdan* has three forms for O.E. þâr :—*thare*, *thore*, *there*, all of which are established by the rhyme :—1805, *thore* : *Egremoure* (cf. 2895, *Egremoure* : *tresoure*, 1003, *Agremore* : *more*) ; 126, *thore* : *lore* ; 430, *thare* : *sware* ;

[1] See Sweet, *Anglia*, iii. 152. [2] Cf. Mall, *Harrowing of Hell*, p. 18.

2245, *there : chere*, 2404 : *bere*; 2604, *there : were* (wǣron), 208 : *were* (worian), &c.

We likewise find *sore* and *sare*[1] (O.E. sâre) :—1196, *sore : more*; 166, *sare : care*; 1377, *sore : thore*.

The O.E. diphthongs *ea* and *eo* and the O.E. *ȳ* (mutated from *êa* or *êo*) appear as *e* in this poem :—1595, *me : see*, 632 : *fee*, 1339 : *free*, 405 : *be*; 1535, *depe : slepe*; 1011, 1523, *dere : here*; 963, *yere : vere*, 1257 : *Olyvere*; 996, *nere : were*; 596, 1528, *nede : spede*; 1702, *eke : speke*; 1726, *leke : speke*; 184, 215, 1208, *shelde : felde*; 2530, *hevene : elevene*, &c.

A brief summary of the grammatical inflexions employed in the poem will also give evidence of a great similarity with the forms used by other East-Midland writers, and will serve to show that the language of the *Sowdan* agrees closely with that of *Chaucer*.

In the declension of substantives the only remnant of case-formation by means of inflexions is the ending used to form the Genitive Singular and the Plural.

The genitive singular of nouns ends in *es* (sometimes written *-is* or *ys*) for all genders :—356, *develes*; 1209, *stedes*; 849, *worldis*; 1804, *worldes*; 3035, *dammes*; 1641, *nedes*; 1770, *shippes*; 1072, *faderis*.

Substantives ending in *-s* in the nominative case, remain unchanged in the genitive case :—1214, 1287, *Ferumbras*; 2006, *Naymes*; 3207, *Charles*; 1639, 1350, *Floripas*.—*Florip*, l. 614, is the genitive case of *Floripe* or *Florip*, l. 2027, 1571.

The nominative plural of all genders is formed by *-es* (*-is*, *-ys*) or *-s* :—919, *knightes*, 1947, 2276, *knightis*; 1384, *horses*, 1401, *horsys*; 429, 2054, *gatis*; 192, *wordes*; 837, *swerdes*; 174, *hedes*; 2289, *ladies*; 3271, *soules*; 26, *bokes*; 606, *peres*; 297, *tours*, &c. Examples of a plural case without *s* are seen in *thinge*, l. 2, 1709 :—O.E. *þing*; *honde*, 987, O.E. *handa*, as well as *hondes*, 1412, 2568; *frende*, 3212, O.E. *frȳnd*, as well as *frendes*, 1011, O.E. *frêondas*. Other plurals which are equally easily explained by their O.E. forms are :—*eyen*, 825, O.E. *êagan*; *shoone*, 1381, O.E. *scêon*; *fete*, 1403, O.E. *fêt*, *fote*, 1427, O.E. *fôtum*, 2673, O.E. *fôta*.

[1] Cf. Schipper, *Alexiuslegenden*, 98/121.

To mark the difference between the definite and indefinite forms of adjectives is a difficult task; as the final *-e* had in most cases already become silent in the poet's dialect, it seems probable that he no longer observed the distinction.

The pronouns are the same as in *Chaucer* and in other East-Midland poems:—*I, me, thou, the; he, hym; sche, her* and *hir; it* and *hit* (cf. note to l. 41); *we, us; ye, you.* The plural of the personal pronoun of the 3rd person is *thai* and *he* (cf. note to l. 2698) for the nominative case; *hem,* and in some doubtful passages (see note to l. 88) *thaym* for the accusative case.

As in *Chaucer,* the pronoun of the 2nd person is often joined to the verb:—*hastow* 1680, *maistow* 1826, *shaltow* 1669, *woltow* 1727, *wiltow* 1151, *artow* 1967, *kanstow* 2335, &c.

Possessive pronouns:—*myn* and *thyn* are used before vowels and before *h; my, thy* before consonants. Only once, l. 90, *my* is placed before a vowel. *His, hire* and *here; our, your; here* and (twice, 623, 1244) *thair.*

The demonstrative pronouns are *this, these* or *thes; that.*

The definite article *the* or *þe,* is used for all cases singular and plural. But we find besides, the following examples of inflexion:—*tho,* 2063, O.E. *þá,* and the accusative sing. *þon,* 108. In l. 2052, *tho* means 'them, those' = Lat. eos. *Tha,* l. 2639, seems to be a mistake of the scribe, it is perhaps miswritten for *þat* (day), cf. l. 619.

Men, 115, 1351, and *me,* 287, are used as indefinite pronouns. *Everyche, every, everychone* occur frequently. Note also *ichoon* 2774, *ilka* 2016; *thilke* 2644, *eche* 1865.

That or *þat, who, whome* are used as relative pronouns. The interrogative pronouns are *who* and *what.*

Verbs. The plural imperative ends in *-eth* or *-th,* which, however, we find frequently omitted, as in l. 194, *prove you,* 2078 *proveth;* 2131 *sende,* 167 *sendith; telle* 1977, *tellyth* 1625, &c.

The *-n* of the infinitive mood is often dropped, as in *Chaucer:*—274, 1588, *sene : bene;* 1124, *see : tre;* 658 : *cite;* 600, *be : cite;* 1225 : *contre;* 1411, *flee : cite;* 3065, *fleen : men;* 1282, *sloo : mo;* 792, *sloone : one,* &c.

The final *-(e)n* of past participles of strong verbs is in most cases dropped, as in *Chaucer*:—3176 *forlorne : borne*, 32 *born*, 3011 *wonne*, 21 *wonnen*, 2756 *comen : nomen*, 155 *come*, 2476 *holpe*, 1362 *bygote*, 1026 *blowe*, &c.

Weak verbs form their past participles in *-ed*, *-d*, *-et*, *-t*, much as in *Chaucer*:—*lerned* 3042, *eyde* 1648, *tooldc* 670, *bogt* 111, *delte* 526, *displaied* 133.

The prefix *i-* or *y-* occurs sometimes, *icome* 784, *come* 155, *istonge* 533, *itake* 49, *taken* 1430, &c.

The present participles end in *-inge* and *ande*, as is often the case in East-Midland works:—2831 *prikande : comande*, 435 *cryande*, 924 *makande*, 3225 *mornynge : kynge*, 2399 *slepynge : honde*, where evidently *slepande* is the true reading.

As in *Chaucer* the 2nd person preterite of strong verbs is sometimes formed by *-est* or *-ist*, *letist* 2167; but we find also regular forms, as in *slough* 1259, where, however, the O.E. *e* (*slôge*) is already dropped.

The *-en* or *-n* of the preterite plural and of past participles is commonly dropped, *ronnen* 3007, *ronne* 2959, *took* 477, *tokene* 2621, *slough* 78, *sloughen* 401, *ido* 327 : *so*, &c.

The *-d* in the past participles and in the preterite of weak verbs is sometimes omitted, as often happens in East-Midland works. Thus we find *comforte* 2242 and *comforted* 312, *commaunde* 57 and *commaunded* 228, *graunte* 607, *liste* 1132, *list* 1966, *discumfite* 1464, &c. On the same analogy we find *light* 1125, 1189, and *lighted* 3109, *worth* 1203, and *worthed* 1163.

As regards the final *-e*'s, it may be remarked that the scribe has added many final *-e*'s, where the rules would not lead us to suspect them, and has often given a final *-e* to words which in other passages of the poem, although similarly used, have no *e*:—*note* 245, 274, *not* 255, 313; *howe* 19, *how* 275; *undere* 61, *under* 713; *bute* 247, *but* 8; *cooste* 202, *coost* 3062; *crafte* 424, *craft* 2335; *ashamede* 1295, *ashamed* 558, &c.

This is due either to carelessness on the part of the scribe, or perhaps to the fact that in the speech of the copyist the final *e*'s had already become altogether silent, so that finding many words ending in *-e* and not knowing its meaning, he considered it as a mere "ornament in writing" (Ellis, *Pronunciation*, i. 338), and sometimes added, sometimes omitted it.

With respect to the composer of the *Sowdan* himself, there may be some doubt left whether in his speech the final *e* had become altogether silent, or was still pronounced occasionally. From the following instances it may be concluded with certainty that the poet very frequently did not sound the final *e*:—757 *boghte : noght*, 3154 *hat : fat*, 961 *wronge : distruccion*, 556 *onlace : was*; cf. also 1383, 1611, 2163; 2795 *spéke we of Ríchard*, 2999 *fought*, 2093, 859 *bringe*, 9, 2547 *kepte*, 834 *wente*, 142 *come*, 713 *wode*.

In other cases there is no certainty whether the final *e* is quite silent or must be slightly pronounced or slurred over, so as to form trisyllabic measures. It must be noted, however, that in supposing trisyllable measures in all these doubtful cases, the number of this kind of measure will increase to a great amount in the *Sowdan*. Therefore I rather incline to think the final *e* silent also in the following instances:—2090 *défende this place*, 1201 *bréke both báke*, 861 *cóme from ál*, 2119 *aske consaile*, 1597 *wóle these traítours*, 1783 *whéns come yé*, 2317 *pásse that brígge*, 1100 *rónne bytwéne*, 2997 *fóught so lónge*, 175 *broke nothinge*, 1658 *bédde with ríght*, 713 *gréne wode síde*, 571 *hóme to Róme that nýght*, 1610 *the fáls jailoúr fedde yoúr prisonére*, 2152 *fáls traitóurs of Fránce*, 921 *chárged the yónge with ál*, 380 *aboúte midnýghte*, 726 *sóne to hím*, 160 *únneth not óne* [Chaucer still pronounces *unnethë*].

Nevertheless there seems to be some instances where the final *e* is to be sounded, as in ll. 298, 2790, 1332, 1619, 2740, 592, 2166, 2463, 1405, 2386, 895, 332, 91.

Final *en* also seems sometimes not to constitute a separate syllable:—1365 *waíten uppon mé*, 459 *bréken our wállis*, 45 *slépen with ópyne ýȝe*, 485 *cómen by the cóst*, 2313 *díden it aboút*, &c.

In all these cases *n* had very probably already fallen off in the speech of the poet, as the following examples lead us to suppose:— 178 *wynne : him*, 1582 *dye : biwry*, 2309 *shewe : trewe*, 2107 *slépe to lónge*, 861 *cóme from ál*, &c.

As regards the final *es* of nouns, the poet seems to have observed the same rules as those followed by Chaucer; viz. *es* is sounded when joined to monosyllabic stems; it does not increase the number of syllables (and therefore is often spelt *-s* instead of *-es*), when the stem has two or more syllables:—197, 277 *goddës*, 665 *nailës*, 445 *tentës*, 2068 *tentïs*, 174, 1799 *hedës*, 2032, 2868 *swerdës*, 2327 *wallës*, 1209 *stedës*, 1770 *shippës*, 2702 *somers*, 2687, 2591 *felowes*, 2660 *felows*, 2412 *maydyns*, 647, 1597 *traytours*, 2036 *orders*, 45 *lovers*, 2612, 3098 *develes*, 1072 *faderis*, 203, 862 *sowdons*, 881 *sarsyns*.

The final *es* of adverbs seems no longer to constitute a separate syllable:—2213 *hónged' els bý*, 2786 *êls had' hé*, 2109 *éllis I may sínge*, 1525 *élles wol' hé*, 2061 *thêns*, 1783 *whens*.

METRE AND VERSIFICATION.

The poem is composed in four-line stanzas. The arrangement of the rhyme is such that the 1st and 3rd lines rhyme together, and the 2nd and 4th together, which gives the following rhyme-formula: *a b a b*. The rhyme-endings employed in one stanza do not occur again in the next following.

But it must be noticed that there seem to occur some instances of eight-line stanzas, one of which, beginning at l. 1587, is built on the model employed by *Chaucer*. Others are arranged differently. Those beginning at ll. 1059 and 1219 show the rhyme-formula *a b a b a c a c*, in that of l. 1411 the 2nd and 4th lines are rhymed together, and the 5th and 7th, whilst the 1st, 3rd, 6th, 8th, all end with the same rhyme. The formula for the stanzas beginning at ll. 807, 879, 1611 is *a b a b c b c b*. In the stanza of l. 939 all the pair lines are rhymed together, and the odd ones also, which is the only instance in the poem of eight consecutive lines having only two rhyme-endings, as generally eight lines show four different rhyme-endings, and three only in the passages cited above. But the whole stanza of l. 939 seems not to be due to the author; he has very probably borrowed it from some other poem.[1]

Turning now our attention to the fact that the lines occurring between the Initials or Capital Letters, which are met with in some passages in the MS., are often divisible by eight, we might feel

[1] See note to l. 939.

inclined to regard this as an additional reason for considering the stanza employed in the *Sowdan* as an eight-line one. Indeed, the portion from the Initial of l. 1679 to the next one of l. 1689 might be taken for one single stanza. The 24 lines from l. 575 (beginning with an Initial) to the next Initial in l. 598 might equally be considered as three stanzas, whilst there are 5 times 8 lines = 5 eight-line stanzas from the Initial of l. 2755 to the next Initial in l. 2795.

In all these instances the supposition of eight-line stanzas would suit the context, as is the case also with other passages. Thus in the following cases it might seem as though eight lines taken together were more closely connected and made better sense than four lines, *e.g.* ll. 583—598, 1703—1710, 1679—1686, 939—962, 1043—1050, 244 ss., 455 ss., 631 ss., 1059 ss.

But, on the other hand, it must be borne in mind that there are also a great many cases where, as regards the sense, four lines can be considered as an independent whole, when, *e. g.*, the speech spoken by a person is contained in four lines, and the words of another person replying to the first follow in the next four lines. Very often also these next four lines contain only a part of the second person's reply, so that the remainder of his reply falls into the following stanza. This 'enjambement' or continuation of the sense, and sometimes of the syntactical construction from one stanza to another, need not, of course, prevent us from admitting the supposition of eight-line stanzas; as, upon the whole, it is met with in all poems composed in stanzas, and as it is frequently used in *Le Morte Arthur* (Harleian MS. 2252, ed. Furnivall), which is written in eight-line stanzas; but as there is no instance known of an eight-line stanza containing four different rhyme-endings, which at this supposition it would be the case with the *Sowdan*, the eight-line stanzas containing either three rhyme-endings, as in *Chaucer*, or two, as in *Le Morte Arthur*, and as in some passages of the *Sowdan* (ll. 1691, 1695, 1699, 1711, 1715), we find Initials placed after four lines, I believe a stanza of four alternately rhyming lines to be the one intended by the composer—a metre which, according to Guest, *History of Eng. Rhythms*, ii. 317—'must have been well known and familiar during the fifteenth century.' The few eight-line stanzas quoted above, may then be owing either to the inadvertence of the poet, who somewhat carelessly employed one of the two rhyme-endings of one stanza a third and fourth time in the following one, or, perhaps also, he intentionally retained that rhyme-ending, and he inserted eight-line stanzas amongst those of four verses as a mere matter of variation. It is perhaps not impossible that the retention of this rhyme-ending was not greatly felt.

As regards the rhymes themselves, they are both monosyllabic or masculine rhymes, and dissyllabic or feminine ones. Frequently they are used alternating with each other, as in the stanzas beginning with l. 2755.

Sometimes we find four feminine rhymes occurring in an unbroken succession, as in ll. 1263-66. But it must be noticed that the number of masculine rhymes is predominant. Thus the stanzas beginning with ll. 3047, 3063, 3123, 1123, 791, 1035, 1271, 1275, 2019, 1311, 1351, 1463, &c., contain only masculine rhyme-endings.

The rhymes are not always full and true; there occur many imperfect ones.

(1) A word in the singular number is often rhymed with a word in the plural number, which therefore has an additional *s* (or *es*):—797, *thinge : tidyngys;* 2647, *fyght : knyghtes;* 2087, *light : knightes;* 1455, *cosynes : kinge;* 2272, *laye : dayes;* 2395, 885, *Ogere : peres;* 2456, *alle : walles;* 2682, *nede : stedes;* 944, *mone : stoones;* cf. also 2376, *wile : beguiled.* In l. 68, *poundis : dromonde;* the rhyme becomes perfect in reading *pounde*, as in l. 2336, instead of *poundis*.

(2) Single *n* is found rhyming with *n*- combinations.

a. n : nd—cf. 814, *ychoon : Mahounde;* 912, *pavilone : Mahounde;* 1201, *crowne : Mahounde.* The rhyme, 162, *Rome : houne*, may be explained in the same manner, for *houne* stands for *hounde*, as it is spelt in ll. 237, 2377, 935, 1756.[1]

β. n : ng—cf. 2349, *Mapyne : endinge;* 86, *Apolyne : tithinge;* 370, *inne : kinge;* 1455, *cosynes : kinge;* 3249, *Genelyne : kinge;* 3171, *serpentyne : endinge;* 959, *distruccion : wronge.*

[1] "This elision of a final *d* in such words as *hond, lond, sheld, held*, &c., is by no means uncommon in ancient poetry, and arises simply from pronunciation."—Morris, *Specimens of Early English*, 320/261.

In 614, *love : vowe*, the second rhyme *vowe* does not contain the consonant *v*.

(3) Rhymes imperfect as concerns the consonants.

m : n—cf. 76, *Rome : one;* 1672, 364 : *done;* 2443, 366, *come : done;* 747, *some : soudone;* 1323, *came : than;* 1488, *came : ranne;* 2128, *tyme : pyne;* 177, *him : wynne;* 2375, *him : tene;* 447, 859, *him : kyn;* 2004, *hyme : skyne;* 2353, *him : inne.*

f : v—cf. 341, *twelve : selve;* 415, *wife : alive;* 1762, *gyfene : lyvene;* 1912, *gife : lyve.* But in all these cases the rhymes are really perfect, they seem only imperfect in consequence of the copyist writing indiscriminately *f* and *v*. Thus the rhyme of l. 341 reappears in l. 1867, *self : twelf.* In l. 2336 we find *gefe*, which is written *geve* in l. 198; *lefe*, l. 764; *safe*, l. 864, are spelt with *v* in ll. 1340, 1529, 2808.

l : n—cf. l. 363, *consaile : slayne.* Quite similar is l. 1251, *felde : sende.*

p : k—l. 820, *stoupe : stroke.* A similar rhyme occurs in *Guy*, l. 10903, *scapid : nakid.*

d : t—l. 2868, *gyrde : sterte;* 1151, *plete : dede.*

d : p—l. 283, *tyde : depe.* But this rhyme is very probably owing to the scribe. For *depe* we ought to read *wide.*

A single consonant rhymes with a double consonant. The only certain instance occurs in l. 311, *tyde : chidde.* For in ll. 312, 317, *dele : welle*, we might read *wele*, as this word is frequently spelt in the poem; cf. ll. 385, 2618, 1173, 1651, &c. For *dedde* in l. 2980 (*rede : dedde*) we may substitute *dede*, which occurs in l. 2510. The rhyme *glad : hadde*, 2687, becomes perfect if we read *gladde*, which is the usual spelling of the word in the poem; cf. ll. 439, 570, 918, &c. Besides, I believe *hadde* to be monosyllabic. *Ferre : nere* l. 1575; in l. 117 we find *fere.*

The rhyme, l. 2654, *sloughe : drowe* can easily be restored in reading *slowe*, which occurs frequently, as in ll. 2401, 2683, 304, 2208, &c. The rhyme *ane : shafe*, 555, seems to be due to some clerical error.

(4) Rhymes imperfect as concerns the vowels.

a : e—2803, *gate : lete;* perhaps we are justified in reading *late*, cf. *Havelock*, 328; l. 2752, *made : dede.* The rhymes *thare : were*, 1383; *bare : there*, 671; *Agremare : there*, 33, are really perfect ones, as we know the poet to have used *thare*, *there*, and *thore* indiscriminately; cf. ll. 208, 2604, 430, 1805, 1003; l. 1436, *ladde : nede;* 2365, *ladde : bedde*, the author probably pronounced *ledde.* For *lefte*, l. 2335 : *craft*, we may read *lafte*, as is shown by l. 424, *lafte : crafte.* In ll. 1781, 544, *tene : than*, the rhyme will be improved by reading *then.*

a : o (cf. p. xxxv)—504, *thane : gone;* 1143, 1079, *Rolande : honde;* 133, *sowdone : Lavan* (where we might read *sowdan*, as in l. 1491); 627, *sowdane : towne;* 2527, 1684, *Roulande : londe.*

i (*y*) *: e.* This rhyme also occurs in *Chaucer;* cf. Ellis, *Pron.* i. 272; see also *Guy*, p. xiv.—l. 21419, *him : hem;* 1299, *dynte : lente;* 523, *strike : breke;* 1643, *mylde : shelde;* 1263, *togedere : thidere;* 1277, *wepenless : iwis;* 344, *shitte : mette;* 2538, *hende : wynde* (read *wende*), &c.; l. 82, *vilane : remedye* (read *vilanye*, as in ll. 179, 2577); but 1015, *vilane : me*, cf. *Guy*, xi, *v*—813, *sle : curtesye;* 895, *we : lye;* cf. Ellis, *Pron.*, i. 271.

The monophthong *y* is rhymed with a diphthong, the second part of which is *y* :—l. 441, *Sarsynes : Romaynes;* 2761, *Apolyne : agayne;* 2105 : *slayne;* 2175 : *eyne;* 2280, *dye : waye* (cf. 1582); 589, *fyne : Bourgoyne.*

o : ou (*ow*).—l. 1023, *wrothe : southe* (which is written *sothe* in ll. 2014, 2024, 2246, 2719); 779, *fonde : grounde;* 260, *clarione : soune;* 879, *lione : crowne;* 2780, *malison : towne*, &c. Cf. also 1264, *endured : covered.*

o : e.—463, *oost : best.* The rhyme is restored in reading *rest* instead of *oost.*

o : i.—l. 966, *sonne : begynne.*

ue : ewe.—l. 2312, *vertue : fewe.* But this rhyme cannot be objected to, as "final French *u* (as in *due*) was diphthongized into *eu* in Chaucerian English."[1]

Other irregularities are :—l. 112, *douȝte : rowte;* 1987, *use : house;* 1131, *thou : lough;* 1200, *moost : goist;* 1730, *dethe : sleith;*

[1] Cf. Mr. Nicol's *Paper in the Academy of June* 23, 1877, vol. xi. p. 564, col. 1, and *Seventh Annual Address of the President to the Philol. Soc.*, p. 2.

2136, *pas : grace ;* 1611, *was : mace* (in which cases *e* is silent) ; 931, 1144, *peris : fiers.*

A line or verse generally contains four accented syllables, separated from each other by one or by two unaccented syllables, so that there are some instances of trisyllabic feet, as in ll. 817, 834, 2035, 2301, 2791, 3020, 3073, 2313, &c. In ll. 692, 695, two accented syllables are put close together without being separated by an unaccented one, which is altogether wanting. In some passages we find lines of three accented syllables alternating with those of four accents, as in ll. 575—582, 763—770, 839—846, 871—878, 2287—2290, &c. But in most cases lines with four accents follow each other in an unbroken succession, as in ll. 1—372, 995—1010, 1026—1029, 1067—1107, 1147—1154, 1731—1734, &c.

A few instances of verses with more than four accented syllables are also to be met with in the *Sowdan.* They are either due to the author and therefore intended, as in l. 37, where the poet almost literally imitates his original,[1] or they may be considered as due to some clerical error, in which case the metre generally can be restored by a slight emendation.

A verse has generally an iambic effect, that is to say, the first foot begins with an unaccented syllable, which is followed by an accented one. Frequently, however, the first accented syllable is preceded by two unaccented ones, as in ll. 41, 75, 127, 151, 367, 849, 1060, 1815, 1819, 2289, 2758, &c. There are some instances of the first foot consisting of a single (accented) syllable only, the unaccented one being altogether wanting, as in ll. 2120, 2288, 2374, 2394, &c.

DATE OF THE POEM AND NAME OF THE AUTHOR.

George Ellis attributes the present poem to the end of the fourteenth or beginning of the fifteenth century. "I think," he says in his *Specimens of Early English Metrical Romances*, ed. Halliwell, p. 380, "it would not be difficult to prove from internal evidence, that the present translation[2] cannot be earlier than the end of the fourteenth or beginning of the fifteenth century."

[1] See the note.

[2] Although l. 25 says that the story of the *Sowdan* "is written in Romaunce,"

Having seen from the summary of grammatical peculiarities that there is a great similarity between the language of Chaucer and that of the composer of this romance, we might be inclined to consider the latter as a contemporary of Chaucer. From some passages of the *Sowdan*, which seem to contain allusions to Chaucerian poetry, we may conclude that the poet must have known the *Canterbury Tales*. Thus ll. 42—46 :—

"Whan kynde corage begynneth to pryke,
Whan ffrith and felde wexen gaye,
And every wight desirith his like,
Whan lovers slepen with opyn yȝe,
As Nightingales on grene tre" . . .

appear to be imitated from the *Prologue of the Canterbury Tales*, ll. 10—12 :—

"And smale fowles maken melodie,
That slepen al the night with open eye,
So priketh hem nature in her corages."

Further on we remark in ll. 939-40 :—

"O thow, rede Marȝ Armypotente,
That in the trende baye hase made þy trone."

some traces of resemblance with the *Knight's Tale*, ll. 1123-26 :—

"And downward on a hill under a bent,
There stood the tempul of Marȝ armypotent,
Wrought al of burned steel, of which thentre
Was long and streyt, and gastly for to see,"

which may still be compared with the first lines of the *Prologue of Queen Anelida and False Arcite* :—

"Thou ferse God of armes, Mars the rede,
That in thy frosty contre called Trace,
Within thy grisly temples ful of drede,
Honoured art as patroun of that place." [1]

Now the *Prologue of the Canterbury Tales* and the *Knight's Tale*, being written in couplets, or lines arranged in pairs, were certainly composed after 1385,[2] or rather after 1389.[3] From the treatment of

this cannot induce us to consider our poem as a mere translation. It is, on the contrary, a free reproduction of a French original.

[1] Cf. also Lindsay's *History of Squyer Meldrum*, l. 390 :

"Like Mars the God Armypotent."

[2] Cf. *Prioress's Tale*, ed. Skeat (Clarendon Press Series), p. xx; and Furnivall's *Trial Forewords*, p. 111.

[3] Cf. *Chaucer*, ed. Morris, i. 205, footnote.

the final e's, which, contrary to Chaucer's usage, seem to have been silent in a great number of cases in the poet's speech, we may further conclude that the *Sowdan* must be somewhat later than the *Canterbury Tales*. Therefore the poet of the *Sowdan* cannot have been merely a later contemporary of Chaucer; I rather think it to be more probable that he must have lived some time after him. This would bring us to the beginning of the fifteenth century as the date of the romance.

As to the name and profession of the poet nothing is known, and we have no clue whatever from the poem.

The present edition of the *Sowdan* is printed from the unique MS. of the late Sir Thomas Phillips, at Middle Hill, Worcestershire, which is now in the possession of the Rev. John E. A. Fenwick, Thurlestane House, Cheltenham. Sir Thomas Phillips purchased the MS. at Mr. Heber's sale.[1] The oldest possessor's name which we find noted, is on the reverse of the last leaf of the Manuscript, where is written, "This is John Eteyes (or Ebeye's) boke, witnes by John Staff"—in a hand *circa temp.* Eliz. or Jac. I. By some notes made by former possessors on the first fly-leaf of the MS., and by the autograph names which we find there, we learn that Geo. Steevens bought the MS. "at Dr. Farmer's Sale, Friday June 15, 1798, for 1: 10. 0." On May 20th, 1800, it was "bought at the Sale of Geo. Stevens, for 3. 4. 6." by "O. Grahm Gilchrist."

A transcript of the MS. made by Geo. Stevens had been presented by him to Mr. Douce. This copy was re-transcribed by Geo. Ellis, who, in 1811, published some extracts with an analysis of the romance in the *Specimens of Early English Metrical Romances.*[2] The same copy has been followed by Halliwell, who in his *Dictionary of Arch. and Prov. W.*, has several quotations[3] from the present romance, which he styles as "*MS. Douce*, 175."

[1] *Bibliotheca Heberiana*, Part xi. p. 162. MSS. Lot 1533.
[2] Ed. Halliwell, p. 379 *et seq.*
[3] For instances, see the following words:—*Atame, alayned, ameved, assorte, avente, forcer*, &c.

The poem of the *Sowdan* was first printed by the Roxburghe Club in 1854.[1] The text of the present edition differs from that of the *editio princeps* in so far as punctuation is introduced, which is altogether disregarded by the MS. and the Roxburghe Club edition. In some passages words which have been written as one in the MS. are separated in the text; thus *a laye*, l. 2694; *a ras*, l. 645, are printed instead of *alaye, aras*. Sometimes also words written separately in the MS. are united by a hyphen, as *be-falle*, 14; *i-wiss*, 71; *i-sought*, 725; *with-oute*, 841; *a-bide*, 818; *a-ferde*, 1337, &c. These slight deviations from the MS., which are always indicated in the foot-notes, seemed advisable on account of the great help they afford the reader in understanding the text. More important emendations and corrections of evident scribal blunders and other mistakes are given in the foot-notes, and will be found explained in the Notes.

The Index of Names will be useful to those who wish to compare the *Sowdan* with any other version of the romance.

The Glossarial Index contains besides the obsolete terms all those words the spelling or the signification of which essentially differs from that now accepted. Words which show only slight orthographical variations from their modern form have not been included, as the reader will have no difficulty in identifying them.

In conclusion I have the pleasant duty of acknowledging the invaluable assistance which Professor Zupitza at all times readily and freely gave me. My best thanks are also due to Mr. Furnivall and to Mr. Napier for their kind advice and suggestions, and to Mr. Herrtage for collating a transcript of the poem with the MS.

EMIL HAUSKNECHT.

Berlin, January, 1881.

[1] London. Printed by William Nicol, Shakspere Press, MDCCCLIV.

ADDITIONS.

Since the *Introduction* was written, I have had an opportunity of seeing the Hanover MS. of the French *Fierabras*. The kind offices of Professor Koner exerted on my behalf secured me the consent of the Administration of the Royal Hanoverian Library to have the MS. sent to Berlin, and their most generous permission to consult it freely in the Reading Room of the University Library.

Having now compared the *Sowdan* more closely with the Hanover MS., I must state that the final result arrived at in my investigation concerning the original of the *Sowdan* (cf. p. xxxii) is in no way altered.

As already stated above (p. xxxii), and as the subsequent examination and the passages of *H* quoted below will serve to confirm, the Hanover version is, generally speaking, the same as the printed version of the *Fierabras*, differing only in slight variations of readings.

The names in which *S* differs from *F*, but agrees with *H*, are already spoken of on p. xxxi. But there are several others in the spelling of which *H* agrees with *F*, but differs from *S*. Thus we find *Balans* or *Balant* in *H* for *Laban* in *S*; *Guarin*, *H*, leaf 80, back, *F* 438 = *Generyse*, *S* 1135; *Agolafres*, *H*, leaf 81 = *Alagolofer*, *S* 2135; *Amiotte*, *H*, leaf 83, back = *Barrokk*, *S* 2939, etc.

As to the subject-matter, there are no instances where *S*, differing from *F*, agrees with *H*. In all points in which *S* differs from *F* we find it also differing from *H*.

Thus the game of blowing a burning coal, in the description of which *S* slightly differs from *F*, is related in *H* with nearly the same words as in *F*. As, besides the small fragment printed by Grœber in the *Jahrbuch*, xiii, and some few remarks in the *Zeitschrift für rom. Phil.*, nothing is known of the Hanover MS., the following passages printed here may serve to show how little *H* differs from *F*. The game of the coal (*S* 1996—2016, *F* 2907—2934) is thus described in *H*, leaf 58 :—

"Veillard, dist Lucafer, vo*us* ni savez juer,
Vo*us* ne savez en Fr*ance* le g*ra*nt charboun soffler.
Certes, ceo dist li dus, mais n'en oie soffler.
Et respont li payen : Mais te feray mostrer.
Ly payen vait le duc au g*ra*nt fowel mener.
Q*ua*nt Rollant l'ad veu, a Berard l'ad mostre
Orc po*r*res boue jeu ver *et* esgarder.
Dahait qui ne laira ly *et* Naimes juer.
Lucafer se beysa pur un tison combrer,
Trestote le plus ardant quil i poet trover,
Par tiel air soffla le fu qil li fist voler.
Puis ad dist a Names 'Ore vo*us* cove*nt* soffler.'
Names prist le tison qui bien se sout aider,
Vers le payen s'en va pur le tison sofler.
Pur ceo le fist ly dus qa ly se volt meller,
Si suffla le tison qe le fist allumer,
Le barbe *et* le menton fist au payen bruler,
Tres pa*r*my le visaie en fist la flame virer,
Qe par un sule petite qe nel fist souuiler.
Q*ua*nt le voit ly payen, le sanc quida deueher.
Il jette a .ij. ses maines, qi le quide frapper,
Mais ly dus le ferry tres pa*r*my le costes,
Qe les oilz de la teste ly fist en fu voler.
Puys l'ad pris par le flank, s'il voit en le fu ruer.
Lichiers, dist dus Names, Dex te poet mal doner,
Tu me quidoies ore come fole cy trover."

The distribution of the relics, in which *S* (cf. note to l. 3238) differs from *F* 6195 *et seq.* is related as follows in *H*, leaf 100 :—

"AU baron seint Dynis fu mult g*ra*nt l'assemble*e*
Au perron au londy fu la messe chante*e*,
Illok fu la corone pa*r*tie *et* dessevere*e*,
L'un moite fu a saint Dynis donee
Et un clow ansieme*nt*, cest ve*r*ite provee,
De la Corone fu un pa*r*tic a Ais porte*e*,
A Compaign*e* est l'ensigne en l'eglise honorce,
Et les altres .ij. clowes a Orliens fu enveie*e*,
Maint p*r*esant fist Charls de France la loie
Des saintisme reliqes, Jhe*s*u de maiestes.
En l'onur de Deu est mainte eglise fonde*e*,
La feste de lendit fu pur iceo estore*e*.
Jaiaz viderout cens ne taille donce.

No tardoit *que* .iiij. ans k'Espaigne fu gaste*e*.
La fu la treison de Rollant *por*pense*e*,
Qe Ganes le vendist a la gent difface,
Puys fu as chiuals sa chars destreinee,
Pinables en fu mortz de suz Lyons en la pre*e*,
La le vengea Terris au trenchant del espee,
Puys fu pendu armes par gule*e* paree,
Toutz iours vegnent traitors a mal destine*e*
Ou aloignee ou apres ia ni aueront duree.
Charles voit a Orliens, la chancheon est finee
Au deu vo*us* commande, tote j'ai ma chancon fine.
De cels romance est bone la fine *et* l'entre*e*,
Et en mileue *et* par*tote* qi bi*en* l'ad escoutee
La beneiceon aez de Deu *et* del vi*r*gine honore. Amen."

The miracle (*F* 6101—6123)[1] of the glove, in which Charles had placed fragments of the thorns, remaining suspended in the air for over an hour, the description of which is omitted in the *Sowdan* (cf. *Dissert.*, p. 29), is related as follows in *H*, leaf 99 :—

"L'EMP*ER*ERS de France fist forem*en*t a loier
Il a fait un table sur .ij. trestes lever.
Et par de sur un paille q*ui* fu fait outre mer.
Illok fist Charlm̄ la corone aporter,
Puis ad fait l'arcevesqe pa*r*tir *et* deviser,
Si ad fait les reliqes m*u*lt bi*en* envoluper,
Dedens son mestre coffres les a fait deffermer,
Et les altres reliqes qe il voudra aporter.
Les petites espignons qil vist esgruner,
De la saint corone qil fist demenbrer,
Trestote les acoillye n*os*tre emp*er*er ber,
Et les mist en son gant qanqil pout trover.
Un chivaler le tent qil vist lez ly ester,
Mais al ne l'ap*er*ceut my qe nele oit parler.
Charlemayn retiret sa mayne, si lesso le gant aler.
Et dex a fait le gant enmy l'air arester
Tant q*ue* d .j. leue en pout home bi*en* aler ;
Kar la presse fu grant, ne l'en puis remenbrer.
Charlemayn comande l'ewe apporter.
De son gant ly sovengre si *quant* il dust laver,
Mais ne seet a ky le comanda abailier,
Par desur la gent le vist en l'air esteer,
L'arcevesqe la monstre *et* tuit l'altre barne.
Ceo fu mult g*r*ant m*er*veille, hom*e* en doit bi*en* parler,
Charls a pris son gant, s'est assis au soper."

H, leaf 37, agrees with *F*, l. 1043, in making Oliver drink of the bottles of balm, which is not mentioned in the *Sowdan*, l. 1190 (cf. p. xxix).

[1] Cf. *Sir Ferumbras*, 185/5988.

Similarly we find *S* 2604 differing from *H*, leaf 62, where we read *Basyns* (= *Basin*, *F* 3313) instead of *Bryer*.

Again *H*, l. 40, agreeing exactly with *F*, l. 1329 *et seq.*, differs from *S* 1279-82 (cf. p. xxix).

Instead of Floripas, *S* 1515, it is Brulans, *H*, l. 49, and *F* 1949, who advises the Soudan not to slay the prisoners.

The names of the twelve peers are the same in *H* as in *F* (cf. p. xxvii); and the whole scene of the peers being sent one after the other on a mission to Laban (cf. note to l. 1665 of the *Sowdan*) is described exactly alike in *F* 2263—2282 and in *H*, leaf 51, back, with the only difference that the names of the peers are given in a different order in both versions, Richard of Normandy, who is sent off as the sixth in *F*, being the second in *H*.

These variations of *S* from *H* clearly exemplify the impossibility of regarding the Hanover MS. as the original of the *Sowdan*. But as on the whole these differences are not of a very significant nature, and as, moreover, part of these variations may perhaps be attributed to the favourite habit of the author of going his own way in the arrangement of the subject-matter and in some minor points, whereas in the essential course of the events he strictly adhered to his source (see above p. xxxviii, and cf. note to l. 2535); and as besides there are several names, the spelling of which differs in *F*, agreeing in *S* and *H*, I think there can be no doubt that the original of the second part of the *Sowdan* was a version similar to the Hanover MS.

If now we compare the Hanover version with the Ashmole *Ferumbras* more closely than has been possible on page xx, there are some instances where *A*, whilst differing from *F*, agrees with *H*.

H.	A.
lf. 27. Ha *Glout*, dist Karlemaines,	163. A *glotoun*, saide þe Emperer
lf. 27. Que puis *vivre* que cest jours fu passes	175. Ke *lyve* he noȝt þys day to be evene
lf. 25, bk. Ses chiuals ad reine à un arbre rasmee Et garda les leges tote contreval li pree	91. Þarto ys stede þan tyeþe he

Nevertheless, the following passage in which *A* agrees with *F*, but differs from *H*, will at once show the impossibility of regarding *H* as the original of *A*.

A.	H.
302. Þanne þer come bifore Charloun, Gweneloun and *Hardree*	lf. 28, bk. Atant se sunt drecie Guinelons et *Alores*

In other instances *A* is found differing from *H* as well as from *F*. Thus the name of *Enfachoun*, *A* 4652, which is *Effraons* in *F* 4900, does not occur at all in *H*, which in the passage corresponding to *F* 4900, as well as in that corresponding to *F* 4913, reads *Affricons li Geans*.

Again, in the story of Myloun, in which *A*, l. 2008 *et seq*., differs from *F*, we find *H* disagreeing from *F*, 2734 *et seq*., and from *A* :—

"Volez vo*us* queor de feme essaier *et* esprover
Del riche duc Milon vo*us* deverez remenbrer,
Qe tant nori Galans qe ly fist adouber,
Puys ly tolly sa feile Gabaen au vis cler,
L'enfes Marsilion en fist desherriter.—
Qu*ant* l'entent Floripas, du sens quida deueer."—(*H*, leaf 56.)

But in most cases in which *F* differs from *A*, *H* agrees with *F*.

Thus we find Ferumbras challenging only *six* French knights in *H*, lf. 26, as in *F*, 84, 105, instead of *twelve* in *A*, l. 102.

In *A*, l. 5204, Floripas, swooning away, is upheld by Oliver, whereas in *F*, 5373, and in *H*, lf. 90, it is Guy who keeps her from falling.

For *Howel of saint Miloun*, *A* 5574, we read *Huon de saint Lis* in *F* 5792, and *Hugon de saint Lis* in *H*, lf. 95, bk.

As in *F* 2912 it is to Berard that Roland speaks in *H*, lf. 57, bk., and not to Olyver, as in *A* 2234.

That Maubyn scales the walls by means of a ladder of leather (*A* 2406) is not mentioned in *F* 3061, nor in *H*, lf. 59, bk.

In *A* 1386 Floripas gives Oliver, who is wounded, a warm draught, which heals every wound; in *F* 2209, as well as in *H*, lf. 51, it is by a bit of the mandrake plant that he is healed.

The maid-attendant mentioned in *A* 1238 (*chamberere*) is a man-attendant in *F* 2083 (*chamberlenc*) and in *H*, lf. 49, bk. (*chamberlayn*).

There is no trace of the additional lines of *A*, ll. 4867—4875, to be found in *H*, lf. 86 bk., nor in *F*, 5094.

Among the relics spoken of in *A*, there is nowhere a mention made of the *signe*. In *H* we find the *signe* always mentioned together with the crown and the nails, just as in *F*. In the passage quoted above from *H*, lf. 100, and in the line which corresponds to *F* 6094, we find *ensigne* instead of *signe;* but *ensigne* certainly must be looked upon as a clerical blunder. In the other passages in which we find "the winding sheet, or shroud, of the Lord" mentioned in *H* it is also called *signe*:—

"Et rendrai la corone et le *signe* honore."
H, lf. 42 = *F*, 1498; and *H*, lf. 45, bk. = *F*, 1805.
"Et les saintismes clowes et le *signe* honores."—*H*, lf. 57 = *F*, 2829.

That the *signe* cannot be the "inscription of the cross" (cf. *Introduction*, p. xxx) is proved by an additional line of the Hanover MS., in which the Archbishop is said to have covered the heads of the French with the *signe*:—

"Puys a trait l'ensigne qui bien estoit ovres
Engenolant l'ad ly Rois tote oue lermes baises,
Plus flairoit ducement que basine enbasines.
Quant Franceis l'ont veu, ele vous effraes,
De pite et de ioy fu chescous enplores.
L'ercevesqe le prist, mult fu bien purpenses,
Et nos Franceis en a les chefs envolupes,
Puis le mist sur le paille qest a or ornes,
Od les altres relikes dont illi out asses."
H, lf. 98, corresponding to *F*, 6094 *et seq.*

Abstaining now from citing any more passages where *H* agrees with *F*, but differs from *A*, I think the few quotations above will suffice to show the impossibility of regarding the Hanover MS. as the original of the Ashmole *Ferumbras*, notwithstanding that there are some resemblances of *A* to *H* (cf. p. xx). Therefore the result arrived at on p. xxi as to the original of the Ashmolean version is in no way altered by the detailed comparison of *A* with *H*.

SKETCH OF THE STORY.

Laban, the Soudan of Babylon, who was residing at Agremore in Spain, went to the chase in a wood near the sea (p. 2). Being tired of hunting he sat down under a tree, and, perceiving a ship drawing near unto the shore, he sent one of his men to hail the vessel and to inquire for news. The interpreter of the vessel informs the soudan that the ship, freighted with a rich cargo at Babylon designed as a present to Laban, had been driven by violent storms to the shore near Rome, where the ship had been robbed, and many of its people had been slain by the Romans. He solicits the Soudan to revenge this insult. Laban promises to make them pay dearly for it (p. 3). He convokes a war-council, and assembles a hundred thousand men and seven hundred sail. Himself goes, with Ferumbras his son and Floripas his daughter, in a dromond richly adorned (p. 4). They disembark in the haven of Rome, slay all Christians, and burn towns, abbeys, and churches. The pope of Rome assembles his council (p. 5). Duke Savaris is to meet the Saracens. With ten thousand men he draws near the Soudan's pavilion on the shore (p. 6); they slay ten thousand Saracens. The Romans, though masters of the field, cautiously retire within the walls of the city. Lukafer of Baldas, having scoured the country, brings ten thousand Christian maidens to the Soudan, who orders them to be put to death (p. 7). Lukafer demands Floripas for his wife, in return for which he promises her father to bring Charlemagne and his twelve peers to the foot of his throne. Floripas agrees to accept him when he has fulfilled his promise. The next morning Lukafer assaults the city, but the ditches being too deep (p. 8), the Saracens are obliged to retire. On the following day the assault is renewed, the ditches are, on Mavon's advice, filled with faggots. After a sharp conflict, where there were ten thousand Saracens slain by the stones of the Romans, the heathens are obliged to withdraw (p. 9). This second repulse makes the Soudan almost mad with vexation; he chides his gods. But Lukafer told him that he had learned from a spy that Savaris would, on the following day, come out again to fight with them. He now intended, when Savaris was engaged in the battle, to unfold a banner made exactly like that of the Romans, and to attempt, by this stratagem, to be admitted within the gates. And so it turned out: the Romans mistaking him for Savaris returning from his sally, he entered the main tower, and slew all therein. Savaris, noticing the artifice of the enemy, and seeing his troop reduced to seventy-two men, turned back, but found the gate shut (p. 10). Estragot, a black giant of Ethiopia, slays him with his steel-mace. The Pope having summoned his council, a senator suggested the necessity of sending messengers to Charlemagne to ask his aid. They all assented, and three messengers (p. 11) left the city by a postern at midnight; they passed the enemy's camp without being noticed by any wight. On the next morning Laban attempted a third assault; he commanded every man to throw pikes and bills over the walls to kill the Romans, and ordered the ships to go up the water with their boats bound to the mast, that they might fight in close combat. Near the tower there stood a bulwark, or "bastile," which was a strong defence to the wall. It was thrown down by stones hurled from an engine. Laban, growing proud from this event, summoned the Romans to surrender. Instead of an answer a Roman hurled a dart at his breast-plate, but his hauberk shielded him. The Soudan, more than mad, charged Ferumbras to destroy them all (p. 12), and enjoined Fortibrance and Mavon to direct their engines against the walls. The great glutton Estragot, with his heavy mace, smote on the gates and brake them in pieces. But as he was entering one of the gates, they let the portcullis fall, which crushed him to the ground, where he lay crying like a devil of hell. The Romans rejoiced, but the Saracens grieved. They withdrew to their tents, leaving behind the corpse of Estragot, whose soul went up to Mahound (p. 13). The Pope called all his people to St. Peter's and proposed to them to attempt a sally with twenty thousand men, to attack the enemy before day-break within their camp, and to leave ten thousand for the defence of the city. In the morning the Pope displayed the banner of Rome, and after a prayer for the preservation of the city, they marched out. But Ferumbras, going his rounds (p. 14), noticed their coming, sounded the alarm, and drew up his troops. Then began a fierce struggle. Ferumbras slew Sir Bryer of Apulia (p. 15) and the worthy Hubert. Nine thousand heathens were killed and eight thousand Romans. Lukafer destroyed eighteen Romans; he also slew Gyndard, a senator of Rome, who had killed ten Saracens. Then came the Pope with a great escort and his banner before him. Ferumbras, supposing him to be the sovereign (p. 16), burst open the thick crowd and threw him down to the ground. But having opened his ventail, he saw his tonsure, and recognized the Pope. "Fie, priest," he said, "what doest thou here in the battle-field?

It would be a shame for me to slay thee. Go home and think of thy choir-service." The Pope, being glad to get off so easily, retired to Rome with five thousand men, fifteen thousand being killed. Charlemagne, having learned from the messenger the great disaster which had befallen the Romans, said he would not desist until he had chased the Soudan and Ferumbras out of Christendom (p. 17). He gave ten thousand pounds of francs to his nephew, Guy of Burgundy, and sent him off with orders to advance against the Soudan by forced marches. Himself would follow as soon as possible. In the mean time Laban reminded Lukafer of his vaunting promise to bring him Charlemagne and his twelve peers in return for his daughter Floripas. Lukafer said he would do all he had promised. With ten thousand men he attacked the city on one side, the other being assaulted by Ferumbras. The combat continued as long as daylight lasted. At night they retired to their tents (p. 18). Then treason was planned by Isres, who by inheritance possessed the guard of the chief gate of the town. He went to the Soudan and offered to betray the city on condition that his life and property should be spared. The Soudan promised it. Ferumbras with twenty thousand men went with Isres, but on entering the gate he caused the traitor's head to be struck off by the portcullis and to be carried on the point of a spear through the city. "Treason," cried the people (p. 19), when Ferumbras advanced into Rome. All the streets were soon covered with dead men. Ferumbras went to St. Peter's, seized the relics, the cross, the crown, and the nails, burned the whole city, and carried away all the treasures and the gold to Agremore in Spain, where the Soudan went back to stay. Three months and three days they spent there in great festivities, making offerings to their gods, and burning frankincense in their honour. They drank the blood of beasts and milk, and ate honey, and snakes fried with oil (p. 20). When Sir Guy, approaching, drew near Rome, he found the whole city in flames. He grieved much that he had arrived too late, and resolved to wait there for Charlemagne, and then to tell him how Laban had burnt the city, and had sent the relics to Agremore, his principal town in Spain. Soon king Charles advanced to rescue Rome with his twelve peers and three hundred thousand soldiers (p. 21). Roland led the vanguard, Oliver the rear, and the king was with the main body. The provisions were conveyed by sea. Guy, seeing the army come, went to meet the king, and told him the mischief done by the Soudan, who, moreover, had made a vow to seek Charles in France in order to afflict him with grief. "He will find me near," said Charles, "and shall pay dearly for it. Unless he consents to be baptized (p. 22), he shall never see Babylon again." They all took ship without delay. Propitious winds drove them into the river Gase, where they landed, thirty miles from Agremore, and laid waste the country. Laban, hearing this news, was astonished at Charles's presumption (p. 23). He assembled all his barons, and charged them to bring him alive that glutton that called himself king of France, and to slay the rest of his army. Ferumbras went forth with many Saracens. He meets with Roland. They deal each other heavy strokes. Oliver cuts off a quarter of Lukafer's shield. The combat lasted the whole day. Well fought the twelve peers (p. 24). Ferumbras charges Oliver. King Charles, seeing this, rides at Ferumbras, and strikes his helm with a heavy mace. Ferumbras cannot approach him on account of the crowd. Charlemagne slew thirty Saracens with his sword Mounjoy. Lukafer of Baldas encountering Charles told him that he had promised the Soudan to bring him Charles and the twelve peers. Charles strikes him on his helmet (p. 25), but Lukafer is rescued by a great throng. Roland, drawing Durnedale, cleared a space around him, and hammered the heads of the Saracens. So did the other peers, and thirty thousand Saracens were slain. At night the pagans quit the field. Ferumbras vows never to desist until he has conquered Roland and Oliver (p. 26) and been crowned king at Paris. Charles went to his pavilion and thanked God and St. Mary of France. He praised the elder knights for having won the victory, and exhorted the young ones to take example by them. They all make merry and go to supper. The Saracens address a prayer to the red Mars Armipotent (p. 27), to grant the Mahometans the victory over the Christians (p. 28). In order to recruit the late losses in his army, the Soudan sent for his vassals, and assembled more than three hundred thousand Saracens at Agremore. He addressed them (p. 29) in order to increase their ardour, ordered a solemn sacrifice to his gods, and charged Ferumbras to march with thirty thousand of his people against the Christian king (whom he wished to teach courtesy), and to slay all his men except Roland and Oliver (p. 30), if they would renounce their gods. Ferumbras led out his troops; until arriving near Charles's camp, he ordered them to halt in a wood, and advanced with only ten of his men to the camp of Charlemagne, and offered to fight at once against six of his peers. If he should conquer them, he would lead them away to his father's hall; but if he should be conquered, he would be Charles's man. The king sent for Roland and ordered him to undertake the combat. Roland refuses (p. 31), because Charles had praised the old knights: they might show their prowess now. Charles, vexed, smites Roland on the mouth, so that the blood springs from his nose, and he calls him a traitor. Roland draws his sword, but the other barons separate them and try to conciliate them. Meanwhile Oliver, who being sorely wounded kept his bed, on hearing of this dispute, had armed himself and went to Charles. He reminds the king of his long services, in reward for which he demands the battle. Charles remonstrates with him. But Oliver insists (p. 32). He rides to the forest, and finds Ferumbras alighted under a tree, to a branch of which his steed was tied. "Arise," he said, "I am come to fight with thee." Ferumbras, without moving, demands his name. "I am Generyse, a young knight lately dubbed." Ferumbras observes: "Charles is a fool to send thee; go and tell him to send me Roland and Oliver and such four other douzeperes. For little honour were it to me to fight with thee." "Spare thy words," replies Oliver, "and take thy arms" (p. 33). Ferumbras is wrath and seizes his helmet, which Oliver assists him to lace. Ferumbras thanks him, courteously bowing to him. They mount their steeds, and rushing together like fire of thunder, they have their lances broken. They draw their swords. Ferumbras smites Oliver on his helmet so that the fire flies. Oliver strikes at the head of Ferumbras, breaks away the circle of his helmet, and the sword glancing off down his back, he cuts off two bottles of balm (p. 34), which he throws into the river. Ferumbras tells him that they were invaluable to a wounded man, and that he should atone for their loss with his life. He strikes at Oliver, who wards off the blow with his shield, but his steed is killed under him. Oliver quickly starts up and tries to kill his adversary's horse, but Ferumbras rides off and ties it to a hazel. "Yield thyself to me," says Ferumbras, "believe on Mahound, and I will make thee a duke in my country, and give thee my sister" (p. 35). "Ere I yield to thee," answered Oliver, "thou shalt feel my strokes." They fight for a considerable time; the blood runs from both their bodies. By mutual consent they stop to take breath. Ferumbras again asks Oliver his name and kin. "Thou must be one of the twelve peers, as thou fightest so well." "I am Oliver, cousin to Charlemagne." "Thou art welcome here," says Ferumbras; "thou slewest my uncle (p. 36); now thou shalt pay the penalty." The fight continued the whole day. At last Oliver, smiting Ferumbras upon the helmet, had his sword broken. He ran to the steed at the tree and seized a sword that was hanging there, but in turning on Ferumbras, he received a blow that made him kneel down (p. 37). But he returns Ferumbras a fearful stroke. Charles, seeing Oliver on his knees, prayed to Christ that he might grant the victory over the pagan. An angel announced to him that his prayer was heard. Charles thanks God (p. 38). The fight begins again. Ferumbras breaks his sword on Oliver's helmet. He runs for another and asks Oliver to surrender. But Oliver aims at him a blow which cuts his hauberk, so that his bowels are laid bare. Ferumbras implores his mercy, and consents to be christened, his gods having proved false. He requested him to take his hauberk (p. 39), to fetch his horse, and to carry him to his own tent. But the Saracens who lay concealed in the wood rush out. Oliver, being surrounded, sets down Ferumbras under an olive-tree, and defends himself with his sword, dealing the Saracens many a hard blow. Then Roland rushed into the throng of the enemy and slew many (p. 40). His horse being killed by arrows and darts, he fights on foot, but his sword breaking, he is taken and led away. Oliver rides to rescue him, but his horse being also killed, he is overpowered and bound. Both were conducted to Lukafer of Baldas (p. 41). Charles sees them, and calls for a rescue. Many enemies were slain by the French barons, but the Saracens had fled with their prisoners, and

Charles is obliged to turn back. Under a holm tree they find Ferumbras, whom the king is going to put to death. But on his requesting to be baptized Charles took pity on him (p. 42), led him to his tent, and ordered a surgeon to attend him. He soon recovered, and bishop Turpin baptized him by the name of Floreyn. But he continued to be called Ferumbras all his life. Afterwards he was known as Floreyn of Rome on account of his holiness. Roland and Oliver being brought to the Soudan, Laban enquires their names. They confess their names (p. 43). The Soudan swears they shall both be executed the next morning before his dinner. But Floripas advises him to detain them as hostages, and to remember his son Ferumbras, for whom they might be exchanged. The Soudan, finding her counsel good, orders his gaoler Bretomayn to imprison them, but to leave them without food (p. 44). At high tide the sea filled their deep cells, so that they suffered much from the salt water, from their wounds, and from hunger. On the sixth day Floripas, who was gathering flowers in her garden, heard them lament. Moved to compassion, she asks her governess Maragound to help her in getting food for the prisoners. Maragound refuses, and reminds Floripas of her father's command. Floripas, thinking of a trick, called to her governess to come to a window (p. 45) and see the porpoises sporting beneath. As Maragound is looking out, Floripas pushes her into the flood. She then asks Bretomayn to let her see the prisoners. The gaoler threatened to complain to her father, but Floripas, having seized his key-clog, dashed out his brains. She then went to tell her father she had surprised the gaoler feeding the prisoners (p. 46) and promising to deliver them, wherefore she had slain him. The Soudan gives the prisoners into her guard. She now proceeded to the prison, asked the prisoners what they wanted, and promised to protect them from any harm (p. 47). She let down a rope, and with her maidens drew up both, and led them to her apartments. There they ate, took a bath, and went to bed. The Soudan knew nothing of his prisoners being in Floripas's chamber. Meanwhile Charlemagne tells Guy that he must go to the Soudan to demand the surrender of Roland and Oliver, and of the relics of Rome Naymes of Bavaria represents that a messenger to the Soudan

(p. 48) would certainly be slain; and that they ought to be anxious not to lose any more besides Roland and Oliver. Then said the king: "By God, thou shalt go with Guy." Ogier the Dane remonstrates, but is ordered to go too. So are Thierry of Ardane, and Folk Baliant, Aleroys, and Miron of Brabant. Bishop Turpin kneels down to implore the king's mercy, but he must go too, as well as Bernard of Spruwse (p. 49) and Brier of Mountdidier. The knights take leave and start. About the same time the Soudan having assembled his council, Sortibrance and Brouland (p. 50) advise him to send twelve knights, and to bid Charles to give up Ferumbras and to withdraw from his country. The knights are despatched; near Mantrible they meet with the Christian messengers. Duke Naymes enquires whither they intend to go (p. 51). Having heard their message, the delegates of Charlemagne cut off their heads, which they take with them to present to the Soudan at Agremore. Laban was just dining when Naymes delivers his message: "God confound Laban and all his Saracens, and save Charles, who commands thee to send back his two nephews and to restore the relics" (p. 52). They then produce the heads of the Soudan's messengers. The Soudan vowed a vow that they should all ten be hanged as soon as he had finished his dinner. But Floripas recommended him to put off his resolution until a general council of his barons had determined on the best way to procure the liberation of Ferumbras. Thereupon the Soudan gives the prisoners into her guard. Floripas leads the knights into her tower (p. 53), where they were glad to find Roland and Oliver. They told each other how they had fared. After washing, they dined off venison, bread, and wine. The following day Floripas asks Naymes his name, and enquires after Guy of Burgundy, whom she had loved for a long time (p. 54), and for whom she would do all she could for their benefit, and would be baptized if he would agree to love her in return. Naymes tells Guy to take her for his wife; but Guy refuses, as he never will take a wife unless she be given him by Charles. But Roland and Oliver persuade him, so that he at last consents. Floripas, holding a golden cup of wine (p. 55), kissed him, and requested him to drink to her after the fashion of her country; she then would drink to him in return. They all make merry, and prepare to assail the Soudan at supper on the follow ing day. Meanwhile Lukafer comes to the Soudan and asks leave to see the prisoners, in order to know how Floripas guards them. Finding the door locked (p. 56), he burst it open with a blow of his fist, and told them he was come to speak to them, and to enquire after Charlemagne. Duke Naymes answers. Lukafer then asks what amusements they have after dinner. Naymes says: "Some joust, some sing, some play at chess." "I will teach you a new game," says Lukafer (p. 57). With a thread he fastened a needle on a pole and put a burning coal upon it. He blew it at Naymes's beard and burnt it. Naymes waxed wroth, and snatching a burning brand from the fire he smites at Lukafer, and throws him into the fire, where he was burnt to charcoal. Floripas applauds this, but points out their danger, and advises them to arm. At supper time she goes to her father (p. 58). As they were sitting at table, the twelve peers rushed in and slew all whom they met. Laban, pursued by Oliver, jumps out of a window on to the sea-shore and escaped without injury. They killed all in the castle, and then drew up the bridges and shut the gates. Laban vowed a vow that he would hang them all and burn his daughter. He sent to Mantrible for troops (p. 59) and engines and besieged Agremore. Floripas recommends the peers to enjoy themselves. In the morning the Soudan attacks the castle, but is repulsed (p. 60). He accuses his gods of sleepiness and shakes them to rouse them out of sleep. Brouland tells him, as the castle is strong and well stored with provisions, the peers will hold it very long; but if he would send orders to Alagolofer, the bridge-keeper at Mantrible, not to allow any one to pass without leave (p. 61), they would get no assistance from Charles and die from hunger. Espiard, the Soudan's messenger, is despatched to Mantrible, and commands the giant not to suffer any one to pass the bridge (p. 62). Alagolofer drew four and twenty chains across the bridge. Meanwhile the Soudan assaults the castle again, but the twelve peers slew three hundred Saracens (p. 63). Laban threatens to hang them, and utters imprecations against Floripas, who returns them. He then calls for Mavon, his engineer, and orders him to direct a mangonel against the walls. Mavon knocked down a piece of the battlements.

Roland and Oliver lament; they are comforted by Floripas (p. 64). Guy kills Marsedage, the king of Barbary, by throwing a dart at him. The Saracens stop the attack to bury Marsedage, and bewail him seven nights and seven days. Then the Soudan more closely blockades the castle (p. 65). The provisions being exhausted, Roland complains of Charles's forgetfulness; but Floripas cheers him up, saying she possessed a magic girdle, which was a talisman against hunger and thirst for those who wore it. They all successively put it on, and felt as if they had feasted (p. 66). Laban wondered at their endurance, but at last remembering the girdle, he induced Mapin to attempt to steal it at night. Mapin entered the chamber of Floripas (p. 67) through a chimney. He finds the girdle and puts it on, but Floripas perceives him and cries out. Roland hurries to her assistance, cuts off Mapin's head, and throws him out through the window into the sea without noticing the girdle. Floripas, seeing her girdle lost, is much grieved; Roland comforts her. They agree to attempt a sally to obtain food (p. 68). In the morning Naymes and Ogier remain in the castle, while the others start and surprise the Saracens sleeping in their huts. They slew three hundred, and carried off as much food as they could bear (p. 69). The Soudan is enraged and is going to burn his gods, but, appeased by his wise men, he sacrifices again, and is assoiled by the priests. Laban holds council (p. 70). A new assault begins, but so many of the assailants were slain by the showers of stones hurled down by the peers that the ditches are filled with dead bodies. The Saracens retire. But soon a second attack ensues. There being no stones, Floripas gave them her father's silver and gold to cast amongst the assailants. The Soudan in alarm for his treasure gives up the assault (p. 71). He is enraged with his gods, and smites Mahound so that he fell on his face; but the priests induce him to kneel down and ask forgiveness (p. 72). Meanwhile Roland exhorted Richard of Normandy to go on a message to Charles, that he might come to their rescue. They all would, the following morning before day-break, make an attack on the Saracens, and meanwhile he should steal off in the darkness. In the morning they sally out. Floripas and her maidens draw up the bridges after them. Richard went off towards Mantrible (p. 73).

The others slay many Saracens; but Guy, overpowered by the Babylonians, is taken prisoner. Laban asks his name. Guy tells him. He is to be hanged. Three hundred Saracens crowding near the gate of the castle, attempted to prevent the other peers from entering. A fearful struggle begins (p. 74), in which Sir Bryer is killed. At last the Saracens take to flight. The peers retire inside the castle, taking the corpse of Bryer with them. Floripas enquires after Guy, and on hearing of his capture, begins to lament despairingly. Roland promises to rescue Guy (p. 75). On the following morning Laban orders Sir Tamper to erect a gallows before the castle, where Floripas could see it. Guy is led bound. Roland calls his companions to arms. They rush forth (p. 76). Oliver cuts down Sir Tamper, Roland kills a king of India, takes his sword and horse, and gives them to Guy, having unbound him. They slay many Saracens, and put the rest to flight. Retiring towards the castle, they see Admiral Costroye, and the Soudan's standard-bearer, escorting a great convoy, destined for the sultan, across a field near the high road (p. 77). Roland calls to them to share the provisions with them. Costroye refuses, and is slain by Roland. Oliver kills the standard-bearer, and the convoy is conveyed into the castle (p. 78). Floripas thanks Roland for bringing back Sir Guy, and proposes that he shall choose himself a mistress from amongst her maidens. But Roland refuses to take any that is not a Christian. The Soudan, on hearing such bad news, again defies his gods, and threatens to throw them into the flames (p. 79). But bishop Cramadas kneels before him and appeases him. The Soudan makes an offering of a thousand besants to his gods. When Richard arrived as far as Mantrible, he found the bridge barred by twenty-four chains, and Alagolofer standing before it. Determined not to leave his errand unperformed, he knelt down and commended himself to God. A hind appears (p. 80) and swims across the river; Richard follows her, and passing over in safety, hurries on to Charlemagne. Meanwhile Genelyn, the traitor, had advised Charles to retire to France, because the twelve peers were all slain. The king believed him, and marched homeward, lamenting for his peers. Richard overtakes him. and is recognized by Charles, who asks him about the others.

Richard tells the king how they are besieged within the castle of Agremore, and are waiting for his assistance. Charles, vowing vengeance on Genelyn (p. 81), turned and marched to Agremore. Richard informed him of the giant who kept the bridge, and how he had passed the river by a miracle. He proposed a plan that twelve knights, disguised as merchants, with their arms hidden under their clothes, should pay the toll, and the bridge being let down, they should blow a horn as a signal for the others to approach. They start and arrive at Mantrible (p. 82). Alagolofer asks whither they are going. Richard says they are merchants on their way to the Soudan, and they are willing to pay the toll. Alagolofer refuses to let them pass, and tells them about the ten knights, who had passed there and done so much mischief to the Soudan; therefore he will arrest them all. Sir Focard draws his sword and smites at him, Richard blows his horn, and Charles advances (p. 83). Alagolofer fights them with a great oak club. Richard seizes a bar of brass and knocks him down. Four men get hold of him and throw him into the river. They loosened the chains; but the Saracens assembling on the walls of the city, many Christians were slain. Alagolofer's wife, Barrock the giantess, comes on with her scythe and mows down all whom she meets. Charles dashes out her brains (p. 84), and with fifteen knights enters the outer gate of the town, thinking his army would follow him. But the gate was instantly closed upon him, and his men came too late. Charles was in great danger; but Genelyn, seeing him shut in, exclaimed that the king and the twelve peers were dead, and proposed to retire, as he wished to be king himself. They were going to return, but Ferumbras (p. 85) calls him a traitor; he rallies the French, and with his axe bursts open the gate. He chased the Saracens and rescued the king. Mantrible is taken with all its engines and treasures. Richard found two children of seven months old (p. 86), and four feet high. They were sons of Barrock, begotten by Astragot. Charles caused them to be baptized, and called the one Roland and the other Oliver. But they soon died for want of their mother's milk The king appoints Richard governor of the city, and hurries on to Agremore with his army and with Ferumbras (p. 87). Laban, being told by a spy that his city was taken and the bridge-ward killed, swears to avenge him. He calls a council, and charges his barons to take Charles alive that he might flay him. Charles approaches. Floripas first recognizes the banner of France and tells the others (p. 88). Roland and all his companions sally forth to meet Charlemagne. Laban draws up all his people in battle-order. The French make a great slaughter of the Saracens. Charles encounters the Soudan; he unhorses him, and would have cut off his head, but for Ferumbras, who requested that his father might be baptized. The Saracens, seeing Laban a prisoner, fly; but the Christians pursue them. Three hundred escaped to Belmarine. Charles leads Laban to Agremore. Floripas welcomes her father (p. 89), but he is enraged at seeing her. She then bids Charlemagne welcome, and presents the holy relics to him. Charles kisses them, and says a prayer; he then thanks Floripas for her assistance to his knights, and for having preserved the precious relics. He orders Turpin to prepare a vessel wherein to baptize the Soudan, and to wash off his sin in the water (p. 90). Turpin leads Laban to the font, but the Soudan strikes at him, spits on the vessel, utters invectives against all Christians, and curses Ferumbras. Charles commands Naymes to cut off his head. He is executed; his soul goes to hell, there to dance with devils. Floripas was baptized with all her maidens, and was wedded to Guy. Charles divided Spain between Guy and Ferumbras (p. 91), and charges Sir Bryer of Bretayne to take care of the relics, and to bring all his treasure to Paris. After taking leave of Guy and Floripas, Charles sails to Monpilier, where he thanks God for the victory (p. 92), and for the relics. He presents the cross to Paris, the crown to St. Denis, the three nails to Boulogne. Charles well remembered the treachery of Genelyn, and ordered him to be drawn and hanged at Montfaucon in Paris (p. 93).

The Romaunce of the Sowdone of Babylone and of Ferumbras his Sone who Conquerede Rome:

From the unique MS. of the late Sir Thos. Phillipps.

God in glorye of myghteste[1] moost,
That al thinge made in sapience
By vertue of woorde and holy goost,
Gyvinge to man grete excellence,
And alle, þat is in erthe, wroght
Subiecte to man and man̄ to the,
That he shoulde with̄ herte and thought
To loue and serve, and noon but the:
For ȝyfe man̄ kepte thy co*m*maundemente
In al thinge and loued the welle
And hadde synnede in his entente,
Than shulde he fully thy grace fele;
But for the offences to God I-doo*n*[2]
Many vengeaunces haue be-falle.
Where-of I wole you telle of oon,
It were to moch̄ to telle of alle.
While þat Rome was in excellence
Of alle Realmes in dignite,
And howe it felle for his offence,
Listinythe a while and ye shal see,
Howe it was wonen and brente
Of a Sowdon, that heathen was,
And for synne howe it was shente;
As Kinge Lowes witnessith þat cas,

God has ordained all things wisely.

He has subjected the earth to man, and man to God.

The man who keeps His commandments and loves Him well,

will feel His grace.
But many who offended Him have felt His vengeance.
I will tell you of one; it would take too long to tell of all.

Listen to me, and ye shall hear how Rome, the former mistress of all nations, came to fall by its sins,

and was destroyed by a heathen Soudan.

King Lewis has borne witness to

[1] *Read:* myghtes [2] *MS.* dōō

that story, which, written in Romance and found in very old chronicles at St Denys in France, relates

As it is wryten in Romaunce
And founden in bokes of Antiquyte
At Seinte Denyse Abbey in Fraunc[e],[1]
There as Cronycles remembrede be,

how Laban, the king of Babylon, who was born at Ascalon, conquered a great part of Christendom.

Howe Laban, the kinge of hie degre,
And syr̛ and Sowdon̛ of hie Babilon̛,
Conquerede grete parte of Christiante,
That was born in Askalon̛.

He was holding his court in the city of Agremore, on the river Flagot,

And in the Cite of Agremare[2]
Vppoñ the Rivere of Flagote
At þat tyme he soiorned ther̛[2]
Fulle roially, wel I wote,

with 12 kings and 14 amirals, and many worthy barons and knights,

With kinges xij and Admyralles xiiij,
With many a Baroñ & Kniȝtis ful boold,
That roialle were and semly to sene;
Here worþynesse al may not be told.

[lf 1, bk] when, in the time between March and May,

Hit bifelle by-twyxte March and Maye,
Whan kynde corage begynneth to pryke,
Whañ ffrith and felde wexen gaye,
And every wight desirith his like,
Whañ lovers slepeñ withe opyñ yȝe,
As Nightyngalis on grene tre,
And sore desire þat thai cowde flye,
That thay myghte withe here louere be:

he went to the chase

This worthy Sowdoñ in this sesoñ
Shope him to grene woode to gooñ,
To chase the Bore or the Venesoñ,
The Wolfe, the Bere and the Bawson.

in a wood near the sea.

He roode tho vppoñ a fforeste stronde
With grete rowte and roialte,
The fairest, þat was in alle þat londe,
With Alauntes, Lymmeris and Racches free.
His huntes to chace he commaunde,
Here Bugles boldely for to blowe,
To fere the beestis in þat launde.

[1] *leaf worn.* [2] *See the note.*

The Sowdoñ woxe wery I-nowe;
He rested him vndere an holme tre
Sittynge vppoñ a grene sete
Seynge a Dromonde com sailyng in þ^r see
Anone he charged to bekyñ him *with* honde
To here of him tidinges newe.
The maist*er* sende a man to londe,
Of diuers langages was gode and trewe,
And saide "lorde, this Dromonde[1]
Fro Babyloyne comeñ is,
That was worþe thousande poundis,
As[2] it mete with shrewes I-wis,
Charged with perle and p*re*cious stones
And riche pelure and spicerye,
With oyle and bras qweynte for the nones
To presente yow, my lorde worthy.
A drift of wedir' vs droffe to Rome,
The Romaynes robbed vs anone;
Of vs thai slowgh ful many one.
With sorwe and care we be bygone.
Whereof, lorde, remedye
Ye ordeyne by youre Barons boolde,
To wreke the of this vilane;
Or certes oure blis is coolde."
The Soudon hirynge this tyþinge,
With egre chere he made a vowe
To Mahounde and to Appolyne,
That thai shulde by it dere I-nowe,
Er that he wente fro theyme.[3]
"Where be ye, my kinges boolde,
My Barons and my Admyral?
Thes tidinges make myn herte coolde,
But I be venged, dyen I shalle.
Sire Ferumbras, my sone so dere,
Ye muste me comforte in this case;

Being weary with hunting, he sat down under a holm tree, and, seeing a dromond sailing on the sea, he charged one to enquire for news concerning the ship. The interpreter of the vessel being sent ashore, informed the soudan, that this dromond, freighted at Babylon, with a cargo of rich furs, spices, oil, brass and pearls, intended as a present to the soudan, had been driven by stress of weather to Rome, where they had been robbed by the Romans. [leaf 3] Therefore he solicited that the soudan would take revenge on those who had done such villainy to him. The soudan, hearing these tidings, made a vow to Mahound and to Apolyn, that they should dearly pay for it. 'Ferumbras, my son,' he said, 'and my daughter Floripas, ye must

[1] *See the note.* [2] *or* Ar [3] *See the note.*

be my comfort in this case.

My ioye is alle in the nowe here
And in my Doghter Dame Florypas.

Order Sortibrance, my counsellor, to be called for, and my chancellor Oliborn,

Sortybraunce, my Counselere,
Lete clepe him forthe to counsaile me,
And Oliborne, my Chauncelere
And noble Clerke of hie degre,

and Espiard my messenger, that he may go to Africa and to Asia and to all the princes, who owe me allegiance, and command them hastily to assemble with shield and lance at Agremore."

And Espiarde, my messangere,
To goon to Assye and to Aufrike,
To kinges, princes ferrʼ and nerʼ,
Barons, Admyralls and Dukes frike,
Comaundinge hem vppoñ her legeaunce
To come in al hast vnto me,
Wel Armed with shelde and launse,
To Egremoure þoñ riche Cite."

In a short time 100,000 men had assembled.

In shorte tyme this message was wroghte
An hundred thouusande on a rowte
That robbery was righte dere boght,
Was never none derrer withoute*n* douȝte.

On the advice of Lukafer, king of Baldas,

The kinge of Baldas, sir Lukaferʼ,
Of Aufryke lorde and governoure,
Spake to the Sowdoñ, that me*n* myghte here,
And saide "sir, for thyn honourʼ,
Do sende for shippes both ferʼ and nere."

the soudan also brought together 700 sail and a [leaf 4] dromond for himself, for Ferumbras of Alexandrie, for the Asiatic king of Chaunder and for Floripas.

Carrikes, Galeis and shippes shene,
vij hundred were gadered al in fere
And a Dromonde for the Sowdeñ kene.
Sir Ferumbras of Alisaundre
In the Dromonde with him was,
Of Assy the kinge of Chaunderʼ,
And his faire doghter Floripas.

There were two masters in that vessel, and two idols placed on the main top, with round maces, therewith to menace the Christians. The sails of red sendal-silk were

Two maistres were in the Dromounde,
Two goddes on hye seteñ thore
In the maister toppe, withe macis rounde,
To manace with the Cristeñ lore.
The sailes were of rede Sendelle,
Embrowdred witħ riche araye,

With beestes and breddes every dele,
That was right curious and gayo;
The Armes displaied of Laban
Of Asure and foure lions of goolde.
Of Babiloyne the riche Sowdon̄,
Moost myghty man he was of moolde,
He made a vowe to Termagaunte,
Whan Rome were distroied & hade myschau*n*ce,
He woolde turne ayen erraunte
And distroye Charles the kinge of Fraunce.

richly embroidered with figures of animals and birds.
Four golden lions, the arms of the soudan of Babylon, were also displayed thereon.
Laban made a vow to Termagant, to destroy Rome, and after that Charlemagne.

Forth̄ thai sailed on the flode,
Tille thai come to the haven of Rome:
The wynde hem served, it was ful goode.
Ther londed many a grymlye gome.
Thai brente and slowen, þat Cristen were,
Town̄, Abbey and holy chirche.
The hethen hade such power there,
That moche woo gan thai there wirch̄.

Having disembarked in the haven of Rome,
they slew all Christians, and burned towns, abbeys and churches.

Tidinggis came to Rome anone
Unto the Pope, that þt tyme was,
That the heþen came to bren and slone.
This was to hem a sory cas.
He lete cal his counsaile to-geder
To wete, what was beste to don̄.
Anone as thai were come þeder',
He asked of hem al ful sone:
"Lordinges, it is vnknowne[1] to you,
That this cursed hathen Sowdon̄
Bre*n*nyth and stroyeth oure pepul nowe,
Alive he leveth vnneth not one.
Seint Petir be oure governoure
And save this worthi Cite of Rome,
And Seinte Poule be oure gydoure
From this cursed hethen̄ houne[2]!"
Ifreȝ he bispake him than̄,

The Pope of Rome, hearing of the heathens laying waste the whole country,
assembled his council.
[leaf 8]
Jeffrez, a senator

[1] *See the note.* [2] *looks like* hound.

of Rome, advised that worthy men should be sent to Charles of Douce France to implore his assistance.

Of Rome he was a Senatoure,
And saide "sendiħ some worthy man
To Charles kinge of hye honoure.
He wolde you helpe with al his myghte,
That noble kinge of Dowse Fraunce."

But Duke Savariz, thinking this to be a wretched piece of timidity,

"Certes" q*uo*d Savaris "þat weren no righte,
It were right a foule myschaunce,
To sende to þat worthy kinge.

as they had not tried anything for themselves,

We have oure hedes yet al hole,
Oure sheldes be not broke no-thinge,
Hawberke, spere, ner poleyne, ner pole.
Where-of shul we playn̄ to him,
That no thinge yet have assaide?
Mecħ uylanye we myght wynne,
That for noght were so sone afrayed.

asked for 10,000 men to be put under his command.

Ten thousande men delyu*er*e me tyte
Tomorue next in-to the feelde,
And I shall prove with al my myghte
To breke there bothe spere and shelde."
Vnto the Senatours it semed welle,
His counsaile goode and honurable.
This worthi Duke was armed in stele
In armes goode and profitable;
He bare a Chek of goulis clere,
An Egle of goolde abrode displayed.
With him many a bolde Bachelere

The next morning the duke addressed his men,

Tho spake Savaryȝ wiħ wordes on hye
And saide "my felowes alle,
This daie prove you men̄ worthy,
And faire you al shal befalle.
Thenke yat Criste is more myghty
Than here fals goddis alle;
And he shal geve vs the victorie,
And foule shal hem this day bifalle."

and directed them to the soudan's

Forħ than rode þat faire Ooste
With right goode chere and randon̄,

Tille than come ful nyȝe the cooste.
Of the Sowdons Pavylon̄

> pavilion near the shore.
> [leaf 6]

Ferumbras was of hem ware
And sprange out as a sparkil of glede;
Of Armes bright a sheelde he bare,
A Doughty man̄ he was of dede.

> Ferumbras, that doughty warrior, becoming aware of them, led

xv thousande came oute there
With him at þat same tyde,
Ayen the Romaynes for to were,
With̄ bobaunce, booste and grete pride.

> 15,000 men against the Romans.

The stoure was stronge, enduryng' longe:
The Romaynes hade there the feelde;
The Sarysyns thai slough̄ amonge,
Ten thousand and mo with spere and sheelde.
Sauariz was wise and ware
And drowe towards þat Citee.
His baner displaied with̄ him he bare
To releve with his meyne.

> 10,000 and more of the Saracens were slain, and the Romans, though victorious, were led back to Rome by the cautious Savaris.

The Pope with his Senatours
Thanked god þat tyme of glorie,
That gafe hem þat day grete honours,
Of hethen that dai to have the victorie.

> The Pope thanked God for the victory.

Lukafere, kinge of Baldas,
The countrey hade serchid and sought,
Ten thousande maidyns faire of face
Vnto the Sowdan hath he broghte.

> Lukafer of Baldas having scoured the country, brought 10,000 maidens to the soudan, who

The Sowdon̄ co*m*manded hem anone,
That thai shulde al be slayn̄.
Martires thai were eu*er*ychon̄,
And therof were thai al ful fayne.

> ordered them to be slain,

He saide "my peple nowe ne shalle
With hem noughte defouled be,
But I wole distroie ou*er* all
The sede over alle Cristiante."

> saying, he would not have his people polluted by them, and he would destroy every Christian seed.

Tho spake lukefere the kinge,
That hethon̄ hounde Baldas,

> Lukafer said to the soudan:

"Grant me thy daughter and I will bring thee Charlemagne and all his twelve peers."

And saide " Sir Sowdan̄, g*ra*unte me one thinge,
Thi doghter Dame Floripas.
The kinge of Fraunce I shal the bringe
And the xij dosipers alle in fere."
The Sowdan saide in þat tokenyng',

Laban assented; but Floripas said, she would only consent to be his darling,

" I g*ra*unte the here, that is so dere."
Tho sayde Floripe " sire, noon̄ haste,
He hath note done as he hath saide.

[leaf 7]

I trowe, he speketh these wordes in waste,
He wole make bute an easy brayde.

when he had taken Charles and the douzepeers.

Whan he bryngith home Charles the kinge
And the xij dosipers alle,
I g*ra*unte to be his derlynge
What so evere therof by-falle.

The next morning the soudan ordered Lukafer to assault the City with 30,000 men.

Than on the morowe the Sowdan̄
Callid to him Lukafer' of Baldas,
To assaile the Cite anone:
" And loke thou tary not in this cas!
Thritty thousande of my menie,
Of Gallopes, Ethiopes and Aufricanes,
Take hem to the walles with̄ the.
Betith̄ down̄ wallis, towris and stones."
Lukafer' blewe his clarion̄
To Assemble the Sarasyns þat tide,
Where-of thai knewe right welle the soune,
Thai made hem redy for to ride,
But whan thai come to the yate,

The Saracens, finding the ditches too deep, cannot pass, and are

The Dikes were so develye depe,
Thai helde hem selfe Chek-mate;
Ouer cowde thai nothir goo nor crepe.
Lukafer' in al the haste

obliged to return.

Turned to the Sowdan agayn̄
And saide " sir, it is alle in waste,
We laboure nowe alle in vayne.
To depe and brode the Dikes bene,
The Towres so stronge be with̄ alle,

That by Mahounde I can note seeñ,
How that we shulde wyne ther to the walle."
Who was woode but the Sowdoñ?
He reneyed his goddis alle.
He clepede his Engyno*ur* sir mavone,
To counsaile he did him faste calle.

The soudan calls for his engineer Mavon,

He tolde him the case of þat myschefe,
How it stode at that ilke tyde.
Mavon Gafe him counsel in breefe
To fille the Dikes þat were depe.[1]

who advised him to fill the ditch

Every man to woode shal gooñ,
Fagotis to hewe and faste bynde,
And fille the Dikes faste anooñ
With alle, that we may ther fynde.

with fagots.

"Gramercy, Mavoñ," q*uo*d Laban thañ,
"Mahoundis benysone thou shalt haue,
Of alle myn Ooste the wiseste man,
With counsaile men for to saue.

Laban thanks his wise engineer.

[leaf 8]

Alle this was done the seconde daye,
Men myght go even to the walle;
On every party the ooste laye,
Thai made assaite[2] then generalle.

The following day, the ditch being filled with fagots, the city was assaulted from all quarters.

The Romaynes ronneñ to the toures,
Thai were in ful grete dowte;
Thai hade many sharpe shoures,
Thai were assailed sore a-bowte.

The Romans ran to the towers, and a sharp conflict ensued.

Wifis and maidyns stones thai bare
To the walles than ful faste,
Thai were in grete drede and care;
The men over the wallis did caste.

Women and maidens carried stones which the men threw over the walls.

Thai slowen many a Sarasyñ,
x *thousande*[3] pepul of hem̃ and moo.
The daie passed to the fyne,
The hethen withdrowe hem tho.
Whan these tidinges came to laban,

10,000 Saracens were slain and the heathens obliged to withdraw.

[1] *Read* 'wide' [2] *sic.?* assaute. [3] *MS.* $\overset{\text{i}}{\text{M}}$

Laban chides his gods and nearly grows mad with vexation.

His goddes he gan chide.
He waxe both blake, pale and wan,
He was nyȝe woode þat same tyde.

But Lukafer told him that, having espied that

Tho Lukafer comfortede him welle
And saide "sir, be not dismayed,
For I have aspied everydele,
Howe thai shalle alle be betrayede.

Savaris would, the following day, come out again to fight with them, he would have a banner made exactly like his, which when Savaris was much engaged in the battle, he would unfold and enter Rome.

Sauariz wole to morowe witħ us fighte,
His baner knowe I ful welle;
I shal have an othere, I you) plighte,
Like to this every dele.
Whan he is moste besy in bataile,
Than wole I with banere displaiede
Ride in to Rome wit*h*out faile,
Thus shal thai al be betrayede.
The Sowdañ was glad of this tidinge,
Hopinge it shulde be so;

And so it turned out;

And even as it was in purposynge,
Right so was it aftir I-do.

the Romans mistaking him for Savaris, returning from his sally,

Wenynge it hade be Sauarye,
Relevinge fro the hethen stour',
Wenynge doth ofte harme wit*h*oute lye,

he entered the main tower, [leaf 9]

He entred to the maist*er* Toure.
The firste warde thus thay wo*n*ne
By this fals contrevede engyne.
Thus was moche sorowe bygoñ,

and slew all therein.

Thai sloughħ all, that were ther-Inne.

Savaris becoming aware of the artifice of the enemy,

Whañ Sauariz saughħ this discomfitur'
Of the Romaynes in that tyme,
And howe harde thañ was here aventur',
Of sorowe þat myghte he ryme

and seeing out of 10,000 Romans no more than seventy-two left,

Of x thousande meñ lefte no moo
But sexty meñ and twelfe,
And whan he sawe this myschief tho,

turned back, but found the gate shut,

He turned homewarde agayn him selue.
By thañ he founde the gate shite

With Sarisyns, that hade it wone ;
And Estragot with him he mette
With bores hede, blake and donne.
For as a bore an hede hadde
And a grete mace stronge as stele.
He smote Sauaryz as he were madde,
That dede to grounde he felle.

and was slain by Estragot, a black giant of Ethiopia.

This Astrogot of Ethiop,
He was a kinge of grete strengtħ ;
Ther was none suche in Europe
So stronge and so longe in lengtħ.
I trowe, he were a develes sone,
Of Belsabubbis lyne,
For ever he was thereto I-wone,
To do Cristeñ men grete pyne.
Whan tidinggis came to the [P]ope,
That Duke Sauaryz was dede slayñ,
Thañ to woo turned alle his hope ;
He dide calle thañ to counsaile
Alle the Senatouris of Rome,
What þinge þat myght hem most availe,
And what were beste to done.

After the death of Savaris, the Pope summoned his council again.

Tho by-spake a worthy man of counsaile,
An Erille of the Senatouris :
"The best counsaile, þat I can

Sending vnto Char'es the kinge[1]
Certifiynge him by your myssangeris
The myschief þat ye are Inne,
That he come with his Dosyperys
To reskue Cristiante fro this heþen."

An earl of the senatours suggested the necessity of dispatching messengers to Charlemagne, imploring him to come to their deliverance.

[leaf 10]

All thai assentede anone therto ;

They all assented.

The lettres were made in haste.
Thre messageres we ordeyñ[2] therto,
That went forthe at the laste.

Three messengers, with letters written in haste,

[1] *This line in a much later hand.* [2] *Read:* were ordeyned

left the city by a postern at midnight, and passed the enemy's camp without being noticed by any wight.

At a posterne thai wente oute
Pryvely aboute mydnyght,
And passed through alle the route.
Of hem was war no wight.

BVt let we nowe the messangeris goon̄,
And speke we of Laban̄,
Howe he dide saile the Cite anoon̄,

Laban commanded every man to throw pikes and bills over the walls, to kill the Romans.

And commaundid, þat every man
Shulde withe Pikeys or witħ bille
The Wallis over throwe,
That he myght the Romaynes kille,
Playnly on a rowe,

He ordered the ships to go up the water, with their boats bound to the mast, that they might fight in close combat.

By water he ordeynede the shippes goon̄,
The bootis bownden to the maste,
That thai myght fight with hem anoon̄,
Honde of honde, þat was here caste.

Near the tower there stood a bastile which formed a principal protection to the city. It was laid low by stones hurled from an engine.

To the Toure a bastile stode,
An engyne was I-throwe—
That was to the Cite ful goode—
And brake down̄ towres both hie and lowe.
Tho sorowede alle the Citesyns
And were ful hevy than̄.

Laban, growing proud, summoned the Romans to surrender.

Tho wox prowde the Sarasyns,
And than bispake sire laban
And saide "yolde youe here to me,
Ye may not longe endure,
Or ellis shall ye al slayn̄ be,
By mahounde I you ensure."

Instead of an answer, a Roman hurled a dart at his breast-plate, but his hauberk shielded him.

A Romayne drife a darte him to
And smote him on the breste plate,
Ne hadde his hawberke lasted tho,
Mahounde had come to late.

The soudan, more than mad, charged Ferumbras to destroy them all,

Tho was the Sowdon̄ more þan̄ wod,
He cried to Ferumbras,
"For Mahoundes loue, þat is so good,
Destroye vp bothe man and place.

Spare no thinge that is alyve,
Hows, Toure ner Walle,
[leaf 11]
Beest, ner man, Childe nere Wife,
Brenne, slo and distroye alle."
Tho Ferumbras ordeynede anone
To bende the Engynes to the town̄
And bete down̄ both̄ Toure and stoon̄.
He cleped forth̄ Fortibraunce and Mavon̄
And saide "be youre Engynes goode?
Shewe forth here nowe your crafte
For Mahoundis love, þat gevith man foode,
That ther be no Toure lafte."

and enjoined Fortibrance and Mavon to direct their engines against the walls.

Tho the grete gloton̄ Estagote[1]
With his myghty mace sware
On the Gatis of Rome he smote
And brake hem alle on thre thare.

The great glutton Estragot, with his heavy mace, smote on the gates and brake them in pieces.

In he entrid at the Gate
The Porte-Colis on him thai lete falle.
He wende, he hade come to late,
It smote him through herte, lyuer and galle.

But as he was entering one of the gates, they let the portcullis fall, which crushed him to the ground,

He lai cryande at the grounde
Like a develle of Helle;
Through the Cite wente the sowne,
So lowde than gan he yelle.

where he lay crying like a devil.

Gladde were al the Romaynes,
That he was take in the trappe,
And sorye were al the Sarsyns
Of þat myschevos happe.

The Romans were glad, but the Saracens grieved.

Sory was the Soudon̄ than̄
And Ferumbras and Lukafer'.
Thai drowe hem tille her tentes than̄,
Thai left him ligginge there.
Mahounde toke his soule to him
And broght it to his blis.
He loued him wel and al his kyn,

They withdrew to their tents, leaving behind the corpse of Estragot, whose soul went up to Mahound.

[1] Estragote

Of þat myghte he not mys.

The Pope called all his people to St. Peter's,

Anone the [P]ope dide somoñ alle ;
The peple of the Cite came,
To Seinte Petris he dide hem calle,
And thidere came every man.

and proposed to them

He saide on hie "my Children dere,
Ye wote wel, howe it is ;
Ayenst the Sarisyns, þat nowe be here,
We mowe not longe endure I-wis.

[leaf 12]

Thay brekene oure walles, oure Toures alle
With caste of his Engyne.
Therefore here amonge you alle
Ye shalle here counsaile myne.
Thai bene withdrawe to here Oost,[1]
And on-armede thay ben alle.

to attempt a sally with 20,000 men, to attack the enemy before day-break within their camp,

Therfore, me thenketh, is beste
To-morowe erly on hem to falle.
We have xxx^{ti} thousande men ;
Twenty thousande shal go witħ me,

and to leave 10,000 for the guard of the city.

And in this Cite leve ten
To governe the comynalte."

The senators assented.

The Senatouris assentede sone
And saide, bet*er* myghte no man seyne.

In the morning

On the morowe this was it done[2] ;
God bringe hem wele home agayne.

the Pope displayed the banner of Rome,

The Pope did display than
The hie baner of Rome,
And he assoiled every mañ
Througħ gracious god in Dome.

and after a prayer for the preservation of the city,

He praide of helpe and socour'
Seinte Petir and Poule also
And oure lady, þat swete floure,
To saue the Cite of Rome from woo.

they marched out.

Forth thai rideñ towarde the Oost.

But Ferumbras, going his rounds,

Ferumbras romede a-boute ;

[1] *Read:* reste [2] *See the note.*

He saw the Romaynes comeñ by the Cost,[1] [discovered their coming,]
Thereof he hade grete dowte.
He blewe an horne, of bras it was; [sounded the alarm,]
The Sarsyns be-goñ to wake.
"Arise vp" he saide in aras,[2]
"We bene elles alle I-take,
And Armes anone, every wight,
To horse with spere and shelde!
Ye may se here a ferefuƚƚ sighte
Of oure enemyes in the felde.
Astopars,[3] goo ye biforne vs, [and drew up his troops.]
For ye be men of myghte;
Ethiopes, Assaynez and Askalous,
Go nexte afore my sighte.
My Fadir and I with Babyloynes,
Ho[4] shal kepe the rerewarde.
King Lukafer with Baldeseynes,
To venge alle, shalle have the Fowarde." [leaf 13]
The Romaynes aspied, þat thai were ware
Of here comynge thañ,
And therfore hade thay moche care.
Natheles on he*m* thai goñ—
Seinte Petir be here socoure!—
And laiden on side, bake and boñ.
There bigan a sturdy shoure [There began a hard struggle.]
Sire [5]Ferumbras of Alisaundre ooñ,[6]
That bolde man was in dede,
Vppon a steede Cassaundre gaye,
He roode in riche Weede.
Sire Bryer of Poyle a Romayne to fraye [Ferumbras slew Sir Bryer of Apulia]
He bare through witħ a spere,
Dede to the grounde ther he lañ
Might he no more hem dere!

[1] *MS.* Oost *corrected to* Cost. [2] *Read:* a rns.
[3] *See the note.* [4] *Read:* Wo [5] *MS.* Berumbras.
[6] *See the note.*

That sawe Huberte, a worthy man,
Howe Briere was I-slayn̄,
Ferumbras to qwite than̄
To him he rode ful even̄.
With a spere vppone his shelde þan̄
Stifly ganne he strike;
The shelde he brake I-myddis the feelde;
His Hawberke wolde not breke.
Many goode strokes were delte.
Ferumbras was a-greved tho,
and the worthy Hubert.
He smote with mayne and mygħte
The nekke asonder, the ventayle also,
That dede he sate vprighte.
There was bataile harde and stronge;
Many a steede wente ther a-straye,
And leyen at the grounde I-stonge,
That resyn never aftyr that day,
9000 pagans were killed,
IX thousand of the payens pride
That day were slayn̄,
and 8000 Romans.
And viij thousande of the Romaynes side,
That in the feelde dede lay*ne*.
Lukafer destroyed eighteen Romans,
Lukafere, þat paynym proude,
Slough Romaynes eyȝtene,
Of werrʼ moche sorowe he coude,
His strokes were over alle sene.
he also slew Gyndard, a senator of Rome, [leaf 14] who had slain ten Saracens.
Gyndarde, a Senatoure of Rome,
Had slayne Sarsenys ten̄,
Tille he met with the cursed gome,
Lukifere slough him than.
Then came the Pope with a great guard and his banner before him.
Tho come the Pope with grete aray,
His baner to-fore him wente.
Ferumbras than gan̄ to assaye,
If he myght that praye entente,
Ferumbras, supposing him to be the sovereign,
Supposynge in this though[t]e,
Ther was the soueravne;
He spared him therfore riħt noħt,

But bare him downñ ther in þe playñ.
Anooñ he sterte on him all ane
His Ventayle for to onlace,
And saugh his crowñ newe shafe,
A-shamed thanne he was.

burst open the thick crowd and threw him down to the ground.

But seeing his tonsure, he was ashamed.

" Fye, preest, god gyfe the sorowe !
What doist thou armede in the feelde,
That sholdest saie thi matyns on morwe,
What doist thou with spere and shelde ?

"Fie, priest," he said, "what doest thou in the battle-field?

I hoped, thou hadiste beñ an Emperoure,
Or a Cheftayne of this Ooste here,
Or some worthy conqueroure.
Go home and kepe thy Qwer' !
Shame it were to me certayne
To sle the in this bataile,
Therfore turne the home agayñ !"

It would be a shame for me to slay thee.

Go home and think of thy choir-service!"

The Pope was gladde þer-of certayne,[1]
He wente home to Rome that nyght
With Five thousande and no more,
XV thousande lefte in the feelde aplight,
Full grete sorowe was therfore.

The Pope retired with 5000 men,

15,000 being killed.

NOwe telle we of the messanger',
That wente to Charlemayne,
Certyfyinge him by lettres dere,
Howe the Romaynes were slayne,
And howe the Contrey brente was
Vnto the Gate of Rome,
And howe the people song 'alas,'
Tille socoure from him come.
"Who" quod Charles, that worthy kinge,
"The Sowdoñ and Ferumbras ?
I nyl lette for no thinge,
Till I him oute of Cristendome chace.
Therefore Gy of Burgoyñ,
Mynne owen nevewe so trewe,

Charlemagne, having learned from the messenger the great disaster which had befallen the Romans,

[leaf 15]

said, he would not desist until he had chased the soudan and Ferumbras out of Christendom.

[1] *Read:* 'without faile.'

He gave 1000 pounds of francs to his nephew Guy of Burgundy,

Take a thausande pounde of Frankis fyne,
To wage wytħ the pepul newe.
Take this with the nowe at this tyme,
And more I wole sende the,

and sent him off with orders to advance against the soudan by forced marches.

Loke that thou spare no hors ne shelde,
But þat he dede be;
And faste hye the thyderwarde,
For I drede thay haue grete nede,

Himself would follow as soon as possible.

And I shalle come aftirwarde
As faste, as I may me spede."

SPeke we of Sir Labañ
And let Charles and Gy be,
Howe he ordeyned for hem thañ
To Distroye Rome Citee.

Laban reminded Lukafer of his vaunting promise to bring him Charlemagne and his douzepeers,

"Sir Lukafer', thou madiste thi boost
To conquer' the Romaynes
And to bringe me the Ooste
Of the xij peris and Charlemayne.

in return for his daughter Floripas.

Vppoñ a condicioñ I graunte the
My doghter, dere Dame Floripas.
Wherefore, I aske nowe of the
To holde coven*au*nte in this cas."

Lukafer said, he would do all he had promised.

"That I saide" q*uo*d Lucafere,
"To Mahounde I make a vowe
To done al þat I hight the ther',
Ye and more th*an*[1] for Florip love."

With 10,000 men he attacked the city on one side,

He ordeyned assaute anone in haste
With x thousande men and moo;

the other being assaulted by Ferumbras.

And Ferumbras at that oþ*er* side faste
Assailed hem with grete woo.

The combat continues as long as daylight lasts.

The saute endured al þat daye
From morowe, tille it was nyght,
To throwe and shete by eu*er*y waye,
While that hem endured the light.

At night they retired to their tents.

Tho wente thai home to thair' tentys,

[1] *See the note.*

Tille it were on the morowe.
Isres in his fals ententes
Purposed treson̄ and sorowe.
He was chief Porter of the Town̄,
By heritage and fee so he shulde be.

Isres, who possessed by inheritance the guard of the principal gate, [leaf 16] planned treason.

He wente to the Sowdan̄,
For the riche Cite betraye woolde he,
And saide "lorde, gife me grace
For my goodes and for me,

He repaired to the soudan and offered to betray the city on condition that his life and property should be spared.

And I wole del*yu*er the this place
To haue and holde for ever in fee.
The keyes of this riche Cite
I haue in my bandon."
"That gr*a*unte I" q*uo*d Laban "the
To be free withoute raunson̄."

The soudan promised it.

Ferumbras made him yare,
With xx^{ti} thousand mon̄ and moo,
With this Isres for to fare,
And to wynne the Cite soo.

Ferumbras with 20,000 men went with Isres.

As sone as he entred was
The chief Gate of alle,
And alle his men in aras,[1]
He lete the Portcolys falle.

On entering the gate,

He smote of the traitourus hede
And saide "god gife him care!
Shal he never more ete brede,
All traitou*r*s evel mot[2] thai fare!
If he myght leve and reigne here,
He wolde betraye me;
For go he west, south̄ or North̄,
Traitou*r* shalle he never be."

he caused the traitor's head to be struck off by the portcullis, and

He dide lete bere his hede on a spere
Through̄-oute this faire Citee.
'Treson, treson̄' thai cried there,
Pite it was to here and see.

to be carried on the point of a spear through the city.
"Treason," cried the people within,

[1] *Read:* 'a ras.' [2] *MS.* met

The people fled by every waye,
Thai durst no-where a-bide.

and all streets were soon covered with dead men.

The hye wey ful of dede men laye,
And eke by every lanys side.

Ferumbras went to St. Peter's, seized the relics, the cross, the crown and the nails,

Ferumbras to Seinte Petris wente,
And alle the Relekes he seased anooñ,
The Crosse, the Crowñ, the Nailes bente;
He toke hem with him everychone.
He dide dispoile al the Cite
Both of tresoure and of goolde,

[leaf 17] burned the whole city,

And after that brente he
Alle þat ever myght be toolde.

and carried away all the treasures and the gold to Agremore, where the soudan went to stay. Three months and three days they spent there in great festivities, making offerings to their gods,

And alle the tresoure witħ hem þai bare
To the Cite of Egremour'.
Laban the Sowdoñ soiourned there[1]
Thre monþes and thre dayes more
In myrtħ and Ioye and grete solas.
And to his goddes offrynge he made,
He and his sone Sir Ferumbras
Here goddis of golde dide fade,

and burning frankincense in their honour.

Thai brente Frankeñsense,
That smoked vp so stronge,
The Fume in her presence,
It lasted alle alonge.
Thai blewe hornes of bras,

They drank the blood of beasts and milk, and ate honey

Thai dronke beestes bloode.
Milke and hony ther was,
That was roial and goode.

and snakes fried in oil.

Serpentes in Oyle were fryed
To serve þe Sowdoñ with alle,
"Antrarian Antrarian" thai lowde cryed
That signyfied 'Ioye generalle.'
Thus thai lived in Ioye and blis
Two monþes or thre.
Lete we now be alle this,

[1] *See the note.*

And of Gye nowe speke we.

NOw speke we of Sir Gȳe
That toward Rome hied witħ his Oost.
Whañ he approched there-to so nyȝe,
That he myght se the cooste,
Alle on a flame þat Cite was,

> When Sir Guy drew near Rome, finding the whole city in flames,

That thre myle al abowte,
Ther durst no mañ, þat ther was,
Come nyȝe the Cite for grete dowte.
That was a sory Cite than,
Sir Gye was in grete care,

> he grieved much

Ther was nowhere a soryer mañ,
For sorowe he sighed ful sare,
And saide "welallas"[1] the while
"For we come ar to late,

> that he had arrived too late.

For by some treson or some gyle
Thai entred in at some Gate.
There is no more but for to abyde,
Tille Charles come, the kinge,

> He resolved there to wait for Charlemagne

In this mede Vnder grene wode side,

> [leaf 18]

To telle him of this titbinge,
Howe Laban hath the Cite brente
And bore the Religes[2] a-waye,
And howe he hath hem to Spayne sente
With Shippes of grete aray,

> and then to tell him, how Laban had burnt the city, and had sent the relics to Agremore,

To Egremour' his chief Cite,
Ther to live and ende;

> his principal town in Spain.

And manassitħ Charles and his baronye.
God gife hem evelle ende!"
Kinge Charles he forgate nought
To come to reskowe Rome,
Alle his Doȝypers were I-sought,

> King Charles advanced to rescue Rome with his douzepeers

Fulle sone to him thay come.
Thre hundred thousande of Sowdeoures

> and 300,000 soldiers.

[1] *MS. is rubbed, but it looks more like* welawai.
[2] *Read:* 'reliqes.'

Kinge Charles with him dide lede,
They were doughty in all stourys
And worthy men of dede.

Roland led the vanguard,

Sir Roulande þat worthy knighte,
He ladde the Fowarde,

Oliver the rear,

And Sir Olyuer', that was so wighte,
Gouerned the Rerewarde.

the king was with the main body.

The Kinge himselfe and his Baronye,
With Dukes And Erilles roialle,
Gouerned alle the medil partye.
By commaundemente generall

The provisions were conveyed by sea.

He ordeynede grete plente
Of Flessh and Fissh, brede and wyne,
In shippes to saile by the see,
To serven him ful wel and fyne.

Guy seeing them come, went to meet the king, and told him the mischief done by the soudan,

Sir Gye aspied his comynge,
He knewe the baner of Fraunce,
He wente anoon ayen the kinge
And tolde him of þat myschaunce,
Howe that the cursed Sowdan
Hath brent Rome and bore the Relekis awaye,
And how he hath slayn alle and some,
That he hath founde of Cristen faye.

who moreover had made a vow to seek Charles in France in order to afflict him with grief.

And more-over he made his a-vowe,
To seke kinge Charles in Fraunce
And do him wo ther I-nowe.
"God gif him moch myschaunce!"—

[leaf 10]

"A" quod Charles "þat nedith noght,

"He will find me near," said Charles, "and shall dearly pay for it.

He shal fynde me nere.
By god, þat dere me boght,
He shal by it ful dere.
I shalle him never leve I-wis
Withinne walle ner withoute,
I swere by god and seinte Denys,

Unless he consents to be baptized,

Tille I have sought him oute;
And but if he will Baptised be

And lefe his fals laye,
Babyloyne shal he never see
For alle his grete aray.

he never shall see Babylon again."

Anoon to shippe every mañ
With vitaile and with store,
Euen towarde the proud Sawdañ
With-outeñ any more.

They all took ship without delay.

Wynde him blewe ful fayre and goode
Into the Ryver of Gaȝe,
Even over the salte flode
And ouer the profounde rase.
XXX legeeȝ from Egremour'
By londe for south it is,
And ther withoute any more
To londe thai wente I-wis,
And brente and sloughen al þat thai fonde,
And stroyed both Toure and towñ.
Thai lefte no thinge on grounde,
That thai ne bete it downñ.

Propitious winds drove them into the river Gase, where they landed, 30 miles from Agremore, and laid waste the country.

Tithinggis were tolde to Laban,
Howe Charles was I-come
And slough bouth childe, wyfe, man
And brente and stroyed alle and some
With thre hundred thousand of Bacheleris,
That were both stoute and gaye,
And with him al his Dosyperis,
Pepul of grete araye.
"And but ye ordeyne remedy,
He wole you brenne and slooñ,
Youe and youre riche Baronye,
He wole leve a-life neu*er*e ooñ."
Whan Laban herde these tidyngys,
His herte woxe alle cooldc
And saide "this is a wonder thinge!
Howe durste he be so boolde?
Litill ke*n*nyth he what I may doo,

Laban, hearing this news,

[leaf 20]

was astonished at Charles's presumption.

He dredith me litil nowe.
But certes he shalle, er' he goo,
To Mahounde I make a vowe.

He assembled all his barons,

Sir Lucafer' and Ferumbras
To him dide he calle
And Mavoñ and Sortebras
And his Barons alle.

and charged them to bring him alive that glutton that called himself king of France,

I charge you vppoñ youre legeaunce,
That ye bringe me that gloton,
That clepeth himselfe kinge of Fraunce,
Hidere to my Paviloñ.

and to slay the remnant.

Kepe him a-live, the remenaunte slo
The xij Peris ychooñ!
I shalle tech him curtesye,
I swere by god Mahounde."

Ferumbras went forth with many Saracens.

Ferumbras anooñ than
Arrayed him for to ride
With proude Sarasyns many a man,
That boldely durst a-bide.

He meets with Roland.

Rowlande met with Ferumbras
And gafe him such a stroke
That al astonyed þerof he was,
It made him lowe to stoupe.

They deal each other heavy strokes.

Ferombras smote him agayne
With myghte and may*n*, with ire
That he stenyed alle his brayne,
Him thought, his eyeñ were alle on fyre.

Oliver cuts off a quarter of Lukafer's shield.

With Lucafer' Oliver' mette,
And hit him on the sheelde
A stroke, that was right wel sette;
A quarter flye in the feelde.

The combat lasted the whole day.

Thus thai hurteled to-gedere
Alle the lefe longe daye,
Nowe hider and nowe theder;
Mony an hors wente ther astraye.

Well fought the twelve peers.

The Dosyperis thay foughten wele,

Duke Neymys and Oger',
With goode swerdes of fyne stele
And so dide Gye and Syr Bryer'.
Ferumbras was euer a-bowte [leaf 21]
To fyghte with Olyvere, (Ferumbras charges Oliver.)
And Olyuer' with-oute dowte
Leyde on with goode chere.
Kinge Charles saugh Ferumbras, (King Charles, seeing this, rides on to Ferumbras,)
To him fast he rode
And it on the helme with his mace, (and strikes his helm with his heavy mace.)
That stroke sadlye abode.
Ferumbras was woode for woo, (Ferumbras cannot approach him on account of the crowd.)
He myght for prees come him to
For no worldis thinge, that myght be tho.
Kinge Charles anoon[1] Ioye oute-drowe, (Charlemagne with his sword Mounjoy slew 30 Saracens.)
And with his owen honde
XXX^ti Sarseynys ther he slowe,
That laie dede vppone the sonde;
Many of hem therfore made joy Inowe.
Sir Lucafere of Baldas, (Lukafer of Baldas, encountering Charles,)
He presed to Charles sone,
And saide "Sir, with harde grace,
What hastowe here to done?
I behight Laban to bringe the to him (told him that he had promised the soudan to bring him Charles and the douzepeers.)
And the xij peris alle;
Now shaltowe come from al thy kyn
Into the Sowdans halle.
Yelde the to me" he saide,
"Thy life shalle I safe."
A stroke on him than Charles layde; (Charles strikes him on his helmet,)
He made the Paynym to rafe.
He smote him on the helme
With mown-Ioye, his gode bronde.
Ne hadde he be reskued than,
He hade slayn him with his honde.

[1] *A modern hand has written in the margin* "Mount."

but Lukafer is rescued by a great throng.

Than came Baldeȝynȝ with thronge
To reskue there here lorde,
And nubens with hem amonge
And Turkes by one accorde.

Roland, drawing Durendale, cleared a space around him and

Tho Roulande Durnedale oute-drowe
And made Romme[1] abowte.
XL of hem ther he slowe,
Tho were thai in grete dowte.
Roulande as fiers as a lioñ

hammered the heads of the Saracens.

With Durnedale[2] tho dinge
Vppon the Sarsyns crowne,

[leaf 22]

As harde as he myght flynge.

So do the other peers,

Duke Neymys and Sir Olyuer',
Gy and Alloreynes of Loreyne,
And alle the noble xij Peris,
Oger' and Bryer' of Brytayne,
Thai foughten as feythfully in þat fight,
The feelde ful of dede men laye.

and 30,000 Saracens were slain.

XXX^ti thousande, I you plight,
Of Sarsenys ther were slayñ.
Al thinge moste haue añ ende,

At night the Pagans quit the field.

The nyghte come on ful sone,
Every wighte retourned to wende;
Ferumbras to his men gan gone
And saide "oure hornes blowe we,
This day haue we a ful ille afraye,
To saie the south and not to lye,
Oure goddis holpe vs not to daye,
What devel þat ever hom eilith.
This bataile was so sharpe in faye,
That many a man it wailyth.

Ferumbras vows, never to desist

Shalle I never in herte be glade to daye,
Till I may preve my myghte
With Roulande, that proude ladde,
Or with Olyuer', that is so lighte,

[1] *See the note.* [2] *Insert:* 'gan.'

That evel hath vs ladde ;
And in Paris be crowned kinge
In despite of hem alle,
I wole leve for no thinge
What so evere byfalle.

unless he be crowned king at Paris.

Kinge Charles with grete honour'
Wente to his Pavilon̄ ;
Of the treyumple he bare the flour'
In dispite of Mahounde.

Charles went to his pavilion and

Almyghty God and Seynte Denyse
He thanked ful ofte sithe
And oure lady Marie of Paris,
That made hem gladde and blith̄.

thanked God and St. Mary of France.

He recomendide the olde Knightes,
That þat daye hade the victorye,
And charged the yonge with al her myghtes
To haue hem in memorye ;
For worthynesse wole not be hadde,
But it be ofte sough̄te,
Ner knigh̄thode wole not ben hadde,
Tille it be dere boghte.

He praised the elder knights for having won the victory and exhorted the young ones

[leaf 23]

"Therfore ye knightes, yonge of age,
Of oolde ye may now lere,
Howe ye shalle both hurle and rage
In felde with sheelde and spere.
And take ensample of the xij Peris,
Howe thai have proved her myght,
And howe thai were both wight and fiers
To wynnen honourys in righte.
These hethen houndes we shal a-tame
By God in magiste,
Let us make myrth̄ in goddis name
And to souper nowe goo we."

to take an example by them.

They make merry and go to supper.

O Thow, rede Marȝ Armypotente,
That in the trende baye hase made þy trone,
That god arte of bataile and regent

Prayer addressed to the red Mars Armipotent,

And rulist alle that alone,
To whom I profre precious present,
To the makande my moone
With̄ herte, body and alle myn entente,
A crown̄ of precious stoones,
And howe to the I gyfe
Withouten fraude or engyne,
Vppon̄ thy day to make offerynge,
And so shal I ever, while þat I live,
By righte þat longith to my laye,
In worshipe of thy reverence
On thyn owen Tewesdaye
With myrr̄, aloes and Frankensense,

to grant the Mahometans the victory over the Christians.

Vppon̄ condicion̄ that thou me graunte,
The victorye of Crystyn̄ Dogges,
And that I may some[1] hem adaunte
And sle hem down̄ as hogges,
That have done me distruccion̄
And grete disherytaunce
And eke slayn my men *with* wronge.
Mahounde gyfe hem myschaunce!"

In the spring of the year

IN the semely seson of the yere,
Of softenesse of the sonne,
In the prymsauns of grene vere,

[leaf 24]

Whan floures spryngyn̄ and bygy*n*ne,
And alle the floures in the frith̄
Freshly shews here kynde,

man ought to show his manhood

Than it is semely therwyth̄,
That manhode be in mynde;
For corage wole a man to kith̄,
If he of menske haue mynde,

and to think of love.

And of loue to lystyn̄ and lithe,
And to seke honur̄ for þat ende.

For none can be a good warrior, unless he knows how to love.

For he was neu*ere* gode werryour̄,
That cowde not loue a-ryght;

[1] *Read:* 'sone.'

For loue hath made many a conquerour’
And many a worthy knighte.
This worthy Sowdan, though he heþen wer’,
He was a worthy conquerour’;
Many a contrey with shelde and spere
He conquerede wyth grete honoure.
And his worthy sone Ferumbras,
That kinge was of Alisaundr’,
And Lucafer’ of Baldas,
That cruel kinge of Cassaundr’,
That wroughten wonders *with* here honde
With myghte and mayne for to fyghte,
And over-ride mony a manly londe,
As men of Armes hardy and wighte.
The Sowdan seyinge this myschief,
How Charles hade him a-greved,
That grevaunce was him no thinge lese,[1]
He was ful sore ameved.
He sente oute his bassatoures
To Realmes, provynces ferr’ and ner’,
To Townes, Citeis, Castels and Tours,
To come to him ther’ he were,
To Inde Maior and to Assye,
To Ascoloyne, Venys, Frige and Ethiope,
To Nubye, Turkye and Barbarye,
To Macedoine, Bulgar’ and to Europe.
Alle these people was gadred to Agremore,
Thre hundred thousand of Sarsyns felle,
Some bloo, some yolowe, some blake as more,
Some horible and stronge as devel of helle.
He made hem drinke Wilde beestes bloode,
Of Tigre, Antilope and of Camalyoñ,
As is here vse to egre here mode,
Whan þai in werre to battayle goon.
He saide to hem "my frendes der’,
As my trust is alle in you,

The soudan was a great conqueror; Ferumbras and Lukafer wrought wonders with their hands.

The soudan sent for his vassals, and assembled more than 300,000 Saracens at Agremore.

[leaf 25]

He addressed them in order

[1] *Read:* 'lefe.'

to increase their ardour,

On these Frenche dogges, that bene here,
Ye moste avenge me nowe.
Thai have done me vilanye,
Mikille of my people have thay slayñ.
And yet more-over thay manace me
And drive me to my contrey agayn;

ordered a solemn sacrifice to his gods,

Wherefore I wole at the bygynnynge
To Mahounde and to my goddis alle
Make a solempne offerynge;
The better shall it vs byfalle.
The laste tyme thai were wrothe,
We hade not done oure dute.
Therefore to saye the southe" ....
There were many hornys blowe,
The preestes senden thikke I-nowe
Goolde, and silver thikke thai throwe,
With noyse and crye thai beestes slowe,
And thought to spede wel I-nowe;
And every man his vowe he made
To venge the Sowdañ of his tene.
Here goddis of golde thai wex alle fade,
The smoke so grete was hem bitwene.
Whan alle was done, the Sowdan than

and charged Ferumbras

Charged Ferumbras redy to be
On the morowe, ere day began,
To ride oute of þat Cite

to march with 30,000 of his people

With xxx^{ti} thousande of Assiens,
Frigys, Paens and Ascoloynes,
Turkis, Indeis and Venysyens,
Barbarens, Ethiopes and Macidoynes,

against the Christian King, whom he wished to teach courtesy,

"Bringe him to me, that proude kinge;
I shal him teche curtesye,
Loke that thou leve for nothinge

[leaf 26] and to slay all his men except Roland and Olive.

To sle alle his other mayne,
Safe Rouland and Olyuere,
That bene of grete renowne,

If thai wole reneye her' goddis ther'
And leven on myghty Mahounde."

if they would renounce their gods.

FErumbras with grete araye
Rode forthe, Mahounde him spede,
Tille he came nyȝe ther' Charles lay
By syde in a grene mede.
In a woode he buskede his men
Prively that same tyde,

Ferumbras led out his troops; until arriving near Charles's camp, he ordered them to halt in a wood,

And with his felowes noon but ten
To kinge Charles he gan ride
And said "sir' kinge, that Arte so kene,
Upon trwes I come to speke with the,
If thou be curteis, as I wene,
Thou wolte graunte a bone to me,

and advanced with only ten of his men to the camp of Charlemagne,

That I mighte fight vppoñ this grene,
With Rouland, Olyvere and Gye,
Duke Neymes and Oger' I mene,
Ye and Duke Richarde of Normandye,
With al sex attones to fight.
My body I profr' here to the
And requyre the, kinge, thou) do me right,
As thou art gentille Lord and fre;

and offered him to fight at once against Roland, Oliver, Guy, Duke Naymes, Ogier the Dane, and Richard of Normandy.

And if I may conquere hem in fere,
To lede them home to my Faderis halle;
And if thai me, I graunte the here,
To be thy man, body and alle.
The kinge Answered with wordis mylde
And saide "felowe, þat nedith nought,
I shalle fynde of myñ a Childe,
That shal the fynde that thou hast sought."

If he should conquer them, he would lead them away to his father's hall; if he should be conquered, he would be his man.

The kinge lete calle Sir Roulande
And saide "thou most with this man fight,
To take this bataile here on honde,
Ther-to God gyfe the grace and myghte!"

The king sent for Roland and ordered him to undertake the combat.

Roulande answered with woordis boolde
And saide "Sir, have me excused!"

Roland refuses,

He saide, certeynly he ne wolde ;
The bataile vttirly he refused.

because Charles had praised the [leaf 27] old knights.

" The laste day ye preised faste
The oolde knightes of her' worthynes.
Let hem goon forth̄, I haue no haste,

" May they show their valour now."

Thai may goo shewen her' prowes."

Charles, vexed, smites Roland on the mouth, so that the blood springs from his nose, and he calls him a traitor.

For that worde the kinge was wrothe
And smote him on the mouthe on̄ hye,
The bloode at his nose oute-goth,
And saide " traitour, thou shalte a-bye."
" A-bye " quod Roulande " wole I noughte,
And traitour was I never none,
By þat lord, þat me dere hath bought ! "

Roland draws his sword,

And braide oute Durnedale þer' anone.
He wolde haue smyten̄ the kinge ther',

but the other barons separate them

Ne hadde the barons ronne bytwene ;
The kinge with-drowe him for fer'
And passed home as it myght beste bene.

and try to conciliate them.

The Barons made hem at one
With grete prayer' and instaunce,
As every wrath moste over-gone,
Of the more myschiefe to make voydaunce.

Meanwhile Oliver, who, being sorely wounded, kept his bed, on hearing of this dispute, had armed himself and went to Charles.

Olyuere herde telle of this,
That in his bedde laye seke sore.
He armede him ful sone I-wisse,
And to the kinge he wente withoute more
And saide " Sir Kinge, a bone graunte me

He reminds him of his long services, and demands the battle.

For alle the servyse, that I haue done,
To fight with þat kinge so free
To morue day, ere it be none."
Charles answered to Olyuer' :

Charles remonstrates with him.

" Thou arte seke and woundede sore,
And thou also my cosyn̄ dere,
Therfore speke thereof no more."—

But Oliver insists.

" Sir Kinge " he saide " I am alle hoole,
I aske you this bone in goddis name."

"Certes" he saide "I holde the a fole,
But I praye, god sheelde the fro shame."
Forth he rideth in that Forest,
Tille he gan Ferumbras see,
Where he was light and toke his rest,
His stede renewed til a grene tre.

Oliver rides to the forest, and finds Ferumbras alighted under a tree, to a branch of which his steed was tied.

"Sir" he saide "reste thou wele!
Kinge Charles sente me hidur.
If thou be curteys knighte and lele,
Rise vp and let vs fight to-geder."

"Arise," he said, "I am come to fight with thee." [leaf 28]

Ferumbras sate stille and lough,
Him liste not to rise oute of the place.
"My felowe" quod he "what arte thou?
Telle me thy name for goddis grace."

Ferumbras, without moving, demands his name.

"Sir" he saide "Generyse,
A yonge knighte late dobbet newe."

"I am Generys," says Oliver, "a young knight lately dubbed."

"By Mahounde" quod he "thou arte not wyse,
For thy comyng shaltowe sore rewe.
I holde Charles but a foole
To sende the hider to me,
I shall the lerne a newe scole,
If thoue so hardy to fighte be.

Ferumbras observes, "Charles is a fool to send thee.

I wende, he wolde haue sende Roulande,
Olyuer and iiij mo Dosyperys,
That hade bene myghty men of honde
Bataile to a-bide stronge and fiers.
With the me liste no playe begynne,
Ride agayn and saye him soo!
Of the may I no worshype wynne,
Though I slough the and such V mo."

Go and tell him to send me Roland and Oliver, and such four other douzepeers. For little honour were it to me to fight with thee."

"Howe longe" quod Olyuer "wiltowe plete?
Take thyn armes and come to me,
And prove þat thou saiest in dede,
For boost thou blowest, and þenkes[1] me."

"Spare thy words," says Oliver, "and take thy arms."

Whan Ferumbras herde him speke so wel,

[1] *Read:* 'as thenketh.'

Ferumbras is wrath and seizes his helmet,

He caught his helme in grete Ire,
That wroght was of goode fyne stele
With Perlis pight, Rubeis and Saphire.

which Oliver assists him to lace.

Olyuer’ halpe him it to onlase;
Gilte it was alle abowte.

Ferumbras thanks him, courteously bowing to him.

Ferumbras þanked him of his grace
And curteisly to him gan lowte.

They mount their steeds,

Thai worthed vp on̄ here stedes,
To Iuste thai made hem preest,
Of Armes to shewe her’ myghty dedis
Thai layden here speres in a-reeste,

rush together like fire of [leaf 29] thunder, and have their lances broken.

To-geder thai ronnen̄ as fire of thonder’,
That both here Launces to-braste.
That they seten̄, it was grete wonder;
So harde it was, þat thay gan threste.

They draw their swords.

Tho drowen̄ thai oute here swordes kene
And smyten to-geder by one assente.
There thai hitten̄, it was wele sene;
To sle eche other was here entente.

Ferumbras smites Oliver on his helmet

Syr Ferumbras smote Olyuer’
Vppon̄ the helme righte on hye
With his swerde of metel cler’,

so that the fire flies.

That the fyre he made oute-flye.

Oliver strikes at the head of Ferumbras,

Olyuer’ him hitte agayn̄ vpon̄ the hede
[1] the hede than fulle sore,

breaks away the circle of his helmet,

He carfe awaye with myghͭt and mayne
The cercle, that sate vppon̄ his crown̄.

and the sword glancing off down his back, he

The stroke glode down by his bake,
The Arson he smot ther awaye

cuts off two bottles of balm,

And the botelles of bawme withoute lake,
That uppone the grene ther thai laye,
That were trussed by-hynde him faste.
Tho Ferumbras was fuƚƚ woo;
Olyuer’ light adown̄ in haste,
The botellis he seased both two,

[1] *Blank in MS. See the note.*

He threwe hem into the River than
As ferr' as he myghte throwe.
"Alas" q*uo*d Ferumbras "what doistowe,[1] manne?
Thou art wode, as I trowe.

which he throws into the river.

Thai were worth an C mt pounde
To a man, þat were wounded sore.
Ther was no p*re*cioso*ur* thinge vppoñ grounde,
That myghte helpe a man more.
Thou shalt abye by Mahounde,
That is a man of myght*es* moost.
I shall breke both bake and crowñ
And sle the, ther thou goist."

Ferumbras tells him that they were invaluable to a wounded man, and that he should atone for their loss with his life.

Tho Olyuer' worth vp agayñ,
His swerde he hade oute I-drawe.
Ferumbras him smote with mayne
And mente to haue him slawe.
He smote as doth the dinte of þondir;
It glased down by his sheelde
And carfe his stedes neke a-sonder,
That dede he fille in the felde.

He strikes at Oliver, who wards off the blow with his shield, but his steed is killed under him.

[leaf 30]

Wightly Olyuer' vp-sterte
As Bacheler, doughti of dede,
With swerde in honde him for to hirte
Or Ferumbras goode stede.

Oliver quickly starts up and tries to kill his adversary's horse,

That Ferumbras aspied welle,
He rode a-waye than ful faste
And tiede him to a grene hasel,
And come ayen to him in haste

but Ferumbras rides off and ties it to a hazel.

And saide "nowe yelde the to me!
Thou maiste not longe endure;
And leve on Mahounde, þat is so der',[2]
And thy life I shalle the ensure.[3]
Thou shalt be a Duke in my contr',
And men haue at thyñ oweñ wille.
To my Sustir shaltowe wedded be,

"Yield thyself to me," says Ferumbras; "believe on Mahound, and I will make thee a duke in my country and give thee my sister."

[1] *MS.* deistowe. [2] *Read:* 'free.' [3] *MS.* ensuce.

It were pite the for to spille!"
"Better" quod Olyuer "shul we dele,

"Ere I yield to thee," answered Oliver, "thou shalt feel my strokes."

By God that is in magiste,
And of my strokes shaltow more fele,
Er I to the shalle yelde me."

They fight for a considerable time

Thai smeten togeder with egre mode,
And nathir of othire dradde;
Thai persed her hauberkes, that were so goode,

the blood ran from both their bodies. By mutual consent they stop to take breath.

Tille both thayr bodyes bladde.
Thay foughten soo longe, þat by assente
Thai drewe hem a litil bysyde,
A litil while thaym to avente,
And refresshed hem at þat tyde.

Ferumbras asks Oliver again his name and kin.

"Generis" quod Ferumbras,
"As thou arte here gentil knighte,
Telle me nowe here in this place
Of thy kyn and what thou hight;
Me thenkith by the now evermore,

"Thou must be one of the douzepeers, as thou fightest so well."

Thou shuldist be one of the xij peris,
That maiste fighte with me so sore,
And arte so stronge, worthy and fiers."
Olyuere answered to hym agayn:
"For fer I leve it not ontoolde,

"I am Oliver, cousin to Charlemagne." [leaf 31]

My name is Olyuere certayn,
Cousyn to kynge Charles the boolde,
To whome I shalle the sende
Qwikke or dede this same daye,
By conqueste here in this feelde,
And make the to renye thy laye."
"O" quod Ferumbras than to Olyuer,

"Thou art welcome here," says Ferumbras;

"Welcome thou arte in-to this place,
I have desyrede many a yere
To gyfe the harde grace.

"thou slewest my uncle,

Thou slough myn uncle Sir Persagyne,
The doughty kinge of Italye,
The worthyeste kinge þat lyued of men,

By Mahounde, thou shalt abye!"
Tho thai dongen̄ faste to-geder’
While the longe day endured,
Nowe hither’ and nowe thider’;
Fro strokes wyth̄ sheeld*es* here bodies þai couered.

> now thou shalt pay the penalty!"
> The fight continued the whole day.

And at the laste Olyuer’ smote him so
Vppon̄ the helme, þat was of stele,
That his swerde brake in two.
Tho wepen̄ had he nevere a dele.

> At last Oliver, smiting Ferumbras upon the helmet, has his sword broken.

Who was woo but Olyuere than?
He saugh noone other remedy.
He saide "sir’, as thou arte gentile man,
On me nowe here haue mercy.
It were grete shame I-wis,
And honur’ were it noon̄,
To sle a man wepenles;
That shame wolde never’ goon̄."
"Nay traitou*r*, thou getiste noon̄.
Hade I here an hundred and moo!
Knele down̄ and yelde the here anoon̄,
And eles here I woole the sloo."
Olyuer’ saugh, it wolde not be,
To truste to moch in his grace.
He ranne to the stede, þat stode by the tr*e*,
A swerde he raught in þat place,
That was trussed on Ferumbras stede,
Of fyne stele goode and stronge.

> He ran to the steed at the tree and seized a sword that was hanging there;

He thought he quyte[1] Ferumbras his mede.
Almoost hadde he abyde to longe;
For in turnynge Ferumbras him smote,
That stroke he myghte welle fele,
It come on hym so hevy and hoote,
That down it made hym to knele.
Tho was Olyuer’ sore ashamede
And saide "thou cursed Sarasyne,

> [leaf 32]
> but in turning on Ferumbras he received a blow that made him kneel down.

[1] *See the note.*

Thy proude pride shall be atamed,
By God and by seinte Qwyntyne.
Thou hast stole on me that dynte,
I shall quyte the thyn̄ hire."

But Oliver returns him fearful stroke.

A stroke than Olyuer' him lente,
That hym thought his eyen̄ wer' on fir'.

Charles, seeing Oliver on his knees,

Kinge Charles in his pavilon̄ was
And loked towarde þat fyghte
And saugh, howe fiers Ferumbras
Made Olyuere knele down̄ right.
Wo was him tho in his herte;

prayed to Christ

To Ihesu Criste he made his mone;
It was a sight of peynes smerte,
That Olyuere kneled so sone:
"O Lord, God in Trinite,
That of myghtis thou) arte moost,
By vertue of thy maieste
That alle knoweste and woste,
Lete not this hethen man
Thy seruaunte ouercome in fyght,
That on the bileve ne kan,
Ihesu, Lorde, for thy myghte!

that he might grant the victory over the Pagan.

But graunte thy man the victorye,
And the Paynym̄ skomfited to be,
As thou arte Almyghty God of glorye!
Nowe mekely, Lorde, I pray to the."

An angel announces him,

To Charles anoone an Aungel came
And broght him tidingges sone,

that his prayer was heard.

That God had herde his praier' than̄
And graunte him his bone.

Charles thanks God.

Thu Charles thanked God aboue[1]
With herte and thought, worde and dede,
And saide "blessed be thou), lorde almyghty,'[1]
That helpiste thy seruaunte in nede."

[leaf 33]

These Champions to-gedir thai gone

[1]—[1] *See the note.*

With strokes grete and eke sure,
They begin again.
Eche of hem donge othir on̄,
Alle the while thai myghte endur'.
Ferumbras brake his swerde
Ferumbras breaks his sword on Oliver's helmet.
On Olyueris helme on hye.
Tho wexe he ful sore a-ferde ;
He ranne for an othir redyly
He runs for another and asks Oliver to surrender.
And saide "Olyuere, yelde the to me
And leve thy Cristen̄ laye,
Thou shalte have alle[1] my kingdome free
And alle aftir my daye."
"Fye, Saresyne" q*uo*d Olyuere than̄,
"Trowest thou, that I were wode,
To forsake him, þat made me man̄
And boght me with his hert blode."
He raught a stroke to Ferumbras,
But Oliver aims at Ferumbras a blow which cuts his hauberk, so
On his helme it gan down̄ glyde,
It brast his hawberke at þat ras
And carfe hym throughe-oute his syde,
His bare guttis men myght̄ see ;
that his bowels are laid bare.
The blode faste down̄ ranne.
"Hoo, Olyvere, I yelde me to the,
Ferumbras implores his mercy, and
And here I become thy man.
I am so hurte, I may not stonde,
I put me alle in thy grace.
My goddis ben false by water and londe,
consents to be christened, his gods having proved false.
I reneye hem alle here in this place,[2]
Baptised nowe wole I be.
To Ihe*su* Crist I wole me take,
That Charles the kinge shal sene,[3]
And alle my goddes for-sake.
Take myn hawberke and do it on the,
He requested him to take his hauberk, to
Thou shalte haue fuƚƚ grete nede.

[1] *Probably an error for* 'half.'
[2] *In the margin the Scribe adds :—*'The merci Ladi helpe.'
[3] *See the note.*

X thousande Saresyns waiten vppon̄ me,
fetch his horse, And therfore go take my stede.
Lay me to-fore the, I the praye,
and to carry him to his own tent. And lede me to thy tente.
[leaf 34] Hye the faste forth in thy way,
That the Saresyns the not hente."
A-noon̄ it was done, as he ordeynede,
And faste forth thai ryden.[1]
But the Saracens, who lay concealed in the wood, rush out. The Saresyns anone assembled,
For to haue with hem foghten.
Ferumbras saugh̄ the feelde thore
Of Sarsynes fully filled;
Oliver, being surrounded, sets Of Olyvere dradde he ful sore,
That Saresyns shulde him haue killed.
He praide, that he wolde let him down̄
"Vndir yonde Olyfe tree,
Foṙ if ye cast me down̄ here, with hors shoon̄[2]
Alle to-treden̄ shalle I be."
down Ferumbras under an olive-tree, and defends himself with his sword, He priked forth and layde him thar',[2]
Out of the horses trase,
And with his swerde by-gan him wer',
For amonge hem alle he was.
A Saresyn̄ smote him with̄ a spere,
That it brake on pecis thre;
His hauberke myght̄ he not der',
So stronge and welle I-wroght was he.
dealing the Saracens many a hard blow. He hit þat Saresyns with his swerde
Through̄ the helme in-to the brayne.
He made an other as sore aferde,
He smote of his Arme with mayne.
Then Roland rushed into the throng of the enemy and slew many; But than̄ come Roulande with̄ Durnedale
And made way him a-bowte.
He slowe hem down̄ in the vale,
Of him hade thai grete dowte.
The prees of Saresyns was so stronge

[1] *Read:* 'soghten.' [2]—[2] *See the note.*

A-boute Roulande that tyde.
Thai sloughen his horsys with thronge,
his horse being killed by arrows and darts,
And dartis throwen on every syde.
Whan Roulande was on his Fete,
he fights on foot,
Than was he woo with-alle.
Many of hem he felte yete
And dede to grounde made hem falle.
At the last his swerde brake,
but his sword breaking,
Than hadde he wepyn noon,
As he smote a Saresyns bake
[leaf 35]
A-sundre down to the Arson.
Tho was he caught, he myght not flee,
he is taken
His hondes thai bounden faste
And lad him forth to here Cite,
and led away.
And in depe prison they hem caste.
Olyuer' sawe, howe he was ladde,
A sorye man than was he;
Him hadde leuer to haue bene dede
Than suffren that myschief to be.
Smertly aftire he pursued tho,
Oliver rides to rescue him,
To reskue his dere brother.
The prees was so grete, he myghte not so,
It myghte be no othir,
Be he was cowþe[1] by verr' force
With LX of Astopartes.[2]
Thai hurte him foule and slough his hors
but his horse being also killed,
With gauylokes and wyth dartis.
Yet on foote, ere he were foolde,
He slough of hem fiftene.
He was not slayn, as god woolde,
But taken and bounded[3] *with* tene.
he is overpowered and bound.
Tho were taken to Lucafer',
Both were conducted to Lukafer of Baldas.
The proude kinge of Baldas,
Both Roulande and Olyuer'.

[1] *Read:* 'caughte.' [2] Ascopartes.
[3] *Miswritten for* 'bounden.'

Gladde was he of that cas.
Kinge Charles was in herte woo,
Charles sees them, and calls for a rescue.
When he saughe his neuewes so ladde,
He cried to the Frenshmen̄ tho:
"Reskue we these knyghtes at nede."
Many enemies were slain,
The kynge himselfe slough many one,
So dede the Barons bolde.
but the Saracens had fled with their prisoners, and Charles is obliged to turn back.
It wolde not bene, thai were agon̄,
Magre who so woolde.
The Saresyns drewe hem to here Cite,
Kinge Charles turned agayne.
Under a holm tree they find Ferumbras.
He saugħ under an holme tre,
Where a knight him semed lay slayn̄.
Thederward he rode witħ swerde in honde.
Tho he saugħ, he was alyve;
He lay walowynge vppon the sonde
[leaf 86]
With blody woundes fyve.
"What arte thow?" q*uo*d Charlemayne,
"Who hath the hurte so sore?"
"I am Ferumbras" he saide certayn̄,
"That am of hethen̄ lore."
"O fals Saresyn̄" q*uo*d the kinge,
whom he is going to put to death.
"Thou shalte have sorowe astyte;
By the I haue lost my two Cosynes,
Thyn̄ hede shalle I of-smyte."
"O gentil kinge" q*uo*d Ferumbrase,
But on his requesting to be baptized,
"Olyuere my maister me hight
To be Baptised by goddis grace,
And to dyen̄ a Cristen̄ knighte.
Honur' were it noon to the
A discoumfite man̄ to slo,
That is conu*er*ted and Baptized wolde be
And thy man bycomen̄ also."
Charles took pity with him,
The kinge hade pite of him than̄,
He toke him to his grace
And assyned anoon̄ a man

led him to his tent, and ordered a surgeon to attend him.

To lede him to his place.
He sende to him his surgyne
To hele his woundes wyde.
He ordeyned to him such medycyñ,

He soon recovered,

That sone myght he go and ryde.
The kinge commaunded bishope Turpyñ
To make a fonte redye,
To Baptise Ferumbras þerin
In the name of god Almyghtye.

and bishop Turpin baptised him, by the name of Floreyn.

He was Cristened in þat welle,
Floreyne the kinge alle him calle,
He forsoke the foule feende of helle
And his fals goddis alle.

But he continued to be called Ferumbras all his life. Afterwards he was known as Floreyn of Rome

Nought for thañ Ferumbras
Alle his life cleped was he,
And aftirwarde in somme place,
Floreyne of Rome Cite.
God for him many myracles shewed,

on account of his holiness.

So holy a man he by-came,
That witnessith both lerned and lewde,
The fame of him so ranne.

Roland and Oliver being brought to the Soudan, Laban enquires their names.

NOwe for to telle of Roulande
And of Olyuere, that worthy wos,[1]
Howe thai were brought to þe Sowdañ
By the kinge of Boldas.
The Sowdañ hem sore affrayned,
What þat here names were.
Rouland saide and noght alayned :

They confess their names.

"Syr Roulande and sire Olyuere,
Nevewes to Kinge Charles of Fraunce,
That worthy kinge and Emperoure,
That nowe are takyn by myschaunce
To be prisoneres here in thy toure."
"A, Olyuer, arte thou here ?
That haste my sone distroyede,

[1] 'was.'

And Rouland that arte his fere,
That so ofte me hatħ anoyed.

The Soudan swears they shall both be executed the next morning before his dinner.

To Mahounde I make a vowe here,
That to morue, ere I do ete,
Ye shulle be slayn̄ botħ qwik in fere,
And lives shalle ye bothe lete."
Tho saide maide Florepas:

But Floripas advises him to detain them as hostages, and

"My fader so dereworth̄ and der',
Ye shulle be avysed of this cas,
How and in what manere
My brothir, þat is to prison̄ take,
May be delyuered by hem nowe,
By cause of these two knightes sake,
That bene in warde here with you.
Wherefore I counsaile you, my fader dere,

to remember his son Ferumbras,

To have mynde of Sir Ferumbras.
Pute hem in youre prison̄ here,
Tille ye haue better space.

for whom they might be exchanged.

So that ye haue my brother agayn̄
For hem, þat ye haue here;
And certeyn̄ elles wole he be slayn̄,
That is to you so lefe and dere."
"A, Floripp, I-blessed thou bee,

The Soudan finds her counsel good,

Thy counsaile is goode at nede,
I wolde not leve my sone so free,
So Mahounde moost me spede,

[leaf 38]

For al the Realme of hethen Spayne,
That is so brode and large.

and orders his gaoler Bretomayn to imprison them,

Sone clepe forth my gaylour Bretomayne,
That he of hem hadde his charge,
"Caste hem in your prison̄ depe,

but to leave them without food.

Mete and drinke gyfe hem none,
Chayne hem faste, þat thay not slepe;
For here goode daies bene a-gone."
Tho were thay cast in prison depe[1];

[1] *Read:* 'dirke.'

Every tyde the see came inne.
Thay myght not see, so was it myrke,
The watir wente to her chynne.

At high tide the sea filled their deep cells.

The salte watir hem greved sore,
Here woundis sore did smerte.
Hungir and thurste greved heme yet more,
It wente yet more nere here herte.

They suffered much from the salt water, from their wounds, and from hunger.

Who maye live withoute mete?
vj dayes hadde thay righ̄t none,
Ner drinke that thay myghัt gete,
Bute loked vppon the harde stone.

On the sixth day,

So on a daye, as God it wolde,
Floripas to hir gardeñ wente,
To geder Floures in morne colde.
Here maydyns from̄ hir she sente,
For she herde grete lamentacioñ
In the Prisoñ, that was ther nye;
She supposed by ymagynacioñ,
That it was the prisoners sory.

Floripas, who was gathering flowers in her garden, heard them lament.

She wente her' nerr' to here more,
Thay wailed for defaute of mete.
She rued on hem anooñ ful sore,
She thought, how she myght hem beste it gete.

Moved to compassion,

She spake to her Maistras Maragounde,
Howe she wolde the prisoneres fede.

she asks her governess Maragound to help her in getting food for the prisoners.

The develle of helle hir confounde,
She wolde not assente to þat dede,
But saide "Damesel, thou arte woode,
Thy Fadir did vs alle defende,
Both mete and drinke and othere goode
That no man shulde hem thider sende."

Maragound refuses, and reminds Floripas of her father's command.

[leaf 39]

Floripe by-thought hir on a gyle
And cleped Maragounde anoon righ̄t,
To the wyndowe to come a while
And se ther a wonder syght:
"Loke oute" she saide "and see a ferr'

Floripas, thinking of a trick, called to her governess to come to a window and see the porpoises sporting beneath. Maragound looking out, is pushed into the flood.

The Porpais pley as thay were wode."
Maragounde lokede oute, Floripe come ner'
And shofed hire oute in to the flode.
"Go there" she saide "the devel the spede!
My counsail shaltowe never biwry.
Who so wole not helpe a mañ at nede,
On evel deth mote he dye!"
She toke withñ hire maidyns two,

Floripas asks Bretomayn to let her see the prisoners.

To Britomayne she wente hir waye
And saide to him, she moste go
To visetēñ the prisoneris that daye,
And saide "sir, for alle loues,
Lete me thy prisoneres seeñ.
I wole the gife bothñ goolde and gloues,
And counsail shalle it beeñ."
Brytomayne that Iaylor kene
Answered to hir sone agayne
And saide "Damesel, so mote I theñ,
Thañ were I worthy to be slayñ.
Hath not youre Fader charged me,
To kepe hem from every wyght?
And yet ye wole these traytours see?

The gaoler threatened to complain to her father,

I wole goo telle him Anooñ right."
He gan to turne him anone for to go,
To make a playnte on Floripas.

but Floripas,

She sued him as faste as she myghte go,
For to gif him harde grace.

having seized his key-clog,

With the keye cloge, þat she caughñ,
Withñ goode wille she maute[1] than,

dashed out his brains

Such a stroke she hym ther' raught,
The brayne sterte oute of his hede þañ.

She then went to tell her father, [leaf 40]

To hire Fader forth she gothñ
And saide "Sire, I telle you here,

she had surprised the gaoler feeding he prisoners and

I saughñ a sight, that was me lothñ,
Howe the fals Iailour fedde your prisoner',

[1] *Read:* 'mente.'

promising to deliver them;

And how the covenaunte made was,
Whan thai shulde delyuered be ;

wherefore she had slain him.

Wherefore I slough him with a mace.
Dere Fadir, forgif it me ! "
"My doghtir dere, that arte so free,[1]

The Soudan gives the prisoners into her guard.

The warde of hem now gif I the.
Loke, here sorowe be evere newe,
Tille that Ferumbras delyuered be."
She thanked her Fadere fele sithe

She now proceeded to the prison,

And toke her maydyns, and forth she goth,
To the prisone she hyed hire swyth.
The prison dore vp she dothe
And saide "sires, what be ye,
That make here this ruly moone ?

asked the prisoners what they wanted,

What you lakkith, tellyth me ;
For we be here nowe alle alone."
Tho spake Roulande with hevy chere
To Floripe, that was bothe gente and fre,
And saide "lo, we two caytyfes here
For defaute of mete dede moste be.
vj dayes be comyn and goon,
Sith we were loked in prison here,
That mete nor drinke hade we noon
To comforte with oure hevy cher.
But woolde god of myghtes moost,
The Sowdon wolde let vs oute goon,
We to fight with alle his Ooste,
To be slayn in feelde anoon.
To murthir men for defaute of mete,
It is grete shame tille a kinge ;
For every man most nedes ete,
Or ellis may he do no thinge."
Tho saide Floripe with wordes mylde,

and promised to protect them from any harm.

"I wolde fayne, ye were now here,
From harme skath[2] I wole you shelde,

[1] *Read:* 'trew.' [2] *Read:* 'harme & skathe.'

And gife you mete with right gode cher'."
She let down a rope,
A rope to hem she lete down̄ goon̄,
[leaf 41]
That aboven̄ was teyde faste.
and drew up both,
She and hir maydyns drewe þer vppon̄,
Tille vp thay hadde hem at the last.
and led them to her apartments.
She led hem into here chambir dere,
That arrayed for hem was right wele,
Both Roulande and Olyvere,
There they ate,
And gafe hem̄ there a right gode mele.
And whan thay hadde eten̄ alle her fille,
took a bath,
A bath̄ for hem was redy there,
Ther-to thay went ful fayre and stille,
and went to bed.
And aftyr to bedde with right gode cher'.
Now Floripas chamber is here prisone,
The Soudan knew nothing of his prisoners being in Floripas' chamber.
Withouten̄ wetinge of the Sowdon̄ ;
Thai were ful mery in that Dongeon̄,
For of hem̄ wiste man̄ never oone.
Now lete we hem be and mery make,
Tille god sende hem gode delyueraunce.
Aftir the tyme, þat thay were take,
Meanwhile Charlemagne
What did Charles, the kinge of Fraunce,
Ther-of wole we speke nowe,
tells Guy that he must go to the Soudan to
Howe he cleped forth Sir Gy
And saide " on my message shaltowe,
Therfore make the faste redy,
demand the surrender of Roland and Oliver, and of the relics of Rome.
To bidde the Sowden̄ sende me my Nevewes both̄
And the Releqes also of Rome ;
Or I shal make him so wroth̄,
He shall not wete what to done.
And by þat god, þat hath me wroght,
I shal him leve Towre ner Town̄.
This bargan̄ shal so dere be bought
In dispite of his god Mahoun̄."

Naymes of Bavaria represents that a messenger to the Soudan should
DUke Neymes of Bauer' vp stert than̄
And saide " Sir, hastowe no mynde,
How the cursed Sowdan̄ Laban

Alle messengeris doth he shende?
Ye haue lost inowe, lese no mo
Onworthily Olyuer' and Roulande."
"By god, and thou shalt with him go,
For al thy grete brode londe."

THo Ogere Danoys, þat worthy mañ,
"Sir" he saide "be not wrotħ!
For he saitħ soutħ."—"go thou) thañ!
By Gode thou shalte, be thou) never so loth."

"ASire" quod Bery Lardeneys,
"Thou) shalte hem se never more."—
"Go thou forth in this same rees,
Or it shalle the repente ful sore."

FOlk Baliante saide to the kinge,
"Liste ye youre Barons to lese?"-
"Certis, this is a wondir thinge!
Go thou also, thou) shalte not chese!"

ALeroyse rose vp anone
And to the kinge þan gañ he speke
And saide "what thinke ye, sir, to done?"—
"Dresse the forth witħ hem̃ eke!"

MIron of Brabane spake an worde
And saide "Sir, thou maiste do þy wille.
Knowist thou not that cruel lorde,
How he wole thy Barons spille?"—
"Trusse the forth eke, sir Dasaberde,
Or I shalle the sone make!
For of all thinge thou arte aferde,
Yet arte thou) neyther hurte ner take."

BIsshope Turpyñ kneled adowñ
And saide "lege lorde, mercy!"
The kinge him swore by seynt Symoñ:
"Thou goist eke, make the in hast redye!"

BErnarde of Spruwse, þat worthy knygħt,
Saide "sir, avyse you) bettc,
Set not of youre Barons so ligħt,

certainly be slain; and that they ought to be anxious not to lose any more besides Rouland and Oliver. Then said the [leaf 42] king, 'By god, thou shalt go with Guy.' Ogier the Dane remonstrates, but is ordered to go too. So are Thierry of Ardane

and Folk Baliant,

Aleroys

and Miron of Brabant.

Bishop Turpin kneels down to implore the king's mercy, but he must go too,

as well as Bernard of Spruwse

Thou maiste haue nede to hem̄ yette."—
"Thou shalte goon̄ eke for alle thy boost,
Haue done and make the fast yare!
Of my nede gyfe thou no coost,
Ther-of haue thou right no care!"

and Brier of Mountdidier.

BRyer' of Mounteȝ, þat marqwyȝ bolde,
Was not aferde to him to speke.
To the kinge sharply he tolde,
[leaf 43] His witte was not worth a leke:
"Woltowe for Angre thy Barons sende
To þat Tiraunte, þat alle men sleith̄?
Or thou doist for þat ende,
To bringe thy xij peres to the deth̄."
The kinge was wroth̄ and swore in halle
By him, þat boght him with̄ his blode:
"On my messange shall ye gon̄ alle!
Be ye never so wroth̄ or wode."

The knights take leave and start.

Thay toke here lefe and forth̄ thay yede,
It availed not agayne him to sayne.
I pray, god gif hem gode spede!
Ful harde it was to comen̄ agayn̄.

The Soudan assembled his council.

NOwe let hem passe in goddis name,
And speke we of the Sowdon̄,
Howe he complayned him of his grame,
And what that he myght beste done.

Sortibrance and Brouland

"Sortybraunnce and Bronlande[1]" seyde he,
"Of counsail ye be fulle wyse.
How shal I do to avenge me
Of kinge Charles, and in what wyse?
He brennyth my Toures and my Citees,
And Burges he levethe me never oon̄.
He stroieth my men̄, my londe, my fees.
Thus shalle it not longe goon̄.
And yet me greveth most of alle,
He hath made Ferumbras renay his laye.

[1] *See the note.*

Therfore my counselors I calle,
To remedy this, howe thay best maye.
For me were lever that he were slayñ,
Thane he a Cristeñ hounde shulde be,
Or witħ Wolfes be rente and slayñ,
By Mahounde myghty of dignyte."
To answerde Sortybraunce and Broulande
advise him
And saide "gode counsaile we shal you gyfeñ,
If thouc wilte do aftyr coven*au*nte,
It shal you profit, while you lyveñ.
Take xij knightis of worthy dede
to send 12 knights, and to bid Charles
And sende hem to Charles on message nowe.
A-raye hem welle in roial wede,
For thȳ honour and for thy prowe.
[leaf 44]
Bidde Charles sende thy sone to the
to give up Ferumbras and to withdraw from his country.
And voyde thy londe in alle haste,
Or ellis thou shalt him honge on a tre,
As hye, as any shippes maste."
"Nowe by Mahounde" *quo*d Laban,
"This counseil is both trewe and goode,
I shalle him leve for no mañ
To parforme this, though he wer woode."
He did his lettris write in haste,
The knight*es* were called to goo þ*er*witħ,
The knights are dispatched.
That thay hyȝe hem̄ to Charles faste
And charke[1] hym̄ vppoñ life and lithe.
Forth thai ride towarde Mantrible þañ,
In a medowe, was fayre and grene,
Near Mantrible they meet with the Christian messengers.
Thai mette witħ Charles messageris teñ.
Duke Neymes axed hem̄, what thai wolde mene,
And saide "Lordynges, whens come ye?
Duke Naymes inquires whither they intend to go.
And whider ye are mente, telle vs this tyde."
"From̄ the worthy Sowdoñ" thañ saide he,
"To Charles on message shalle we ride,

[1] *Sic in MS. Query*—'charge.'

Euel tithyngg*es* we shalle him telle,
Fro Laban, that is lorde of Spayne.
Farewele, felowes, we may not dwelle."

Having heard their message,

"A-byde" q*uo*d Gy "and turne agayne,
We wole speke with you), er ye goon,
For we be messengeris of his.
Ye shal aby everichone,
So God brynge me to blis."
Anoon here swerdes oute thay brayde
And smoten down right al a-boute.
Tille the hethen were down layde,
Thai reseyued many a sore cloute.

the delegates of Charles cut off their heads, which they take with them to present to the Soudan at Agremore.

Thai smyten of here hedes alle,
Eche man toke one in his lappe.
Fal what so euer byfalle,
To the Soudon wole they trappe.
Tille thai come to Egremoure,
Thai stynte for no worldes thinge;
Anone thai fonde the Sawdan thore,

[leaf 45] The Soudan was just dining.

At his mete proudely sittynge,
And þat maide fair' Dame Floripas
And xiiij princes of grete price
And kinge Lukafer' of Baldas,
Thas was both bolde, hardy and wyse.

Naymes delivers his message:

Doughty Duke Neymes of Bauer'
To the Sowdone his message tolde

'God confound Laban and all his Saracens, and save Charles,

And saide "god, þat made heven so cler',
He saue kinge Charles so bolde
And confounde Laban and all his men,
That on Mahounde byleved,[1]
And gife hem evel endinge! amen.
To morue, longe er it be even,

who commands thee to send back his two nephews and to restore the relics.'

He co*m*maundith the vppon thy life
His Nevewes home to him sende,
And the Religes[2] of Rome withoute strife;

[1] *Read:* 'byleven.' [2] *Read:* 'reliqes.'

And ellis getist thou an evel ende !
xij lurdeynes mette vs on the waye ;
Thai saide, thay come streight fro the.
Thai made it both stoute and gay ;
Here hed*is* here maistowe see.
Thai saide, thai wolde to Charles gooñ,
Evel tidingg*es* him to telle.
Loo here here heddis eu*er*ychone,
Here soulis bene in helle."

They then produce the heads of the Soudan's messengers.

"O" q*uo*d Lavane "what may this be,
To suffr' this amonge my knight*es* alle ?
To be rebuked thus here of the
At mete in myn oweñ halle !
To Mahounde myghty I make a vowe,
Ye shall be hanged alle ten,
Anoon as I have eteñ I-nowe,
In presence of alle my meñ."

The Soudan vowed a vow that they should all ten be hanged as soon as he had finished his dinner.

Maide Floripas answered tho
And saide "my derworth Fadir der' !
By my counsaile ye shal not so,
Tille ye haue your Barons alle in fer',
That thai may se what is the best,
For to delyu*er*e my brother Sir Ferumbras.
And aftirward, if þat ye liste,
Ye may gife hem ful evel grace."

But Floripas recommended him to put off his resolution, until a general council of his barons had determined on the best way of the liberation of Ferumbras.

"Gramercy, doghter, thou saieste welle,
Take hem alle into thy warde.
Do feter hem faste in Ireñ and stele
And set hem in strayȝte garde.
Thus was I neuer rebukede er nowe ;
Mahounde myghty gyfe hem sorowe !
Thay shalle be flayn and honged on a bowe,
Longe ere tyme[1] to morowe."

[leaf 46]

The Soudan gives them into her guard.

Florip̄ toke these messangeris
And ladde hem vp in-to here tour',

Floripas leads the knights into her tower, where

[1] *Read:* 'I dyne.' *See the note.*

they were glad to find Roland and Oliver.

There thai founde two of here feris.
Thay thanked thereof god of honoure.
Tho sayde Duke Neymys of Bauer᾽:
"Gladde men we be nowe here,
To fynde Roulande and Olyuer᾽
In helthe of bodye and of goode cher᾽."
Thai kissed eche other with herte gladde
And thanked god of his grace;

They told each other how they had fared.

And eche toolde othir, howe thay sped hadde,
And howe thay come in-to that place
By helpe of mayde Floriꝑ̄ hire self,
"God kepe hir in honoure!
For thus hath she brought vs hider alle twelfe,
To dwelle in hir owen̄ boure."

After washing,

Tho thay wessh and wente to mete,
And were served welle and fyne
Of suche goode, as she myght gete,

they dined off venison, bread and wine,

Of Venyson̄, brede and gode wyne.
There thai were gladde and wel at ease;
The Soudon̄ ne wist it noght.

and then went to sleep.

Aftyr thay slepe and toke her ese,
Of no man than̄ thay ne roght.

The following day, Floripas asks Naymes his name,

On the morowe Floriꝑ̄, that mayde fre,
To Duke Neymes spake in game:
"Sir gentil knigħt," tho saide she,
"Telle me, what is your name."
"Whi axe ye, my lady dere,
My name here to knowe alle?"
"For he[1] spake with so bolde chere
To my Fadir yestirdaye in his halle.

and enquires after Guy of Burgundy, [leaf 47]

Be not ye the Duke of Burgoyne, sir Gȳ,
Nevewe unto the kinge Charles so fre?"
"Noe, certes, lady, it is not I,
It is yondir knight, þat ye may see."

whom she had loved for a long time, and for

"A, him have I loved many a day;

[1] *Sic in MS. Read:* 'ye.'

And yet knowe I him noght.
For his loue I do alle that I maye,
To chere you with dede and thought.

whom she would do all she could for their benefit,

For his love wille I cristenede be
And lefe Mahoundes laye.

and would be baptised,

Spekith to him nowe for me,
As I you truste maye;
And but he wole graunte me his loue,
Of you askape shalle none here.

if he would agree to love her in return.

By him, þat is almyghty aboue,
Ye shalle abye it ellis ful dere."
Tho wente Duke Neymes to Sir Gye
And saide "This ladye loveth the,

Neymes tells Guy

For thy loue she maketh us alle merye,
And Baptizede wole she be.
Ye shalle hir take to your wedded wife,
For alle vs she may saue."

to take her for his wife,

"By God" quod Gye "þat gafe me life,
Hire wole I never haue,

but Guy refuses,

Wyle I neuer take hire ner no woman,
But Charles the kinge hir me gife.
I hight him, as I was trewe man,
To holden it, while I lyve."

as he never will take a wife, unless she be given him by Charles.

Tho spake Roulande and Olyuer,
Certyfyinge him of her myschefe,
Tellinge him of the parelles, þat þay in wer,
For to take this lady to his wedded wife.

Rouland and Oliver persuaded him.

"But thou helpe in this nede,
We be here in grete doute.
Almyghty god shalle quyte thy mede,
Elles come we nevere hennys oute."
Thus thay treted him to and fro;
At the laste he sayde, he wolde.

so that he at last consented.

Floripas thay cleped forth tho;
And brought fourth a Cuppe of golde,
Ful of noble myghty wyne,

Floripas, holding a golden cup of wine,

[leaf 48]

And saide "my loue and my lorde,
Myn herte, my body, my goode is thyn̄,"

kissed him,

And kissed him with̄ that worde,

and requested him to drink to her after the fashion of her country.

And "sir" she saide "drinke to me,
As the Gyse is of my londe;

She also drinks to him.

And I shalle drinke agayn̄ to the,
As to my worthy hosbonde."
Thay clipped and kissed both̄ in fere

They all make merry.

And made grete Joye and game,
And so did alle, that were ther',
Thai made ful mery alle in same.
Tho spake Floripas to the Barons booldo
And saide "I haue armur' I-nowe;
Therfore I tel you, what I wolde,
And þat ye dide for your prowe.

For the following day

To morue, whan̄ my Fadir is at his souper',
Ye shalle come in alle attonys;
Loke ye spare for no fere,
Sle down̄ and breke both̄ bake and bones;
Kithe you knightis of hardynesse!
Ther is none helpe, but in this wyse,
Then moste ye shewen̄ youre prowes,
And wynne this Castel in this guyse."
Thai sayden alle, it was welle saide,
And gladde thay were of this counsaile.

they all prepare to assail the Soudan at supper.

Here armur' was forth̄ layde,
At souper the Sowdon̄ to assaile.

Lukafer comes to the Soudan and asks leave to see the prisoners, in order to know the manner of their detention.

Kinge Lucafere prayde the Sawdon̄,
That he wolde gif him lysence,
To the prisoners for to goon̄,
To see the maner of her presence.
He gafe him lefe, and forth he wente
Vp vnto Floripas Toure.
To asspie the maner was his entent',
Hem̄ to accuse agayne honoure.

Finding the door locked, he burst it

Whan̄ he come, he founde the dore fast I-stoke,

He smote there-on with his fist,
That the barr' begañ to broke.
To make debate, wel him list.
"Who artowe" q*uo*d Floripas[1]
"þat maketh her' such araye[1]?"
"I am kinge Lucafere of Baldas,
The Sowdoñ sente me hidir in faye;
To seeñ his prisoneris is my desire
And speke with hem everychoñ,
To talke with hem by the fire
And speke of dedis of Armes amonge."
Tho saide Duke Neymes "welcome be ye
To us prisoners here!
What is your wille, nowe telle ye;
For we be meñ of feble chere."
"I woolde wete of Charles the kinge,
What mañ he is in his contre,
And what meyne he hath, and of what thinge
He rekyneth moost his dignyte."
Duke Neymes saide "an Emp*er*oure
And kinge he is of many a londe,
Of Citeis, Castels, and many a Toure,
Dukes, Erles, Barons bowynge to his honde."
"But saye me, felowe, what is your vse,
To do in contr' aftyr the none.
And what is the custome of your hous,
Tille meñ to souper shalle gone?"
"Sir, so*m*me meñ iouste[2] with sper' and sheldc,
And so*m*me meñ Carol and singe gode songes,
Some shote with dartis in the feelde,
And so*m*me play at Chesse amonge."
"Ye bene but foulis of gode dissporte;
I wole you tech a newe play.
Sitte down here by one assorte,

open with a blow of his fist.

[leaf 49]

He told them that he was come to speak to them,

and to enquire after Charlemagne.

Duke Naymes answers.

He then asks what amusements they have after dinner.

Naymes says, 'Some joust, some sing, some play at chess.'

'I will teach you a new game,' says Lukafer.

[1] *These two lines are written as one in the MS.*

[2] MS. iuste.

And better myrthe never ye saye."

> With a thread he fastened a needle on a pole and put a burning coal upon it.

He teyde a tredde on a pole
With an nedil ther-on I-fest,
And ther vppoñ a qwik' cole.
He bade every man blowe his blast.
Duke Neymes hade a long berde,

> He blew it at Naymes's beard and burnt it.

Kinge Lucafer' blewe eveñ to hym̄,
That game hade he never before lered.
He brent the her' of Neymes berde, to the skyne.

> Naymes waxed wroth, and [leaf 50] snatching a burning brand from the fire

Duke Neymes thañ gan wex wroth̄,
For he hade brente his berde so white
To the Chymneye forth he goth
And caught a bronde him with̄ to smyte.

> he smites at Lukafer and throws him into the fire,

With̄ a goode wille he him smote,
That both his eyeñ bresteñ oute.
He caste him in the fire al hote;
For sothe he hadde a righ̄t gode cloute.
And with a fyre forke he helde him doune,

> where he was roasted to charcoal.

Tille he were rosted to colis ilkadele.
His soule hade his god Mahouñ.

> Floripas applauds this,

Florip̄ bade him̄ warme him wele.
"Sires" tho saide Floripas,
"Entendith nowe al to me!
This Lucafer' of Baldas
Was a lorde of grete mayne.

> but points out their danger,

My Fadir hade him euer yn cher'
I telle you for sothe everydele,
He wolde anooñ aftyr him enquer',

> and advises them to arm.

And therefore loke, ye arme you well!"
Florip wente in, as the maner was,

> At supper time she goes to her father.

To here Fadir at souper tyme.
No man spake worde of kinge Baldas,
Ner no man knewe of his sharp pyne.
The xij peris armed hem wel and fyne
With swerdes drawe and egr' chere.
While thay mery[1] drinkyng' the wyne

[1] *Miswritten for* 'were'?

And sittinge alle at here souper.
Thai reheted the Sowdon̄ and his Barons alle
And maden̄ orders wondir fast,
Thai slowe down̄ alle, þat were in the halle,
And made hem wondirly sore a-gast.

[As they were sitting at table, the twelve peers rushed in and slew all whom they met.]

Olyvere egerly sued Laban̄
With sverd I-drawe in his honde.
Oute at the wyndowe lepte he þan̄
Vppon̄ the salte see stronde,[1]
And he skaped away from̄ hime,
But woo was he þerfore,
That he went awaye with̄ lym̄
To worche hem sorowe more.

[Laban, pursued by Oliver, jumps out of a window on to the sea-shore and escaped without injury.]

Roulande than̄ came rennynge
And axed, where was Laban.
Olyuere answerede moornynge
And saide, howe he was agoon̄.

[leaf 51]

Tho thai voided the Court*es* at the last
And slowen̄ tho, that wolde a-byde,
And drewe the brigge and teyed it fast,
And shitte the gatis, that were so wyde.

[They killed all in the castle, and then drew up the bridges and shut the gates.]

Laban, that by the ebbe escapede,
Of harde, er he come to londe,
He alle astonyed and a-mapide,[2]
For sorowe he wronge both̄ his honde
And made a vowe to Mahounde of myght,
He wolde that Cite wynne
And never go thens by day nor nyght,
For foo, for frende, ner for kynne.
"And tho traytouris will I do honge,
On a Galowes hye with-oute the gate;
And my Doghter, þat hore stronge,
I-brente shal be there-ate.

[Laban vowed a vow that he would hang them all and burn his daughter.]

To mauntryble he gan sende anoon̄
Aftir men and tentis goode,

[He sent to Mantrible for troops and]

[1] *MS.* strowde. [2] *Read:* 'a-*w*apide.'

engines,

And Engynes to throwe with̄ stoon̄
And goode armur' many foolde.

and besieged Agremore.

The sege he did leyen a-bowte
On every side of that Cite.
To wallis with Engynes thai gan rowte,
To breke the Toures so fre.

Floripas recommends the peers

Tho saide Florip̄, "lordingges goode,
Ye bene biseged in this toure,
As ye bene wight of mayne and moode,
Proveth here to saue youre honour'.
The toure is stronge, drede you nought,
And vitayle we have plente.
Charles wole not leve you vnsought;
Truste ye welle alle to me.

to enjoy themselves.

Therefore go we soupe and make merye,
And takith ye alle your ease;
And xxx[ti] maydens lo here of Assyne,[1]
The fayrest of hem ye chese.
Take your sporte, and kith you knyghtes,
Whan ye shalle haue to done;

[leaf 52]

For to morowe, when the day is light,
Ye mooste to the wallis goon̄
And defende this place with̄ caste of stoon̄
And with shotte of quarelles and darte.
My maydyns and I shaƚƚ bringe goode wone,
So eueryche of us shalle bere hir parte."

In the morning the soudan attacks the castle,

On morowe the Sowdon̄ made assaute
To hem, that were with̄-Inne,
And certes in hem was no defaute,
For of hem̄ myght thay nought wynne.
Here shotte, here cast was so harde,
Thay durste not nyȝhe the walle.

but is repulsed.

Thay drowen̄ hem bakwarde,
Thay were beten̄ over alle.
King Laban̄ turnede to his tentes agayn̄,

[1] *Read:* 'Assye.'

He was nere wode for tene,
He cryede to Mahounde and Apolyne
And to Termagaunte, þat was so kene,
And saide "ye goddes, ye slepe to longe,
Awake and helpe me nowe,
Or ellis I may singe of sorowe a songe,
And of mournynge right I-nowe.
Wete ye not wele, that my tresoure
Is alle witħ-inne the walle?
Helpe me nowe, I saye therfore,
Or ellis I forsake you alle."
He made grete lamentacioñ,
His goddis byganne to shake.
Yet that comfortede his meditacioñ,
Supposinge thay didde awake.
He cleped Brenlande to aske counsaile,
What was beste to done,
And what thinge myght hiñ moste avayle,
To wynne the Cite sone.
"Thou wotist welle, þat alle my tresour'
Is there in here kepinge,
And my doughter, þat stronge hore.
God yif her evelle endyng'!"
"Sir" he saide "ye knowe welle,
That Toure is wondir stronge.
While þay haue vitayle to mele,
Kepeñ it thay wole fulle longe.
Sende to Mauntreble, your' cheif Cite,
That is the keye of this londe,
That noñ passe, where it so be,
With-oute youre speciall sonde,
To Alagolofur', þat geaunte stronge,
That is wardeyne of þat pas,
That no man passe that brigge alonge,
But he have special grace.
So shalle not Charles witħ his meyne

He accuses his gods of sleepiness, and shakes them to wake up.

[leaf 53] Brouland tells him, as the castle is strong and well stored with provisions, the peers will hold it very long;

but if he would send orders to Alagolafre, the bridge-keeper at Mantrible, not to allow any one to pass without leave, they would get no assistance from Charles, and die from hunger.

Reskowe than̄ Agramoure.
Than̄ thay shalle enfamyched be,
That shalle hem rewe ful sore."—
"Mahoundis blessynge have thou and myne,
Sortybraunce, for thy rede."—

Espiard is despatched to Mantrible,

"Espyarde, messangerʼ myne,
In haste thou most the spede
To my Cite Mavntreble,
To do my message there,
To Alogolofrʼ, þat giaunte orrible.
Bydde him his charge wele lere,
And tel him, howe that the last daye
Ten fals trayt*our*s of Fraunce
Passed by that same waye
By his defaute with̄ myschaunce,
Charginge him vppon̄ his hede to lese,
That no man by the brigge,[1]
Be it rayne, snowe or freze,
But he his heede down̄ ligge."
Espiarde spedde him in his waye,
Tille he to Mauntrible came,
To seke the geaunte, ther he laye
On the banke bysyde the Dame,
And saide "the worthy Sowdon̄,
That of alle Spayn̄ is lorde and sirʼ,

and commands the giant

Vppon̄ thy life co*m*maundeth the anoon̄,
To deserue bett*er* thyn hire.
The laste day thou letist here passe
Ten trattoures of douse Fraunce.
God giffe the evel grace,
And hem̄ also moche myschaunce!
He charged the vppon̄ life and deth̄,
To kepe this place sikerlye;
While in thy body lasteth̄ the breth̄,

not to suffer any one to pass the bridge.

Lette noon̄ enemye passe therʼ-bye."

[1] *See the note.*

Alagolofur rolled his yen̄
And smote with his axe on̄ the stone
And swore by Termag*a*unte and Apolyne,
That ther-by shulde passe*n* never one,
But if he smote of his hede,
And brought it to his lorde Laban̄,
He wolde never ete no brede,
Nere never loke more on man̄.
xxiiij[ti] Cheynes he didde ou*er*-drawe,
That noo man passe myghٖt,
Neyther for loue nere for awe,
No tyme by daye, nere by nyghte.
"Go, telle my lorde, I shalle it kepe ;
On payne of my grete heede
Shalle ther no man̄ goo ner crepe,
But he be take or dede."
This geaunte hade a body longe
And hede, like an libarde.
Ther-to he was devely stronge,
His skynne was blake and harde.
Of Ethiope he was bore,
Of the kinde of Ascopartes.
He hade tuskes, like a bore,
An hede, like a liberde.
Laban nolde not forgete
The saute to renewe,[1]
To wynne the Toure, he wolde not lete.
Here trumpes lowde thay blewe.
Every man wente to the walle,
With pikeys or witħ bowe.
Thai made assaute generallę,
The walles downe to throwe.
But thay witħ-inne bare hem̄ soo,
Thay slowe of the Saresyns iij hundred'.
Thay wroghten̄ hem both care and woo,

Alagolafre drew 24 chains across the bridge.

The soudan assaults the castle again.

[leaf 55]

but the 12 peers slay 300 Saracens.

[1] *These two lines are written as one in the MS.*

Vppoñ her fightinge thay wondride.
Tho cryed Labañ to hem on hye,

Laban threatens to hang them, and utters imprecations

" Traytours, yelde you to me,
Ye shall be hongede els by and bye
Vppoñ an hye Galowe tree."
Tho spake Florip̃ to the Sowdoñ
And sayde " thou fals tyraunte,
Were Charles come, thy pride wer' done

against Floripas, who returns them.

Nowe, cursede myscreaunte.
Alas ! that thou ascapediste soo
By the wyndowe vppoñ the stronde.
That thy nek' hade broke a-twoo !
God sende the shame and shonde ! "—
" A ! stronge hore, god gife the sorowe !
Tho[u] venemouse serpente.
Withe wilde horses[1] thou shalt be drawe to morowe,
And on this hille be brente,
That al men may be war' by the,
That cursed bene of kynde.
And thy love shalle honged be,
His hondes bounde him byhynde."

The soudan calls for Mavon, his engineer, and orders him to direct a mangonel against the walls.

He called forth Mavoñ, his Engynour',
And saide " I charge the,
To throwe a magnelle to yon tour',
And breke it downe on thre."

Mavon knocked down a piece of the battlements.

Mavon set vp his engyne
With a stooñ of .vj. C wight,
That wente as eveñ as eny lyne,
And smote a cornell downñ right.

Roland and Oliver lament;

Woo was Roulande and Olyuer',
That þat myschief was be-falle,
And so were alle the xij peres ;

they are comforted by Floripas.

But Florip̃ thañ comforte hem alle :
" Sires " she saide " beith of goode chere !
This Toure is stronge I-nowe.

[1] *See the note.*

He may cast twies or thries or he hit ayen *þer*,[1] [leaf 56]
For sothe I telle it you.
Marsedage, the roialle kinge,
Rode in riche weede,
Fro Barbary co*m*myng,
Vppoñ a sturdy stede,
Cryinge to hem vppoñ the walle:
"Trayto*u*ris, yelde you here!
Brenne you alle ellis I shalle,
By myghty god Iubyter'."
Gy aspied, that he came ner',
A darte to hime he threwe ful eveñ,
He smote him throwe herte & liver in fer'.
Dame Floripe lough with loude steveñ
And saide "Sir Gye, my loue so free,
Thou kanste welle hit the prikke.
He shall make no booste in his contre;
God giffe him sorowe thikke!"
Whañ Labañ herde of this myschief',
A sory mañ was he.
He trumped, his mene to relefe;
For to cease that tyme mente he.
Mersadage, kinge of Barbarye,
He did carye to his tente,
And beryed him by right of Sarsenye
With brennynge fire and riche oynemente,
And songe the Dirige of Alkaroñ,
That bibill is of here laye,
And wayled his deth everychoñ,
vij nyghtis and vij dayes.
Anooñ the Sowdoñ, south to say,
Sente iij hundrid of knightis,
To kepe the brigge and the waye
Oute of that Castil rightis,
That nooñ of hem shulde issue oute,

Guy kills Marsedage the king of Barbary, by throwing a dart at him.

They stop the attack

to bury Marsedage,

and bewail him 7 days and nights.

Then the soudan more closely blockades the castle.

[1] *See the note.*

To feche vitayle by no waye.
He charged hem to wacche wel aƚƚ abowte,
That thay for-famelid' myght dye.
[leaf 57]
Thus thay kepte the place vij dayes,
The provisions being exhausted,
Tille alle hire vitaile was nyȝe spente.
The yates thai pas the streyte weyes.
Tho helde thai hem with-in I-shente.
Tho spake Roulande with hevy chere
Woordes lamentable,
Whañ he saugħ the ladies so whiȝte of ler',
Faile brede on here table,
Roland complains of Charles's forgetfulness;
And saide "Charles, thou curteys kinge,
Why forgetist thou vs so longe?
This is to me a wondir thinge;
Me thinkitħ, thou doiste vs grete wronge,
To let vs dye for faute of mete,
Closed thus in a dongeoñ.
To morowe wol we asaye what we koñ gete,
By god, that berithe the crowñ."
but Floripas cheers him up,
Tho saide Floripas "sires, drede noghte
For nooñ houngr' that may befalle.
I knowe a medycyne in my thoughte
To comforte you with alle.
saying she possessed a magic girdle which was a talisman against hunger and thirst for those who wore it.
I have a girdil in my Forcer',
Who so girde hem̄ ther-with aboute,
Hunger ner thirste shal him neu*er* dere,
Though he were vij yere witħ-oute."
"O" q*uo*d Sir Gy "my loue so trewe,
I-blessed mote ye be!
I pray you, that ye wole us alle hit shewe,
That we may haue oure saule.
She yede and set it fortħ anooñ,
They all successively put it on and felt as if they had feasted.
Thai proved alle the vertue,
And diden it aboute hem̄ eu*er*ychoñ.
It comforted alle both moo and fewe,
As thai hade bene at a feste.

So were thay alle wele at ease,
Thus were thai refresshed both moost & lest
And weren bifore in grete disese.
Laban̄ wondred, how thai myght endur'
With-outen̄ vitaile so longe.
He remembred him on Floripas senctur',
And of the vertue so stronge.
Tho wiste he welle, that throgh famyne
Might he hem̄ never wynne.
He cleped to him fals Mapyne,
For he coude many a fals gynne:
He coude scale Castel and Toure
And over the walles wende.
"Mapyne" he saide "for myn̄ honoure,
Thou mooste haue this in mynde:
That hore, my doghter, a girdil hath she,
From̄ hounger it savyth hem̄ alle,
That wonnen may thay never be,
That foule mote hir bifalle!
Kanstowe gete me that gyrdill by craft,
A thousande pounde than̄ shal I gefe the;
So that it be there not lefte,[1]
But bringe it hithir' to me.
Thou kanste see by nyghte as welle
As any man doth by daye.
Whan thay bene in here beddes ful still,
Than go forth thider right in thy waye.
Thou shalt it in here Chamber fynde,
Thou maist be thereofe sure."
"Sir, there-to I wole me bynde,
If my life may endure."
Forth wente this fals Mapyne
By nyght into the Tour'—
God gife him evel endinge!—
Euen in to Floripas bour'.

Laban wondered at their endurance,
but at last remembering the girdle,
[leaf 58]
he induced Mapyne
to attempt to steal it at night.
Mapyne entered the chamber of Floripas through

[1] *Read:* 'lafte.'

a chimney;
By a Chemney he wente inne;
Fulle stilly there he soughte it.
he finds the girdle and puts it on,
He it foūnde and girde it aboute him,
And aftyr ful dere he boght it;
For by the light of a lampe ther'
but Floripas perceives him
Floripas gañ him aspye,
Alle a-frayed oute of hir slepe for fere,
and cries out.
But lowde than gan she crye
And saide "a thefe is in my boure,
Robbe me he wole or sloo."
Roland hurries to her assistance, [leaf 59]
Ther-with come Rouland fro his tour'
To wete of hir woo.
He founde Mapyne bysyde hir bedde,
Stondinge amased for drede,
To the wyndowe he him ladde,[1]
cuts off Mapine's head, and throws him out through the window without noticing the girdle.
And there he smote of his hedde,
And caste him oute in-to the see.
Of the gyrdille was he not war';
But whañ he wist, the girdel hade he,
Tho hadde he sorowe and care.
Floripas, seeing her girdle lost, is much grieved;
Floripe to the Cheste wente
And aspyed, hire gyrdel was gooñ,
"Alas!" she saide, "alle is it shente!
Sir, what haue ye done?
He hath my girdel aboute hym̃.
Alas! þat harde while!
A rebelle hounde doth ofte grete tene;
Howe be we alle begilede."
Tho spake Roulande with cher' boolde,
Roland comforts her.
"Dameselle! beyth noughte aferde!
If any vitaile be aboute this hoolde,
We wole hem wynne withe dinte of swerde
They agree to attempt a sally to obtain food.
To morowe wole wee oute-gooñ
And assaye, howe it wole it be.
I make a vowe to god alone,

[1] *See the note.*

Assaile hem wole we!
And if thay haue any mete,
Parte withe hem̄ wole we.
Or elles strokes thay shal gete
By God and seynte Mary myn̄ avour’![1]
In the morne, er the larke songe,

In the morning

Thai ordeynede hem to ride
To the Saresyns, þat hade so longe
Leyen hem besyde.
Duke Neymes and Oger’
Were ordeynede to kepe the place.

Naymes and Ogier remain in the castle,

The x othir of the xij peres
Wente oute to assaye here grace.

the others start

Thay founden̄ hem in logges slepynge,
Of hem hade thay no thought.

and surprise the Saracens still sleeping in their huts.

Thai slowen̄ down̄ þat came to honde,
Mahounde availed hem noghte.

[leaf 60]

In shorte tyme the ende was made,
Thay ten slough iij hundred ther’.
Tho founde thai vitaile, thay were glad,
As moche as thay myghte home ber’.

They slew 300 and carried off as much food as they could bear.

Duke Neymes and Oger’, that kept the tour’,
Say hem with̄ here praye.
Thai thanked god hye of honoure,
That thai spedde so þat day.
Thay avaled the brigge and lete him yn,
Florip̄ and here maydyns were gladde,
And so were thay, that were with-yn;
For alle grete hounger thay hadde.
Thai eten̄ and dronken right I-nowe
And made myrth̄ ever amonge.
But of the Sowdon̄ laban speke we nowe,
Howe of sorowe was his songe.

WHan tidyngges came to him,
That his men̄ were slayn̄,
And howe thai hade stuffed hem̄ also[1]

[1] *See the note.*

With vitaile in agayne,
The soudan is enraged,
For sorowe he woxe nere wode.
He cleped Brenlande and Sortybraunce.
And tolde hem̄ with̄ angry mode
Of his harde myschaunce.
"Remedye ordeyne me,
Ye be chief of my counsaile;
That I of hem may vengede be,
It shalle you bouth availe.
O ye goddes, ye faile at nede,
That I have honoured so longe,
and is going to burn his gods,
I shalle you breñ, so mote[1] I spede,
In a fayre fyre ful stronge;
Shalle I neuer more on you bileve,
But renaye you playnly alle.
Ye shalle be brente this day er eve,
That foule mote you befalle!"
The fire was made, the goddes were broght
[leaf 61]
To have be caste ther-inne.
but, appeased by his wise men,
Tho alle his counsaile him by-sought,
He shulde of þat erroure blynne,
And saide "Sir, what wole ye done?
Wole ye your goddis for-sake?
Vengeaunce shalle thañ on you come,
With sorowe, woo and wrake!
Ye moste make offrynge for youre offence,
For drede of grete vengeaunce,
With oyle, mylke and ffrankeñcense
By youre prestis ordynaunce."
he sacrifices again,
Tho he dide bere hem in ayeñ,
And to hem made dewe offerynge.
and is assoiled by the priests.
The prestis assoyled him of þat synne,
Ful lowly for him prayinge.
Laban holds council.
Tho he cleped his counselers
Brulande and Sortybraunce,

[1] *MS.* mete.

Axynge, howe he myght destroy*e* the xij peres,
That Mahounde gife hem myschaunce.
Thay cowde no more ther-oñ,
But late saile ayeñ the toure.
With xx^ti^ thousande thai gañ goñ,
And bigo*n*ne a newe shoure

A new assault begins,

To breke downñ the Walles,
With mattok*es* and with pike,
Tille iiij hundred of hem alle
Lay slayne in the dike.
So stronge was the cast of stoone.
The Saresyns drewe hem abakke,
Tille it was at hye none;
Tho go*n*ne thay ayeñ to shake.

but the ditches are filled with assailants, who were slain by the showers of stones hurled down by the peers.
The Saracens retire.
A second attack ensues.

Tho fayled hem cast, þat were *with*-inne;
Tho cowde thai no rede,
For stoone was ther noone to wy*n*ne.
Tho were thay in grete drede.

There being no stones,

Than saide Florip, "beith not dismayde!
Ye shalle be holpe anooñ.
Here is syluer vessel and now,"[1] she sayde,
"That shulle ye prove goode wooñ."
She set it forth, thay caste oute faste
Alle that came to honde.

Floripas gave them her father's silver and gold to cast amongst the assailants.

[leaf 62]

Off siluer and goolde vessel thay made waste
That wast[2] downñ vppoñ the sonde.
Whañ thai saugh that roial sight,
Thai leften alle here dede;
And for the tresoure thay do fight,
Who so myghte it awey lede.
Tho the Sowdoñ wexe nere wode,
Seinge this tresoure thus dispoyled,
That was to him so dere and goode
Laye in the dike thus defouled.
He bade that thai shulde leue

The soudan in alarm for his treasure gives up the assault.

[1] ? I now. [2] *Read:* 'went.'

And turne hem̄ agayne in haste.
He wente home tille his tente than
With grete sorowe and mournyng' mode.
To-fore his goddis whan̄ he came,
He cryed, as he were wode:

He is enraged with his gods,

"O fals goddis, that ye beth̄,
I have trustid to longe youre mode.
We[1] were lever' to suffr' dede,
Than̄ lif this life here lenger nowe.
I haue almoste loste the breth̄,
xij fals traytou*r*s me overe-lede,
And stroyen alle þat I haue.
Ye fals goddis, the devel youe spede!
Ye make me nowe for to rave;
Ye do fayle me at my nede."

and smites Mahound

In Ire he smote Mahounde,
That was of goolde fulle rede,

so that he fell on his face;

That he fille down̄ to the grounde,
As he hade bene dede.
Alle here bisshopes cryden̄ oute
And saide "Mahounde, thyn̄ ore!"
And down̄ to the erthe wele lowe thay loute,
Howlynge and wepynge sore,
And saide "Sire Sowdon̄, what haue ye done?
Vengeaunce shalle on the falle,
But thou) repente the here anone."

but the priests induce him

"Ye" q*uo*d he "I shrewe you) alle!"
Thai made a fyre of frank'encense
And bleweñ hornes of bras,

[leaf 63]

And casten in milke hony for the offence,
To-fore Mahoundes face.

to kneel down and ask forgiveness.

Thay counsailed Laban to knele a down̄
And aske forgevenes in that place.
And so he didde and hade pardon̄
Throgh prayere and specialle grace.

[1] ? Me.

Meanwhile Roland

Then[1] this was done, þan sayde Roulande
To his Felowes xj:
"Here may we not longe holde londe,
By God that is in heven.
Therefore sende we to Charles, the kinge,
That he wolde reskowe vs sone;

exhorted Richard of Normandy to go on message to Charles, that he might come to their rescue.

And certyfye him of oure strayȝte beinge,
If ye thinke, it be to done.
Richard of Normandye, ye most goon,
I holde you both wyse and hende.

They all would the following morning, before day break, make an attack on the Saracens, and meanwhile he should steal off in the darkness.

And we shalle tomorowe, as stil as stoon,
The Saresyns a-wake, er ye wynde.[2]
And while we be mooste bysy in oure werke,
And medel with hem alle in fere,
Stele ye a-waye in the derke!
And spede you faste, ye were there!"

In the morning they sally out.

On the morowe aftir the daye
Thay were armede ful ryghte,
Thai rode forth stilly in here way,
God gouerne hem, mooste of myght!

Floripas and her maidens draw up the bridges after them.

Floripe and here maydyns kept the tour
And woonde vp the brigges on hye,
And prayde god, to kepe here paramour,
The Duke of Burgoyne, *Sir* Gye.
She preyde to Rouland, er he wente,
To take goode hede of him,
That he were neyþer take nere shente,
As he wolde her loue wynne.
On thay set with herte stronge
And alle hem sore afrayed.

Richard went off towards Mantrible.

Richard the whiles away he wronge,
Thile[3] thai were alle dismayede.
Towarde the Mountrible he hyed him faste,
To passe, if that he myghte. [leaf 64]
Thedir he came at the laste.

[1] ? 'When.' [2] *Read:* 'wende.' [3] ? 'while.'

God kepe him for his moch̄ myght!
The others slay many Saracens;
His xij[1] felowes besyed hem̄ soo
That many of hem̄ thay sloughe.[2]
Gye slowe the kinge of Babyloyne tho;
but Guy, overpowered by the Babylonians, is taken prisoner.
The Babyloynes of his hors him drowe,
And with force him drowe there
And bounde his hondes ful fast.
A newe game thai gan̄ him lere,
For in depe prison̄ thay him caste.
But Laban̄ wolde him first se,
To wete what he was.
Laban asks his name.
"Telle me thy name nowe" q*uo*d he,
"Thy songe shalle be 'alas.'"—
Guy tells him.
"Sire" he saide "my name is Gye,
I wole it never forsake.
It were to me grete vilanye
An̄ othir name to take."—
"O fals traytou*r*" q*uo*d Laban̄,
"My doghtir, þat stronge hore,
Hath me for-sake and the hath tan̄,
Thou shalte be honged therfore."
He is to be hanged.
Roulande made grete moone,
It wolde noon̄ other be.
Homwarde thai gan̄ goon̄,
300 Saracens crowding near the gate of the castle, attempted to prevent the other peers from entering.
.iij.c Saresyns ther saye he,
That kepte the pace at the brigge-ende,
Armed wel in goode araye,
That thai sholde not in wende,
But be take or slayn̄ þat daye.
Roulande to his felowes saide:
"Beth alle of right gode chere!
And we shal make hem alle afrayde,
Er' we go to oure soupere."
A fearful struggle begins.
There byganne a bykeringe bolde
Of x Bachelers that tyde,

[1] ? xj.

[2] *See the note.*

Agayne iijc meñ I-tolde,
That durste righte wel a-byde.
Tho was Durnedale set a werke, [leaf 65]
XL of hethen he sloughe,
He spared neþer' lewde ner clerke,
And Floripas ther'-of loughe.
The shotte, the caste was so stronge,
Syr Bryer was slayñ there

Sir Bryer is killed.

With dartes, gauylokes and speres longe,
xx^ti on hym there were.
Roulande was woo and Olyuer',
Thay sloughen alle that thai mette.
Tho fledde the Turkes alle for fer',

At last the Saracens take to flight.

Thay durste no longer lette
And saide, thai wer' no men,
But develis abrokeñ oute of helle,
".iij. hundred of vs agayñ hem teñ.
Oure lorde Mahounde hem qwelle!
XL of vs here be ascaped,
And hardde we be bistadde."—
"Who so wole of hem̃ more be iaped,
I holde him worsse than madde."
Tho Roulande and Olyuer'
Madeñ grete woo and sorowe,
And tokeñ the corps of Sir Bryere

The peers retire inside the castle, taking the corpse of Bryer with them.

And beryed it on the morowe.
Floripe asked Roulande anoone
"Where is my loue Sir Gye?"—

Floripas enquires after Guy,

"Damesel" he saide "he is gooñ,
And therfore woo am I."—
"Alas" she saide "than am I dede,

and on hearing of his capture, begins to lament despairingly.

Nowe Gye my lorde is slayñ,
Shall I neuer more ete brede
Tille that I may se him̃ agayñ."—
"Be stille" q*uo*d Roulande "and haue no car',

Roland promises to rescue Guy.

We shal hym̃ haue ful wele.

Tomorowe wele we thiderward far'
With spere and shelde of stele.
But we bringe him to this Tour'—
Leeve me elles no more—
With victorye and grete honour',
[leaf 66] Or thay shalle abye it ful sore."
On the morowe, whan tha daye was clere,
Laban ordeynede Gye honged to be.

On the following morning Laban orders Sir Tamper to erect a gallows before the castle, where Floripas could see it.

He cleped forth Sir Tampere
And badde him do make a Galowe tre,
"And set it eveñ by-fore the tour',
That þilke hore may him see;
For by lord Mahounde of honour',
This traitour there shalle honged be.
Take withe the .iij. hundred knightes
Of Ethiopis, Indens and Ascopartes,
That bene boolde and hardy to fight
With Wifles, Fauchons, Gauylokes[1] and Dartes;
Leste þat lurdeynes come skulkynge oute,
For ever thay haue bene shrewes.
Loke eche of hem̄ haue such̄ a cloute,
That thay neuer ete moo Sewes."

Guy is led bound.

Forth thay wente with Sir Gye,
That bounde was as a thefe faste,
Tille thay come the towr' ful nye;
Thai rered the Galowes in haste.
Roulande perceyued here doynge

Roland calls his companions to arms.

And saide "felows, let armes[2]!
I am ful gladde of here comynge,
Hem shall not helpe her charmes."

They rush forth.

Oute thai ridēn a wele gode spede,
Thai ix towarde hem alle.
Florip with̄ here maydyns toke gode hede,
Biholdinge over the tour' walle.
Thai met first with̄ Sir Tamper',

[1] *MS.* Gamylokes. [2] *Read:* 'as armes.'

God gife him evelle fyne!
Such a stroke lente hym Olyuer',
He clefe him down̄ to the skyne.

Oliver cuts down Sir Tamper;

Rouland bare the kinge of Ynde
Ther with his spere frome his stede.
.iiij. fote it passed his bak byhynde,
His herte blode þer' didde he blede.

Roland kills a king of India,

He caught the stede, he was ful goode,
And the swerde, þat the kinge hadde,
And rode to Gye, there he stode,

takes his sword and horse,

[leaf 67]

And onbounde hym̄ and bade him be gladde.
And girde him with̄ that goode swerde,
And lepen vppon̄ here stedes.
"Be thou" he saide "righte nought̄ a-ferde,
But helpe vs wightly at this nede."

and gives them to Guy, having unbound him.

An hundred of hem sone thay slowe
Of the beste of hem alle;
The remen*au*nte a-way fast thay flowe,
That foule motte hem byfalle!

They slay many Saracens, and put the rest to flight.

Rouland and his Felowes were glad
That Gye was safe in dede.
Thay thanked god, that thay[1] him hadde
Gyfen thay*e*[1] such̄ grace to spede.
As thay wente towarde the Tour',
A litil bysyde the hye waye,
Thai saugh comynge with grete vigour'
An hundred vppon̄ a laye.[2]

Retiring towards the castle,

Costroye ther was, the Admyrall,
With vitaile grete plente,
And the stondarte of the Sowdon̄ Roial.
Towarde Mauntrible riden̄ he,
.iiij. Chariotes I-charged with̄ flessh and brede,
And two other' with wyne,
Of divers colouris, yolowe, white and rede,
And iiij Somers of spicery fyne.

they see admiral Costroye and the soudan's standard-bearer escorting a great convoy, destined for the sultan, across a field near the high road.

[1] *See the note.* [2] *MS.* 'alaye.' *See the note.*

Tho saide Roulande to Olyuerʼ:
"With these meyne moste we shifte,
To haue parte of here vitailes herʼ,
For therof us nedith by my thrifte."—
Roland calls to them
"Howe, sires" he saide "god you see!
We pray youe for youre curtesye,
to share the provisions with them.
Parte of your Vitaile graunte me,
For we may nother borowe ner bye."
Tho spake Cosdroye, that Admyral,
Costroye refuses,
"Ye gete none here for noght.
Yf ye oght chalenge in speciall,
It most be dere I-boght."—
"O gentil knightes" quod Olyuere,
"He is no felowe, þat wole haue alle."
"Go forth" quod the stondart, "thou getist noon here,
Thy parte shalle be fulle smalle."—
[leaf 68]
"Forsoth" quod Roulande "and shift we wole,
Gete the better, who gete maye!
To parte with the nedy it is gode skille,
And so shalle ye by my faye."
and is slain by Roland.
He rode to the Admyral with his swerde
And gafe him suche a cloute,
No wonder thogh he were aferde,
Both his eyȝen braste oute.
Olyuere met withe the proude stondarde,
Oliver kills the standard-bearer.
He smote him through the herte.
That hade he for his rewarde;
That wounde gan sore smerte.
Thai were slayn, that wolde fight
Er durste bikure abyde.
Thai forsoke her parte anoon right,
It lefte alle on that on side.
The convoy is conveyed into the castle.
Forth thai drewen þat vitaile
Streight in-to the Toure.
There was no man durst hem assayle
For drede of here vigourʼ.

Floripe hem resceyved *with* honour'
And thanked Roulande fele sythe,
That she saugħ Gye hir paramour',
That wolde she him qwite and kith*e*.
Thai eteñ and dronken and made hem gladde,
Hem neded ther aftyr fulle sore
Of suche, as god hem sente hade,
I-nowe for iiij moonþes and more.
Florip saide to Roulande than,
"Ye moste chese you a love[1]
Of alle my maydyns, white as swañ."—
Q*uo*d Rouland "þat were myscheve;
Oure lay wole not, þat we *with* youe dele,
Tille that ye Cristyñ be made;
Ner of your play we wole not fele,
For thañ were we cursed in dede."

Floripas thanks Roland for bringing back Sir Guy, and proposes that he shall choose himself a mistress from amongst her maidens. But Roland refuses to take any that is no Christian.

NOwe shall ye here of Labañ.
Whan tidyngg*es* to him wer' comeñ,
Tho was he a fulle sory mañ.
Whan he herde, howe his vitaile were nomeñ,
And howe his men were slayne,
And Gye was go safe hem̃ froo, [leaf 69]
He defyed Mahounde and Apolyne,
Iubiter, Ascarot and Alcaroñ also.
He commaundede a fire to be dighŧ
With picche and Brymstoñ to breñ.
He made a vowe with alle his myghŧ,
"Thai shal be caste ther-Inne!"
The prestes of her' lawe ther-oñ,
Thai crideñ oute for drede
And saide "alas, what wole ye done?
The worse than moste ye spede!"
The Sowdoñ made a grete othe
And swore by his hye trone,
That though hem were never so lotħ,

The soudan, on hearing such bad news, again defies his gods, and threatens to throw them into the flames.

[1] *Read:* 'leve.'

Thai sholde be brente Ichon̄.

But bishop Cramadas kneels before him and appeases him.

Tho came the bisshope Cramadas
And kneled bifore the Sowdon̄,
And charged him by the hye name Sathanas,
To saven his goddes ychon̄:
"For if ye brenne youre goddes her',
Ye wynnyn̄ her malison̄,
Than wole no man do you' cher',
In feelde, Cite, ner' in town̄."
The Sowdon̄ was astonyed þan
And gan him sore repente
Of the foly, that he bygan̄,
And els hade he be shente.

The soudan makes an offering of 1000 besants to his gods.

A thousande of Besauntes he offred þaym to,
By counsail of sir Cramadas,
To please with̄ his goddys tho,
For fere of harde grace.
The Sowdone commaunded euery daye
To assaile the tour' with̄ caste.
But thay with-in gafe not an Eye,
For thai wroghte in wast.

NOwe speke we of Richarde of Normandy,
That on message was sente,
Howe he spede and his meyne.

When Richard arrived as far as Mantrible, he [leaf 70] found the bridge barred by 24 chains, and Alagolafre standing before it.

Whan he to Mauntrible wente,
He founde the brigge Ichayned sore;
xxiiij^ti^ were ouere-drawen̄.
Alagolofure stode there byfore,
That many a man hade slawene.
Whan Richard saugh̄, ther was no gate,
But by flagot the flode,

Determined not to leave his errand unperformed, he knelt down and commended himself to God.

His message wolde he not lete;
His hors was both̄ bigge and goode.
He kneled, bisechinge god of his grace,
To save him fro myschiefe.

A hind appears

A white hende he saugh̄ anoon̄ in þat place,

That swam̄ over' the cliffe.
He blessed him in godis name
And folowed the same waye
The gentil hende, þat was so tame,
That on̄ þat othir side gan playe.
He thanked god fele syth*e*,
That him hade sente comforte.
He hied him in his message swiþe,
To speke with̄ Charles his lorde.
But I shalle you' telle of a trayto*ur*,
That his name was called Genelyne,
He counseiled Charles for his honour'
To turne homewarde ageyn̄.
He saide "the xij peres bene alle dede,
And ye spende your goode in vayne,
And therfore doth̄ nowe by my rede,
Ye shalle see hem no more certeyn̄."
The kinge bileved þat he saide,
And homwarde gan he fare.
He of his xij Dosiperes was sore dismayed,
His herte woxe right fulle of car'.
Rycharde of Normandy came prikande
And hertly to ride begane.
Kinge Charles aspyed him comande;
He co*m*maunded to abide eu*er*y man̄.
"What tidingg*es*?" q*uo*d the kinge to Richarde,
"Howe fare my felowes alle?"
"My lorde" he saide "god wote, ful harde,
For thai be byseged with-in ston-walle,
Abydynge youre helpe and your' socour',
As men þat haue grete nede.
For Ihe*s*ues loue, kinge of honour',
Thiderward ye you' spede!"
"O Genelyne" q*uo*d the kinge,
"Nowe knowe I thy treson̄,
I shalle the qwite, be seynte Fremounde,

and swims across.

Richard follows her, and, passing over in safety,

hurries on to Charlemagne.

Meanwhile Genelyn, the traitor, had advised Charles to retire to France, because the 12 peers were all slain.

The king believed him, and marched homeward, lamenting for his peers.

Richard overtakes him, and is recognised by Charles,

who asks him about the others.

Richard tells the king, how they are besieged within the castle, and are waiting for his assistance.

Charles, vowing vengeance on [leaf 71] Genelyn,

Whan̄ this viage is don̄."

turned and marched to Agremore.

The kinge turned him ageyn̄,
And alle his Ooste him witħ,
Towarde Mountrible certeyne.
And[1] graunte him gree and grith!
Richarde him tolde of that place,
Howe stronge it was I-holde

Richard informed him of the giant, who kept the bridge,

With a geaunte foule of face,
The brigge hath chayned many folde;
The River was both depe and brode,
Ther myght no man̄ over-ryde.

and how he had passed the river by a miracle.

"The last tyme that I over-rode,
By myracle I passed þat tide.
Therfore sir, I shal you telle,
Howe ye mote governe you here.

He proposed a plan,

In yonde wode ye moste dwelle
Priuely in this maner’,

that 12 knights disguised as merchants, with

And xij of vs shalle vs araye
In gyse of stronge marchauntes,
And fille oure somers withe fog and haye,
To passe the brigge Curraunte*s*.

their arms hidden under their clothes,

We shalle be armed vnder the cote
With goode swerdes wele I-gyrde,

should pay the toll,

We moste paye tribute, wele I wote,
And elles over we may not sterte.

and the bridge being let down,

But whan̄ the chaynes be lete down̄
Ouer ther for to passe,
Than wole I, þat ye come on̄,
In haste to that same place.
Whan̄ I see tyme for to come,

should blow a horn as a signal for the others to approach.

Than̄ shalle I my horne blowe.
Loke, ye be redy alle and some,
For that shaƚƚ ye welle knowe."

They start and arrive at Mantrible.

Forth thay wente in þat araye
To Mountrible, that Cite.

[1] *Read:* 'God.'

Alagolofur’ to hem̄ gan seye, — *Alagolafre asks whither they are going.*
“Felawes, wheder wole ye?”
Richarde spake to the geaunte
And saide “towarde the Sowdon̄, — *Richard says, they are merchants on their way to the Soudan,*
With dyu[e]rs chaffer’ as trewe marchaunte,
We purpose for to goon̄,
To shewen him of pellur’ and Gryse,[1]
Orfrays of Perse Imperyalle, — [leaf 72]
We wole the yefe tribute of assaye — *and they are willing to pay the toll.*
To passe by lycence in especyaƚƚ.”
“Licence gete ye noon̄ of me,[2] — *Alagolafre refuses to let them pass,*
I am charged that noone shaƚƚ passe,
For x lurdeyns of Fraunce were her’; — *and tells them about the 10 knights,*
God yefe hem evell grace!
Thay passed this way to Egramour’; — *who had passed there and done so much mischief to the Soudan;*
Thay haue done the Sowdon̄ grete tene,
Thay have wonne his toure and his tresour’,
And yet holde thai it, I wene.
Wherfor’, felawes, I arest you) alle, — *therefore he will arrest them all.*
Tille I knowe, what þat ye bene.”
Sire Focarde brayde oute his swerde with̄-alle, — *Sir Focard draws his sword and*
Wel sore he gan to tene
And saide “fye on̄ the Sarasyne!
For alle thy grete harde hede
Shaltow never drinke wat*er* ner wyne,
By god! thou shalte be dede.”
He smote at him with̄ egre chere — *smites at him.*
But he gafe thereof right nought.
“Alas” q*uo*d Richard “thou combrest vs her’,
By god, that me der’ hath̄ boghte.”
The cheynes yet wer’ alle faste,
The geaunte wexe nere wode,
Richard blewe his horne in haste, — *Richard blows his horn,*
That was both shrille and goode.
Kinge Charles hied him anoon̄ — *and Charles advances.*

[1] *Read:* ‘gray.’ [2] *See the note.*

Towarde the brigge so longe;
The Geaunte faught with hem̄ alone,
He was so harde and stronge.

Alagolafre fights them with a great oak club.

With a Clog' of an̄ Oke he faugh̄t,
That was wele bound with stele.
He slough al þat ever' he raugh̄t,
So stronge was his dinte to dele.

Richard seizes a bar of brass and knocks him down.

Richard raught him with̄ a barr' of bras,
That he caught at the gate.
He brake his legges, he cryed "alas"
And felle alle chek'-mate.
Loude than̄ gan̄ he to yelle;
Thay herde him yelle through̄ þat Cite,
Like the grete develle of helle,

[leaf 73]

And saide "Mahounde, nowe helpe me!"

4 men get hold of him

iiij men him caught ther',
So hevy he was and longe,

and throw him into the river.

And cast him ouer in-to the river'.
Chese he, whither[1] he wolde swy*m*me or gong'!

They loosened the chains;

Anoon̄ thay brast the Chaynes alle,
That ouer the brigge were I-drawe.

but, the Saracens assembling on the walls of the city, many Christians were slain.

The Saresyns ronnen̄ to the walle,
Many Cristen̄ men were ther' I-slawe.

Alagolafre's wife, Barrock the giantess, comes on with her scythe and mows down all whom she meets.

Than came forth Dam barrok', the bolde,
With a sithe large and kene,
And mewe a-down̄ as þikke as shepe in folde,
That came byforne hir by-dene.
This Barrok' was a geaunesse,
And wife she was to Astragote,
She did the Cristen̄ grete distresse,
She felled downe alle þat she smote.
There durst no man hire sithe abyde,
She grenned like a develle of helle.

Charles dashes out her brains,

Kinge Charles with a quarel þat tide
Smote hir, that she lowde gan̄ yelle,

[1] ? 'whether.'

Euer[1] the founte through-oute the brayn̄;
That cursede fende fille down̄ dede.
Many a man hade she there slayn̄,
Might she never aftyr ete more brede!
Charles entred in the firste warde

and with 15 knights enters the outer gate of the town,

With xv knightis and no moo;
Of hym his oste toke no garde,
He wende his oste hade entred also.

thinking his army would follow him.

The Sarysyns ronne to the gate,
And shet it wonder faste.

But the gate was instantly closed upon him, and his men came too late.

Charles men̄ come to late;
Tho was Charles sore agaste.
Betwene two wardes he was shit,
Defende he him if he can̄!
The Sarysyns with him thay mette,

Charles was in great danger;

Grete parel was he in than̄.
Tho Genelyne saie, the kinge was inne

but Genelyn, seeing him shut in,

And the yates faste I-stoke,
Ther myght no man̄ to him wynne,
So was he faste with̄-inne I-loke,
To his frendes he gan speke
And saide "the kinge is dede,

[leaf 74] exclaimed that the king and the 12 peers were dead, and proposed to retire,

And alle xij peres eke.
On peyne" said he "to lese myn hede,
Let vs hye to Fraunce warde!
For I wele be crownede kinge,

as he wished to be king himself.

I shalle you alle wele rewarde,
For I wole spare for no thinge."
Anoon̄ thay assented to Genelyne,
Thay saugh, ther was no better rede.
The Frenssh men̄ drewe hem̄ al ayene,

They are going to return,

Thay wende the kinge hade bene dedde.
Tho Ferumbras with̄ his meyne than̄

but Ferumbras

Came for to seke the kinge,
And saugh hem turne euery man̄;

[1] *Read* 'over.'

Him thought, it was a wondir thing.
"Where is the kinge?" q*uo*d Ferumbras.
Q*uo*d Genelyne "with-in the walle,
Shaltowe neuer' more seen his face!"
"God gyf the an yvel falle!

calls him a traitour,

Turne agayne, thou traytoure!
And helpe to reskowe thy lorde.

rallies the French,

And ye, sires, alle for your' honour'!"
Thay turned agayne with that worde.

and with his axe bursts open the gate.

Ferumbras with axe in honde,
Myghtyly brake up the gate,
Ther myght laste him noon yron bonde,
He hade ner'-honde I-come to late.
The kinge hadde fought so longe with-ynne,
That onnethe myght he no more.
Many ther were abouten him,
His men were wounded ful sore.
Ferumbras came with gode spede,

He chased the Saracens and rescued the king.

He made the Sarasyns to fle.
He reskowed the kinge at his nede,
XL Sarasyns sone killed he.
Thai ronnen a-weye by every side,
Thai durste nowher' rowte.
In shorte tyme was falled her pride,
Thay caught many a sore cloute.

Mantrible is taken,

That Cite was wonne that same daye,
And every tour' ther-ynne
Of Mountreble, þat was so gaye,

[leaf 75]

For alle her' soubtile gynne,

with all its engines and treasures.

Fulle of tresour' and richesse,
Of Siluer and goolde and perr',
And clothes of goolde, wroght of Saresynes,
Of riche aray and roialte.

Richard found 2 children of 7 months old and

Richarde, Duke of Normandy,
Founde ij Children of .vij. monþes oolde,[1]

[1] *See the note.*

xiiij fote longe wer' thay,
Thay wer' Barrakes so*nn*es so boolde;
Bygote thay wer' of Astragot.
Grete joye the kinge of he*m* hade.

4 feet high. They were sons of Barrock, begotten by Astragot.

Hethen̄ thay wer' both̄, wele I wote,
Therfore hem̄ to be cristenede he bade.
He called þat one of hem Roulande,
And that other he cleped Olyuer':
"For thai shalle be myghty men of honde."

Charles caused them to be baptized, and called the one Roland and the other Oliver.

To kepen̄ hem, he was fulle chere.
Thay myght not leve, her Dam was dede;
Thai coude not kepe hem forth̄.
Thai wolde neyþer ete butt*er* nere brede,
Ner no men̄[1] was to hem worthe.
Her' Da*m*mes mylke they lakked ther',
Thay deyden for defaute of here dam.

But they soon died for want of their mother's milk.

Kinge Charles made hevy cher',
And a sory man̄ was than.
The kinge lete ordeyne anoon̄,
The Cite to be gouerned
Of the worthyest of hem̄ ychon̄,
That weren of werr' best lerned.
Duke Richarde of Normandy,
He was made chief gou*er*nour';
And ij C with him in hys company
To kepe the brigge and tour'.

The king appoints Richard governor of the city,

Forth̄ he rode to laban̄ than̄,
With his Ooste and Sir' Ferumbras.

and hurries on to Agremore with his army and with Ferumbras.

A spye to the Sowdon̄ fast ran
And tolde him al that cas,
How Charles was come with his ost,
And Mountrible hade he wonne,
"Alagolofur slayn̄ is for alle his bost,
This game was evel begon̄."
Whane laban herde of his comynge,

[1] *Read:* 'mete.'

Him thought his herte gan breke.
[leaf 76] "Shalle I never be withoute moornynge,
Tille I of him be wreke."
He co*m*maunded to blowe his Claryons
To assemble alle his Ooste.
His counsaile to him he lete calle

Laban, being told by a spy that his city was taken and the bridge-ward killed,

And tolde, how kinge Charles was in þat coost,
Hadde wonne Mountrible and slayñ his men
"And dishirytħ to disheryte me,
And proudely manessith me to fleeñ,
Or drive me oute of this contr*e*.
Me mervaylythe moch of his pride.
By Mahounde, moost of myghŧ!
Ye and my sone withe him doth ride,
To the develle I hem bedighŧ.

swears to avenge him.

But I be venget of hem both
And honge hem̄ on a tree,
To myghty Mahounde I make myne othe,
Shalle I never Joyfulle be.

He calls a council, and charges his barons to take Charles alive that he might flay him.

Therfore I charge you' in alle wyse
That thay be taken or slayñ.
Thane shalle I py*n*ne heme at my gyse
And doñ hem alle qwike be flayñ."

Charles approaches.

On the morowe, whan it was day,
Kinge Charles was in the felde,
Byfore Agremour' in riche aray
On stede witħ sper' and sheelde.

Floripas first recognises the banner of France

Floripe lay on the tour' oñ hye
And knewe the baner' of Fraunce.
To Roulande she gan faste crye
Tidynges of goode chaunce:

and tells the others.

"Kinge Charles is comen and Ferumbras,
Here baners botħ I do see,
With alle her oste yonder' in þat place;
Welcome to vs thay alle be."
Roulande and Olyuere

Arayed hem for to ride ;
And here felawes alle in fer’,
To Charles thay goñ that tyde.

Roland and all his companions sally forth to meet Charlemagne.

Laban come forth with his mayne,
Saresyns, that were ful felle,
Turkes, Indens, and Arabye
Ye and of the Ethiopes like the develes of helle.
There were stronge wardes sette
By ordynaunce of dyuers batáyle.

Laban draws up all his people [leaf 77] in battle-order.

Whan thay to geder were met,
Eythir othir sore gañ assayle.
Ther were Saresyns al to-hewe ;
Roulande sloughe many one.
Thay lay so thikke dede on rewe,
That onneþe myghte men ride or gooñ.

The French make a great slaughter of the Saracens.

Kinge Charles met with Labañ
And bare him downñ of his stede,
He lighted downñ and ceased him thañ,
He thought to qwite him his mede.
He brayde oute Mowñjoye wythñ gode wille
And wolde have smeten of his hede,
Ferumbras prayde him to abyde stille,
To crysteñ him, er he wer’ dede.

Charles encounters the Soudan, unhorses him, and would have cut off his head, but for Ferumbras, who requested that his father might be baptized.

The Saresyns saughe Laban take,
Thay fleddeñ away fulle faste.
Lenger durste thay no maistryes make,
Thai were so sore agaste.
The Cristeñ hem chased to and fro,
As a grehounde doth the hare.
.iij. c. ascaped with moche woo,
To Belmore gan thay far’.

The Saracens, seeing Laban a prisoner, fly ; but the Christians pursue them. 300 escaped to Belmarine.

Kinge Charles ladde Labañ
In-to Agremour’ Cite.
And whañ þat he ther’ came
A ful sory man was he.
His doghter welcomed him

Charles leads Laban to Agremore. Floripas welcomes her father,

With right gode cher’.[1]

but he is enraged at seeing her.

He loked on hir al grymme,
As he wode wroth wer’,
And saide "fye on the, stronge hore,
Mahounde confounde the!"
Charles saide "here-of no more,
But let us nowe mery be!"—

She then bids Charlemagne welcome,

"Sir" she saide thanne,
"Welcome ye be into this tour’!

and presents the holy relics to him.

Here I presente to you, as I can,
Relikes of grete honour’,
That were at Rome I-wonneñ
And broght into this halle.
That game was evel bygonneñ,

[leaf 78]

It sithen rewed us alle."

Charles kisses them, and says a prayer;

Kinge Charles kneled adowñ
To kisse the Relikes so goode,
And badde ther’ añ orysoñ
To that lorde, þat deyde oñ rode.

he then thanks Floripas for her assistance to his knights,

And þanked Floripe withñ al his herte,
That she hade saued his meyne
And holpe hem oute of peynes smerte

and for having preserved the precious relics.

And kepte the Relekes so fre.
Kinge Charles did calle bisshope Turpyñ

He orders Turpin to prepare a vessel, wherein to baptize the Soudan

And bade him ordeyne a grete fat,
To baptyse the Sowdoñ yne;
"And loke what he shalle hat.
Unarme him faste and bringe him ner’,
I shal his godfader be.
Fille it fulle of water’ cler’,
For Baptysed shalle he be.
Make him naked as a Childe,

and to wash off his sin in the water.

He moste plunge ther-inne.
For now most he be meke and mylde,
And I-wassh awaye his synne."

[1] *These two lines are written as one in the MS.*

Turpyn toke him by the honde
And ladde him to the fonte.
He smote the bisshope with̄ a bronde
And gaf him an evel bronte.

Turpin leads Laban to the font, but the Soudan strikes at him,

He spitted in the water cler'
And cryed oute on hem alle,
And defied alle þat cristen̄ wer'.
That foule mote him by-falle!

spits on the vessel, utters invectives against all Christians,

"Ye and thou, hore serpentyne,
And that fals cursed Ferumbras,
Mahounde gyfe hem both̄ evel endyng',
And almyghty Sathanas!

and curses Ferumbras.

By you came all my sorowe,
And al my tresure for-lorne.
Honged be ye both er tomorowe!
In cursed tyme were ye born̄."
Ferumbras saide to the kinge,
"Sir, ye see, it wole not be,
Lete him take his endynge,
For he loueth not Cristyante."
"Duke Neymes" q*uo*d Charles tho,
"Loke þat execucion̄ be don̄,
Smyte of his hedde! god gyfe him woo!
And goo we to mete anoone."

Charles commands Naymes to cut off his head. [leaf 79]

It was done as the kinge co*m*maunde,
His soule was fet to helle,
To daunse in þat sory lande
With develes, þat wer' ful felle.

He is executed; his soul goes to hell, there to dance with devils.

Dame Florip was Baptysed than̄
And here maydyns alle,
And to Sir Gye I-maryed.
The Barons honoured hir alle.

Floripas was baptized with all her maidens, and wedded to Guy.

Alle the londe of Spayne
Kinge Charles gyfe hem̄ two,
To departe bitwyxt hem twayne,
Ferumbras and Gȳ also.

Charles divided Spain between Guy and Ferumbras,

And so thay livede in ioye and game,
And bretherñ both thay wer’,
In pees and werr’ both I-same,
Ther’ durste no mañ hem der’.
Kinge Charles turned home agayñ
Towarde his contre,

and charges Sir Bryer of Bretayne to take care of the relics,

He charged Sir Bryer’ of Bretayne
His tresourer’ for to be :
To kepe the Relikes of grete pris

and to bring all his treasure to Paris.

And his other tresour’,
And bringe hem safe to Parys,
There to a-bide in store.
He saide “farewell, Sir Ferumbras,

After taking leave of Guy and Floripas,

Ye and Gye, my dere frende !
And thy wyf Dame Floripas !
For to Fraunce nowe wole I wende.
Be ye togeder as breth[e]rñ botħ !
No mañ ye neditħ to drede,
Be ye nevere to-gedere wrotħ,
But eyther helpe othir at his nede.
Vysityth me, whañ ye haue space ;
In-to Fraunce makitħ your disporte,
God wole you sende the bett*er* grace,
In age to do me comforte.”
Thai toke leve of the kinge,
With ful hevy cher’,
And turned agayñ botħ mornynge,
With wepynge water cler’.

he sails to Mounpeler,

Kinge Charles with the victory
Sailed to Mou*n*peleres,

[leaf 80] where he thanks God for the victory,

And thanked almyghty god in glorye,
That he hade saued his Dosiperes,
And fende him of the Saresynes
The hyer honde to have,
For alle here strenghe[1] and her’ Engynes

[1] *Read :* ‘strengthe’

and for the relics.

The Relikes of Rome to saue.

He presents the cross to Paris,

At oure lady of Parys
He offred the Crosse so fre;

the Crown to St. Denis, the three nails to Boulogne.

The Crowñ he offred at seynte Denyse,
At Boloyne the nayles thre.
Alle his Barons of him wer' gladd,
Thai gafe him grete presente.
For he so wele hade I-spedde,
Thay did him grete reuerence.

Charles well remembered the treachery of Genelyn,

The kinge hade wel in mynde
The tresone of Genelyne,
Anooñ for him he dide sende
To yefe him an evel fyne:
"Thou traitour unkynde" quod the kynge,
"Remembrist thou not how ofte
Thou hast me betrayed, þou fals Genelyne?
Therfore thoue shalt be honged on lofte!—
Loke that the execucioñ be doñ,

and ordered him to be drawn and hanged at Montfaucon in Paris.

That throgh Parys he be drawe,
And honged on hye on mount Fawcoñ,
As longeth to traytoures by lawe;
That alle men shall take hede,
What deth traytourys shaƚƚ fele,
That assente to such falshede,
Howe the wynde here bodyes shal kele."

Thus Charles conquered the Soudan of Babylone.

Thus Charles conquered Labañ,
The Sowdoñ of Babyloyne,
That riche Rome stroyed and wañ
And alle the brode londe of Spayñ.
[1] . . . .[an]d of his Barons
. . . .[hi]s pride
. . . . .eligons
. . . . .þat tyde
. . . . .on Charles soule
. . . . .s also

[1] *A corner of the leaf torn off.*

. . . . .Peter and Poule
[leaf 81] God lete hem never wete of woo !
But brynge here soules to goode reste !
That were so worthy in dede.
God give joy to all who read this romance. And gyf vs ioye of the beste,
That of here gestes rede !

Here endithe the Romaunce of the Sowdon of Babyloyne and of Ferumbras his sone who conquerede Rome, And Kynge Charles off Fraunce withe xij. Dosyperes toke the Sowdon in the feelde And smote of his heede.

NOTES.

Page 1, line 1. *myghteste*, evidently an error of the scribe for *myghtes*, cf. ll. 1635, 1312, 3068, 2546, 1200, 2059; and *Syr Ferumbras*, l. 2719.

"Nov help hem þe heȝ kyng of hevene,
Þat art of miȝtes most."

God in glorie occurs again in l. 3229; cf. the French expression *Damedeu de glore; Fierabras* 2332.

p. 1, l. 2. *made* and *wroght* in l. 5 are the 2nd person sing. preterite, which in all other instances in this poem ends in *-est*. But perhaps we might suppose a change of person here, and regard *made* and *wroght* as the third person. For examples of the change of person see *Syr Ferumbras*, ll. 2719, 4393, and *Guy of Warwick*, ed. Zupitza, l. 2324.

p. 1, l. 7. *shulde to love; to* before an infinitive, governed by an auxiliary verb, is pretty common in Middle English works. See Zupitza's note to Guy, 1925.

p. 1, l. 9. *ȝyfe*. This is the only instance of ȝ being written in the present poem at the beginning of a word. *ȝife* is written *if* in all other passages of the poem, cf. ll. 550, 651, 763, and 1061, etc. As to the pronunciation of ȝ in the middle of a word, it is doubtful, whether it had still preserved its ancient guttural sound, or not, as the same words are written sometimes with it and sometimes without it, and are often made to rhyme with words in which ȝ or *gh* would be etymologically incorrect; e. g. *nye*, which is spelt *nyȝe* in l. 2284, rhymes with *Gye*, in l. 2657. We even find *whiȝte*, in l. 2289, instead of *white* (l. 2008: *smyte*). At the end of a word ȝ has the sound of *s*.

p. 1, l. 13. *idoone*. The prefix *i-*, O.E. *ge-*, sometimes occurs in this poem, but more frequently it is not written; see *Introduction*, p. xxxviii.

p. 1, l. 14. cf. l. 2516.—ll. 1—14 may be said to contain the moral of the whole poem, which we know the romance writers to be very fond of placing at the beginning of their works. "La moralité de tout un poème," says Léon Gautier, in his *Epopées Françaises*, I. 233, "est quelquefois exprimée dans ses premiers vers."

p. 1, l. 16. *moch* = *much* (as in l. 754) is the usual spelling in this poem. We likewise find *meche*, l. 179, and *mikille*, l. 1016.

p. 1, l. 19. *his* refers to *Rome*.

p. 1, l. 22. Laban, the father of Ferumbras, is styled *sowdan* only in this poem, and once in the *Destruction de Rome*, l. 1436:

"Les noveles en vindrent al *soldan* diffaié."

The French, the Provençal and the English version of *Sir Ferumbras* all agree to call him *amyral* or *amirans*.

p. 1, l. 24. The mention of King Louis and of the abbey of St. Denis (l. 27) seems to be an imitation of the *Destruction*, l. 7 *et seq.*:

"Le chanchon est perdue et le rime fausee,
Mais . . li *rois Louis*, dont l'alme est trespassee
—Ke li fache pardon la verge honoree—
Par lui et par Gautier est l'estoire aunee
Et le chanchon drescie, esprise et alumee
A *saint Dynis* de France premierement trovee."

St. Denis also occurs in the beginning of the French *Fierabras*, l. 4:

"A *Saint Denis* en France fu li raules trouvés."

Cf. besides note to l. 26. *witnessith* = attests, testifies; cf. Stratmann, p. 645. It occurs again in l. 1489.

p. 2, l. 25. *Romaunce*, the French or *Romance* language. We often find the authors of romances, both of translations and of imitations from the French, referring to the original; cf. *Syr Eglamour of Artoys*, sign. E i:

"His own mother there he wedde,
In Romaunce as we rede."

Again, fol. ult.: "In Romaunce this cronycle is."

[Quoted by Warton, *History of English Poetry*, II. 146, footnote.]

p. 2, l. 26. *bokes of antiquyte*. This is to be regarded as one of those frequent assertions of the authors of these poems, who in order to give more credit to their tales, thought it necessary to affirm their antiquity and celebrity in old times. Cf. Gautier, *Epop. Fr.*, II. 87: "Il fut de bon ton d'annoncer, au commencement de chaque poème, qu'on avait trouvé la matière de ce poème dans quelque vieux manuscrit latin, dans quelque vieille chronique d'abbaye, surtout dans les manuscrits et dans les chroniques de Saint-Denis. On se donnait par là un beau vernis de véracité historique. Plus les trouvèrent ajoutaient aux chansons primitives d'affabulations ridicules, plus ils s'écriaient: 'Nous avons trouvé tout cela dans un vieux livre.'"

p. 2, l. 27. *Seinte Denyse* is the genitive depending on *abbey*.

p. 2, l. 28. *there as* = where, or where that. See Koch, *Englische Grammatik*, II. § 511.

p. 2, l. 29. *Laban*. So the father of Ferumbras is called in the *Destruction de Rome*, where only in six passages (ll. 891, 899, 1116, 1194, 1174, 981) we find the form *Balan*, which is the only one used in the French *Fierabras*, in the Provençal version, and in the English

Syr Ferumbras. — *of hie dègre;* this kind of expletive occurs again in l. 100: *clerk of hie degre;* cf. also l. 168: *king of hie honour.*

p. 2, l. 31. *Cristiante* = the company of Christians, the countries inhabited by Christians, cf. ll. 235, 374. It signifies "the religion taught by Christ" in l. 3182. *Cristiante* and *Christendom* are used promiscuously in Middle English writers.

p. 2, l. 33. *Agremare: there.* The rhyme becomes perfect by reading *Agremore: thore,* which we find in l. 1805; cf. also l. 1003 *Agremore: more* (*i. e.* negro), and ll. 672, 775, 2140, 2895.

p. 2, l. 34. *Flagot.* See *Index of Names*, s. v. Flagot, and cf. note to l. 1723.

p. 2, l. 37. This line is too long, nevertheless it seems to be correct as it stands, clearly imitated from several passages of the *Destruction de Rome.*

l. 420. "Ensamble ou li issirent xv roi corone. Et xiiii amaceours . ."
l. 1155. "Bien i ad xxx rois et xiiii amaceours."
l. 689. "xxx roi sont ou li et xiiii amaceours."
l. 163. "Et xiiii amaceours."

p. 2, l. 41. *hit* instead of *it* is found again in l. 2309; in all the other instances *it* is spelt as in modern English.

p. 2, l. 42. *pryke,* to spur a horse, to excite, to spur or to stimulate. It is O.E. *prician,* which occurs in Ælfric's Grammar, ed. Zupitza, p. 174 (*pungo = ic pricige*). This and the following line are imitated from Chaucer; cf. C. T. Prologue, ll. 10, 11, and see *Introduction*, p. xlvi. *Kynde* = naturalis, ingenuus; *kynde wit* = common sense. *Kynde* is O.E. *cynde* (Modern English *kind*).

p. 2, l. 73. *frith* means "forest," or more correctly "enclosed wood." The original sense of *forest* is "unenclosed wood" (see Diez, *Etymol. Wörterbuch*, I. 185). Stratmann, *Dict.* p. 228, *s. v.* frið, seems to be right in connecting *frith* with O.E. *frið*, *freoðo* = pax, tutela, saeptum. Morris, *Allit. Poems*, Glossary, derives it from the Gaelic *frith.* "*frith* is still used in Provincial English, meaning unused pasture-land, brushwood" (Halliwell).

p. 2, l. 45. *yȝe* (O.E. êagum): *flye* (O.E. flêogan). With regard to the power of ȝ, see the note to l. 9, and cf. the spelling *eyen* in ll. 826, 1302, 2012.

p. 2, l. 46. *tre* may be singular (O.E. *tréowe*) as well as plural (O.E. *trêowum*).

p. 2, l. 49. The following lines (49—53) correspond with ll. 94—100 of the *Destruction*, which run as follows:

"Li admirals d'Espaigne s'est ales desporter
As puis sur Aigremore, avec li. M. Escler;
La fist ses ours salvages a ses hommes berser.
La veissies meint viautre, maint brachet descoupler,
Payens et Ascopars as espees jouer,
Coure par le marine et chacier maint sengler,
Maint ostour veisies et maint falcon voler."

p. 2, l. 50. *shope*, literally "shaped:" *he shope him*, "he got himself ready, he planned, devised, intended." The phrase is of frequent occurrence in Chaucer.

p. 2, l. 52. *bawson*, badger. For the use of badgers, see Skeat's note to *Specimens of English Literature*, p. 383.

p. 2, l. 56. *Alaunts*, a kind of large dogs of great strength and courage, used for hunting the wolf, the bear, the boar, &c. Cf.

"Aboute his chare wente white alauntz
Twenty and mo, as grete as any stere,
To hunte at the lyoun or at the bere."

Chaucer, ed. Morris, II. 66/1290.

According to Diez (*Etymol. Wörterb.*, I. 12, *s. v.* "alano") *alaunts* means "Albanian dogs." *Lymmeris*, "blood-hounds." Halliwell quotes the following passage: "A dogge engendred betwene an hounde and a mastyve, called a lymmer or a mongrell." *Lymmer* is the French *limier*, O.Fr. *liemier*, which etymologically means a dog that a courser leads by a lime, *i. e.* a thong or leash. *Lime* is the same word as French *lien*, a leash; Latin *ligamen*. *Lymmer* is preserved in Modern English *limer*, a "lime-hound."

p. 2, l. 56. *Rache* and *brache* are both retained in the modern speech; *rache* seems to be particularly used in Scotland. "*Brache* is said to signify originally a bitch hound — the feminine of *rache*, a foot-scenting dog" (Morris, *Gawayne*, Gloss. p. 89). *Rache* is, according to Stratmann, O.Icel. *rakki; brache* is O.Fr. *braque*, M.H.Ger. *braccho*. Cf. also Halliwell's Dict. *s. v.* "brach." The French *racaille* is etymologically connected with *rache;* see Diez, *Etym. Wörterb.*, II. 407.

p. 2, l. 57. *commaunde* for *commaunded* (l. 228), formed on the same analogy as *comforte* (l. 2242) for *comforted* (ll. 312, 2117), *aliȝt* for *alighted; gerde* for *girded; graunte* (l. 607) for *graunted*, etc.

p. 2, l. 59. *fere*, O.E. *fǣran* (Mod. Eng. *fear*), is an active verb, meaning "to frighten, to terrify." It is still found in this sense in Shakespeare.—*launde: commaunde.* The very same rhyme occurs again in l. 3189, where *launde* is spelt *lande*. The rhyme need not cause any difficulty, cf. Guy, p. xi. κ. Or must *launde* be taken here for *lande* = saltus? Cf. Morris, Gloss. to *Allit. Poems*, *s. v.* launde.

p. 3, l. 62. *set*, means "seat, sedes"; O.Icel. *set*, O.H.G. *sez*, M.H.G. *sitz*. This stanza as it stands seems to be incorrect, there being no rhyme to *sete;* possibly a line has been lost after l. 63.

p. 3, l. 67. The subject of the sentence is wanting. For more instances see Zupitza's note to *Guy*, l. 10. It is to be observed that for the most part the subject wanting is of the same person as the object of the preceding sentence.—*he was god and trew of divers langages* = "he well knew, understood them perfectly."

p. 3, l. 68. *dromonde: poundis.* Read *dromounde* (which occurs l. 125): *pounde* (see l. 2336).

p. 3, l. 69. We find *fro* and *from* in this poem. Both belong to the Midland dialect. *Fro* is confirmed by the rhyme *fro : so* (l. 2760). It is derived from the Scandinavian *fra;* Mod. Eng. has retained it in "froward," and in the phrase "to and fro." The same word enters as a prefix into composition in O.E. compounds, as *fr-ettan,* etc. *Babyloyne,* the author pronounced *Babyloyne* as well as *Babylòne* (either rhyming, cf. ll. 30, 3260).

p. 3, l. 74. *qweynte,* "famous, excellent," cf. Skeat, *Etymol. Dict.* p. 482, *s. v.* quaint. *for the nones,* "for the nonce, for the occasion." Cf. Zupitza's note to *Guy,* 612; it is often used as a kind of expletive.

p. 3, l. 75. *to presente you.* The *Destruction de Rome* has: "vous qui-dai presenter."

p. 3, l. 76. French: "Uns vens nous fist à Rome parmi le far sigler." *Destr.* l. 120.

p. 3, l. 77. Cf. *Destr.* ll. 115-16. See *Introduction,* p. xxiii.

p. 3, l. 78. About the rhyme *Rome: one,* see *Introduction,* p. xliii.

p. 3, l. 79. *bygone,* "afflicted, pressed hard;" literally it means, "overrun, covered." Cf. Shakespeare, *Julius Cæsar:*

"Even such a one,
So pale, so spiritless, and woe-begone."

p. 3, l. 82. *vilane : remedye.* Read *vilanye,* as in l. 2577, where it rhymes with *Gye,* see *Introduction,* p. xliv, and Ellis, *Pronunciation,* I. 271.

p. 3, l. 83. *colde,* used here and in l. 91 in nearly the same sense as in the expressions collected by Zupitza, in his note to *Guy,* 1149.

p. 8, l. 84. *tithynge.* So with *th* in ll. 1787, 714, 783; in ll. 65, 91, 149, 324, etc., we read *tidinge.* There are several instances where *d* and *th* in the middle of a word seem to be promiscuously used in this poem; as *hithire* l. 1265, *hider* 1869 (cf. also *dogdir* 2580, and *doghter* 96, 124, etc.).

p. 3, l. 86. Mahounde, Appolyn and Termagant are the principal deities (cf. ll. 2105, 2177, 2761) of the Mahometans, who were considered as pagans = *payens* (ll. 535, 1040) or *paynym* (ll. 539, 866, etc.). Other idols of the Saracens are mentioned in ll. 2761-2 of the *Sowdone.* Compare also Gautier's note to l. 8, of his *Edition critique de la Chanson de Roland,* and Skeat, *Prioress's Tale* (Clarendon P.S.), 161/2000.

p. 3, l. 88. *theyme* instead of *hem* occurs only three times in the poem (ll. 88, 1237, 2787). There must be some corruption here, as there is no rhyme to *theym.* The last stanza ends at l. 87, and the next one begins at l. 89. As far as the sense is concerned we could easily do without this line; it ought perhaps to be regarded as spurious.

p. 3, l. 93. *Ferumbras* is spelt differently in the different versions of the romance. In the *Sowdan* we always find *Ferumbras,* in the Ashmole MS. *Ferumbras* and *Fyrumbras.* He is called *Fierabras* in the French

Ferabras in the Provençal version; the *Destruction* has *Fierabras*, but more frequently *Fierenbras*. In Caxton's *Life of Charles the Great* his name is *Fyerabras*, Skelton has *Pherumbras*, Lyndsay *Pharambras*, and in Barbour's *Bruce* we read *Ferambrace*; see *Introduction*, pp. xxv and xxxii.

p. 4, l. 99. *Oliborn*. This name does not occur in any other version of this poem. The same is the case with regard to *Espiard*, l. 103. None of the French versions gives any name to the Soudan's messenger. In the Ashmole MS. l. 3823, the messenger is called *Malyngryas*.

p. 4, l. 102. *Assye* = Asia. This name does not occur in the other versions of the poem; cf. note to l. 1000.

p. 4, l. 103. Cf. the *Destruction*, l. 202:

"Par tote la terre sont li baron mande"

ferre and nere, cf. ll. 117, 996, and the note to l. 528 of *Syr Ferumbras*.

p. 4, l. 104. *frike*, "quick, bold," O.E. *frec*. See Stratmann, *Dictionary*, p. 225.

p. 4, l. 108. *þon*. Compare *Introduction*, p. xxxvii.

p. 4, l. 109. The passage is not clear. Perhaps there is some corruption here and we ought to read: *anon rowte*, "assembled quickly, immediately"; *rowte* would then be the preterite formed on the analogy of *lighte*, *graunte*, *commaunde*, etc. See *Introduction*, p. xxxviii.

p. 4, l. 110. *Destruction*, l. 217:

"Par C fois M payen."

p. 4, l. 112. *douȝte : route*. See *Introduction*, p. xliv, and note to l. 9.

p. 4, l. 113. *Lucafer* is the name of the Saracen King in all the versions of this romance but in the French one, where with the single exception of one passage (l. 2242 *Lucafer*), he is always called *Lucifer*, cf. *Introd.* p. xx.

p. 4, l. 114. *lorde and governoure*. This repetition of the same idea by two synonymous words, the one of English and the other of French origin, is very common in M.E. writers. Thus we read in this poem, l. 2164 *lorde and sire*, l. 225 *serchid and sought*, ll. 3199, 1936 *joye and game*, l. 742 *wel and fine*.

p. 4, l. 118. A *carrik* was a kind of large ship, called *caraca* in Italian, *carraca* in Spanish and Portuguese, *carraque* in French, *kraecke* in Dutch. The etymology is not clear. See Diez, *Etymol. Wörterb.*, I. 112. Halliwell has '*carrack*, a Spanish galleon. Sometimes English vessels of great value and size were so called.'

p. 4, l. 119. *Destruction*, l. 385:

"Par vii fois sont C mil, si l'estoire ne ment."

p. 4, l. 124. *his faire daughter Floripas*. Floripas is described as follows in the *Destruction*, ll. 252-262:

"Aitant es vous la bele ou il n'out qu'enseignier
Vestue d'un diapre, onke ne vi tant chier,

Ses crins sur ses epaules plus lusoient d'or mier,
Sa char out bele et blanke plus que noifs en fevrier,
Les oes avoit plus noirs que falcon montenier,
Et le colour vermaile con rose de rosier,
La bouche bien seant et douce pour baisier,
Et les levres vermailes come flour de peskier;
Les mameles out dures com pomme de pomnier,
Plus sont blanches que noifs que chiet apres fevrier;
Nuls hom ne porroit ja sa grant bealte preisier."

Compare also the French *Fierabras*, ll. 2007, *et seq.*

p. 4, l. 128. This line is clearly imitated from the *Destruction*, ll. 331-2:

"En sa main .i. baston que contremont bailie,
Et manace François pour faire les loye."

Cf. *Introduction*, p. xxiii.

p. 5, l. 131. *breddes*, "birds"; *l* and *r* very often change their place in a word. Thus we find *worlde* and *wrolde*, *crafti* and *carfti*, etc.

p. 5, l. 132. *sowdon* and *sowdan* are used promiscuously in the rhymes.

p. 5, l. 146. *Destruction*, ll. 445-6:

"N'i remeigne chastels, dongeons ne fermete
Moustiers ne abbeie que ne soit embrase."

p. 5, l. 150. Compare the *Destruction*, ll. 503-4:

"L'apostoile de Rome ad la novele oie
Ke payen sont veuu els plains de Romanie."

p. 5, l. 157. *unknowne* makes no sense. Perhaps we ought to read *yknowne* or *not unknowne*. In the *Destruction*, ll. 509-513—

"Seignours, ke le feromes, franke gent segnorie?
Li admirals d'Espaigne a no terre seisie;
Il en ont ja gastee une moult grant partie:
Au bref terme serra ceste terre exillie;
Qui bon consail saura vienge avant si nous die."

p. 5, l. 160. *unneth*, O.E. *unéaðe*, "uneasily, scarcely." Chaucer has *unnethë*, the final *e* being almost always sounded. See *Introduction*, p. xxxix.

p. 5, l. 163. *gydoure* evidently means "guide, conductor, commander."

p. 5, l. 164. *houne* = hounde. On the elition of final *d*, see Skeat, *Specimens of Early English*, 320/261, and *Preface to Havelok*, p. xxxvii.

p. 5, l. 165. *Ifreȝ*. There is no person of this name in any other version. Perhaps this Ifres may be identical with Jeffroi, mentioned as a senator of Rome in the *Destruction* (ll. 1122, 1139, 1367).

p. 6, l. 170. About the phrase "douce France" compare Léon Gautier's note to l. 15 of his *Edition critique de la Chanson de Roland.*

p. 6, l. 171. *Savaris*. The author has found this name in the *Destruction*, l. 540.

p. 6, l. 173. *Kinge: thinge*. In my dissertation on the language and the sources of the Sowdan of Babylon, p. 4, bottom, I have shown that *i* or *y*, which corresponds to O.E. *y*, the *umlaut* of *u*, rhymed with original *i* in this poem, which proves that the author wrote in the East Midland dialect. But among the examples collected there (p. 5), I ought not to have cited *kinge*, because this word is not peculiar to the East Midland speech, but occurs with the same form in all dialects. See *Introduction*, p. xxxv.

p. 6, ll. 175-6 are imitated from the *Destruction*, ll. 546-7. See *Introduction*, p. xxiii.

p. 6, l. 176. *ner*, the common form for *nor* (267, 1633) in this poem. "*Polaynes* are knee-pieces in a suit of armour. This term for genouillercs is found in the household book of Edward I." (Morris, *Glossary on Sir Gawayne*, *s. v.* polaynes).

p. 6, l. 181. *tyte*, "soon, quick." The editor of the Roxburghe Club edition of the *Sowdan* curiously confounds *tyte* with *tightly* = "adroitly," occurring in Shakespeare, *Merry Wives*, I. 3. *Tyte* is derived from O.Icel. *tiðr*, "creber," the neuter of which *titt*, used adverbially means "crebro, celeriter." See Stratmann, p. 561, *s. v. tid.*

p. 6, l. 189. *Chek* = "cotton, linen or woollen cloths, woven or printed in checkers." (Latham, *Dictionary*, 1876.)

p. 6, l. 191. A line seems to be wanting here. There is no rhyme to *displayed.*

p. 6, l. 201. *randon*, "rapidity, force." About the etymology see Diez, *Etym. Wörterbuch*, I. 342, and Skeat, *Etym. Dict.*

p. 7, l. 202. *than* seems to be an error for *thay.*

p. 7, l. 214. *Sarysyns.* There are several spellings of the name of this people in the poem: *Sarsyns, Sarsenys, Sarisyns, Sarasyns.*

p. 7, l. 222. *that day* occurs again in l. 223. The author probably only wrote it once; the repetition is most likely due to the scribe.

p. 7, l. 224. The following lines are imitated from the *Destruction*, ll. 613-619; see *Introduction*, p. xxiii.

p. 7, l. 228. The French text (*Destruction*, l. 624) has:

> "Maintenant soient tot occis et descoupe.
> Ne voil que mi serjant en soient encombre."

p. 8, l. 247. The original meaning of *brayde* is "start, blow," but this makes no sense here, nor can it mean "a boast," as the editor of the Roxburghe Club edition explains it. But Mid. Eng. *brayde*, as well as O.E. *brægd* or *bregd*, often signifies "deceit, craft, a cunning trick, a fraudulous contrivance, a stratagem or artifice." See Mätzner's *Wörterb.* and Halliwell's *Dict.* This, I think, is also the meaning of *brayde* in l. 247. Floripas has been engaged to Lukafer who had promised the Soudan, her father, to bring the emperor Charlemagne and all his twelve peers to the foot of his throne, in return for the hand of his daughter. Floripas, not at all enamoured of the king of Baldas, but obeying the will of her father, said she would only agree to accept him when he had fulfilled these conditions. But she does not believe that Laban thinks of ever fulfilling them, she is persuaded that those words, those promises made by Laban, are only a *brayde*, i. e. a stratagem or artifice devised by him in the hope of winning her hand before the performance of his promise. This signification of *braide* has been retained in the Mod. Eng. adjective *braid*, "crafty, deceitful."

p. 8, l. 257. The *Ethiopes*, "Ethiopians," are not mentioned in the other versions of this romance. On the rhyme *Aufricanes : stones* cf. *Introduction*, p. xxxv.

p. 9, l. 278. *Destruction*, l. 908:

"Sortibrans a mande Mabon l'engineor."

p. 9, l. 283. *depe : tyde*. The rhyme becomes perfect if we read *wide* instead of *depe*.

p. 9, l. 286. French text gives, l. 934:

"Si emplirons les fossés."

p. 9, l. 289. Cf. *Destruction*, l. 627. "Mahon te benoie," and l. 925, "Mahon te doint honour."

p. 9, l. 293. *Men myght go even to the walle*, compare the *Destruction*, l. 918:

"K'om poet aler al mure."

and l. 958:

"K'om pooit bien au mur et venir et aler."

p. 9, l. 295. *assaile*, evidently a mistake. Read *assaute*, as in l. 2205.

p. 9, l. 298. *shour*, "fight, attack." See Zupitza's note to *Guy*, l. 9206. *sharpe shoures*, as in the *Destruction of Troy*, l. 5804, "sharp was the shoure." Cf. also l. 950 of this poem, "bataile was sharpe."

p. 9, l. 300. *stones thai bare*, etc. *Destruction*, l. 967:

"Ces dedens ou grans pieres firent grant lapide."

p. 9, l. 303. French text gives (l. 975):

"Maintes pieres del mur ont contreval rue."

p. 9, l. 306. In the *Destruction*, l. 977:

"L'asalt dureit cel jour jusque a la nutee."

p. 9, l. 307. French: "Payen se sont retrait." *Destruction*, l. 979.

p. 10, l. 311. For *tyde : chidde* see *Introduction*, p. xliii.

p. 10, l. 312.

"Lucafer li traitre traison ad pense,
Qu'il se contrefera les armes del cite;
Et tote si pense sont a Labam demonstre.
'Sire admirail d'Espaigne,' ceo dist li diffaies,
'La cite est moult fors, et François sont doute;
Ils defendront le mur, ja mais n'iert entre,
Que par une voidie que jeo ai porpense.
Il ad dedens un conte de mult grant crualte,
Savaris ad a non, est de grant parente;
Chescon jour il s'en ist, s'est oue nous melle,
De la gent dieffae, mainte teste a coupe."—*Destr.*, ll. 986-96.

p. 10, l. 317. *Destruction*, l. 997.

"J'ai bien conu ses armes et les ai avise."

p. 10, l. 331. *Destruction*, l. 1011:

"Tantost le mestre porte aurons moult bien ferme."

p. 10, l. 332. *Destruction*, l. 1057:

"Mais tot le premier bail ont Sarrasin poeple."

p. 10, l. 336. *discumfiture*, "defeat." See below, note to l. 1320.

p. 10, l. 339. *ryme*, "to speak loudly, to cry." O.E. *hrêman* or *hrŷman*. See Stratmann, p. 322.

p. 10, l. 340. French text (l. 1063):

"De V. M. ne remendrent que iiiC sans fausser."

See note to l. 67.

p. 10, l. 341. *twelfe : selve ; f* and *v* very often stand for one another, see *Introduction* on p. xliii.

p. 10, l. 344. *shite : mette.* See Ellis, *Pronunc.*, I. 272, and *Introduction*, on p. xliv. Cf. also ll. 2054, 2963, 2960. *by than* = then; see Mätzner's *Wörterb.* p. 217(2).

p. 11, l. 346. *Estragot* or *Astragot.* This name is not to be found in the other versions, it only occurs in the *Sowdan* and in the *Destruction*; cf. *Destr.* l. 1090-4:

"Estragot le poursuit uns geans diffaies

. . . .

Teste avoit com senglers, si fu rois corones.
El main tient .i. mace de fin ascier trempe,
Un coup a Savaris desur le chef done."

p. 11, l. 360. French text reads:

"Et la novele en ont l'apostoile conté."—*Destr.* l. 1101.

p. 11, l. 363. *consaile : slayne.* See *Introduction*, p. xliii.

p. 11, l. 364. See above, l. 78.

p. 11, l. 368. *erille* is not derived from the Erse, as the editor of the Roxburghe Club edition supposes. It is simply another spelling for *erle*, which occurs in l. 1986. O.E. *eorl*, Mod. Eng. *earl.*

p. 11, l. 369. There must be a gap of some lines here; between this and the following line a space has been left of about the width of one line; l. 370 is written in a much later hand.

p. 11, l. 376. *lettres* translates the French "li brief" (*Destr.* l. 1121), *in haste* = French "isnelement" (*Destr.* l. 1119).

p. 11, l. 377. *we ordeyne* makes no sense. Read *were ordeyned*, as in l. 2396. Cf. the *Destruction*, l. 1133:

"Tot troi sont coiement de la cite hastés."

p. 12, l. 379. *at a posterne.* On the posterns compare Skeat, *Spec. of Eng. Literature*, 359, 165.

p. 12, l. 380. *aboute mydnyghte.* French: "Tote la nuit alerent ou la lune clarté." *Destr.* l. 1136.

p. 12, l. 394. *honde of honde*, "hand to hand."—In the Glossary of the Roxburghe Club ed. we read: "Cast. Wherewithal to throw." This is the sense of *cast* in l. 2471; but it occurs with two other meanings. In l. 394 *cast* signifies "device, plot, intention," as often elsewhere. In ll. 460, 2091, 2099, 2467, 2603, 2792, it means "the act of throwing, the throw."

p. 12, l. 400. *hevy*, "afflicted, sorrowful." So in ll. 3037, 3224.

p. 13, l. 427. *Estagote*, miswritten for *Estragote*, cf. ll. 346, 352, and *Destr.* l. 1090. *brake on three*, cf. ll. 2234, 1388, 1269.

p. 13, l. 441. *Sarsyns : Romaynes.* See *Introduction*, p. xliv.

p. 14, l. 464. *oost* does not rhyme with *beste*. Both the sense and the rhyme will be improved if we read *rest* for *oost*.

p. 14, l. 473. As it stands, the line makes no sense. *This* is written indistinctly in the MS., so that we may read either *this* or *thus*; the sense requires the latter, which I think is the true reading. Or else we may keep *this* and write *idone* instead of *it done*.

p. 15, l. 488. *aras*. Read *a ras*, and see note to l. 1349.

p. 15, l. 491. *and armes* makes no sense, as we are hardly entitled to take *armes* for the 2nd person plural imperative; which in this poem always ends in *-eth*. See *Introduction*, p. xxxvii. I think we must change *and* into *as*. For the explanation of the phrase "as armes," see note on l. 2660.

p 15, l. 495. The *Ascopars* or *Ascopartes* are mentioned in the *Destruction* as the subjects of the Soudan. The name of this people is not to be found in any other version. *Astopars* is merely a clerical error for *Ascopars*, which may be easily accounted for by remembering that in the MSS. the characters *c* and *t* are very often formed almost alike. The true spelling *Ascopars* is found in ll. 2196, 2648; cf. also the *Destruction*, ll. 98, 426. Nothing is known of the origin and the home of the Ascoparts. That they must have been men of great bodily strength follows from l. 496, "for ye be men of mighte," and l. 2645, "that bene boolde and hardy to fighte." Compare also what is said about them by Donne, in his first satire:

> "Those Askaparts, men big enough to throw
> Charing-cross for a bar."

It is worthy while to note that a giant, called Askapard, occurs in the romance of Sir Bevis of Hamptoun. See Ellis, *Metr. Romances*, ed. Halliwell, p. 263.

p. 15, l. 500. *Ho* is evidently a mistake for *we*. *rere-warde*, "rear-guard;" the van is called *fowarde*, ll. 502, 732, the main body *the medyl partye*, l. 735.

p. 15, l. 504. *than : gon.* See *Introduction*, p. xxxv.

p. 15, l. 510. *oon* makes no sense. I suspect the reading of this and the following stanza is quite corrupt. If ll. 510 and 511 should belong to different stanzas, the *enjambement*, or continuation of the sense from one stanza to another, would be unusually strong. I am therefore inclined to think that originally a stanza began at l. 510, and that there is a line wanting after l. 509, which contained the rhyme to *bon* (l. 508). The scribe noticing the absence of rhyme tried to restore it himself. Adding *oon* to l. 510, he made it rhyme with *bon* (l. 508). Having thus destroyed the rhyme of ll. 510 and 512 (*Alisaundre : Cassaundre*, as in l. 984), he added *gaye* to l. 512, which now rhymed to l. 514, where he still added *to fraye.* In order to get a rhyme to l. 518, he changed in l. 516 the original *laye* (: *Romayne*) into *lan* ("he ceased, stopped"), and wrote "*to*" *the grounde* instead of "*on*" (cf. l. 1186) or "*at*" (cf. ll. 533, 435) *the grounde*, connecting thus these words with l. 515, whereas originally they belonged to *there he laye*, or—as *there* also may have been added by the scribe—to *he laye.* If now we read *with mayne* instead of *ful evene*, in l. 521, we get a perfect rhyme to l. 519; l. 520 having lost its rhyming line, he made it rhyme, by adding *than* to l. 522, which originally rhymed to l. 524. Now to get a rhyme to l. 524 he composed and inserted himself l. 526. Therefore I think the original reading of these two stanzas ran as follows:

510 Sir Ferumbras of Alisaundre
  That bolde man was in dede,
Uppon a steede Cassaundre
  He roode in riche weede.
514 Sir Bryer of Poyle a Romayne
  He bare through with a spere;
Dede on the ground [there] he laye,
  Might he no more hem dere.
518 That saw Huberte, a worthy man,
  Howe Briere was islayne,
Ferumbras to quite than
  To him he rode with mayne.
522 With a spere uppone his shelde
  Stiffly gan he strike;
The shelde he brake imiddis the feelde,
  His hawberke wolde not breke.
526 Ferumbras was agreved tho, &c.

On the rhyme *Romayne : laye* (l. 514) cf. ll. 536, 890.

p. 15, l. 514. *Bryer of Poyle* does not occur in any of the other versions.

p. 15, l. 516. *lan*, preterite of *lin*, "to cease;" more common in the compound *blin*, contracted from * *be-lin.*

p. 15, l. 517. *might he no more hem dere.* On the order of words, cf. ll. 2954, 649, 2435.

p. 16, l. 520. *qwite*, "to requite, reward, retaliate, pay off." See below note to l. 780.

p. 16, l. 531. On *stronge* (O.E. strang): *istonge* (O.E. gestungen), see *Introduction*, p. xxxv.

p. 16, l. 532. *astraye*, "out of the right way or proper place, running about without guidance." O.French *estraier*, which is derived from Latin *ex strada*, see Diez, *Etym. Wörterb.* I. 402; II. 296.

p. 16, l. 541. *werre*, "war," seems to owe its origin to the French *guerre*, as it is not found in O.E. It appears for the first time in the *Saxon Chronicle*,—*he coude*, "he knew, had endured." See Mätzner's *Grammatik*, II. 262.

p. 17, l. 555. It is evident that *all ane* must be a corruption. Perhaps the conjecture of the editor of the Roxb. Club edition, supposing *all rafe* to be the true reading, may be right. But he is certainly wrong to identify this *rafe* with the *rafe* in l. 866, which, being the infinitive mood of a verb, cannot be taken for an adjective or adverb, which the sense seems to require in l. 555. Halliwell, *s. v.* Raff, gives: "in raff = speedily." There is a Danish adjective, *rap*, "brisk, quick." Cf. Skeat, *Etym. Dict.* s. v. *raffle* and *rap*.

p. 17, l. 570. *certaine* spoils the rhyme. The rhyme becomes perfect if we read *without faile*, as in l. 322.

p. 17, l. 573. *aplight*, "on plight, on my word." See Zupitza's note to *Guy*, l. 8541. It is often used as an expletive.

p. 17, l. 580. *who the sowdan*, etc. = who is the Sowdan. The verb of the sentence is wanting; cf. note to l. 2156.

p. 17, l. 587. French text gives:

> "Et Guion de Bourgoyne ad a lui appelé
> Fils est de sa soror et de sa parenté
> Cosins, vous en irrés. . ."
>
> *Destr.* ll. 1179, *et seq.*

p. 18, l. 613. *hight* = (1) "was called," (2) "promised," (3) "called" (partic. past). It is the preterite tense of *haten*, *hoten*, or *hat* (l. 3154). Cf. Zupitza's note to *Guy*, l. 169.

p. 18, l. 614. *than* seems to be a corruption, and I think must be left out. *Florip* is the genitive of *Florip*, which occurs as a nominative in ll. 2075, 1527. There is another nominative *Floripas* which forms the genitive *Floripas*, ll. 1659, 2350.

p. 19, l. 625. *Isres*, the name of the "chief porter of the town," who betrayed the city, only occurs in the *Sowdan*; in the *Destruction* the same treachery is committed by *Tabour*, *D.* 1203.

> "Uns traitre del cit que del porte out les cles."

p. 19, l. 636. *bandon*, literally "proclamation," means "power, disposal." See Skeat, *Etym. Dict.* s. v. *abandon*.

p. 19, l. 647. French:

> "Le chief al portier trenche," *Destr.* l. 1236.

p. 19, l. 648. In the *Destr.* l. 1244-5:

> "Dieux" fist il "te maldie, et que t'ont engendre,
> Kar traitour au darain averont mal dehe."

p. 19, l. 650. *met*, a mistake for *mot*, which we find in ll. 1582, 2334, 3170.

p. 20, l. 663. Cf. the *Destr.* l. 1260:

"Al moustier de saint Piere est Fierenbras alés."

p. 20, l. 665. *the crosse, the crown, the nailes bente.* The relics mentioned in the *Destruction* are the crown of thorns, the cross, the nails, and the "signe," which, as I have shown in my *Dissertation* (pp. 45, 46), does not mean "inscription of the cross," but is the Greek *σινδών*, and signifies "the shroud, or winding-sheet, of the Lord, suaire, sudatorium." In the French *Fierabras*, as well as in *Syr Ferumbras*, no mention is made of the cross.

p. 20, l. 673. *thare* instead of *there* would improve the rhyme. See *Introduction*, p. xxxv.

p. 20, l. 678. *fade*, O.E. fadian, "dispose, suit." *Stratmann*, p. 187.

p. 20, l. 679. *frankencense* = "pure incense." Compare Skeat, *Etym. Dict.*

p. 20, l. 686. *roial*, "excellent." Cf. "roial spicerye," *Chaucer*, ed. Morris, III. 135/142.

p. 21, l. 699. *Alle on a flame that cite was*; cf. the French:

"Kant il vindrent a Rome si virent luy porte ouerее
La flambe en la cite moult granment alumee.
Pour grant chalour qu'i fu n'i povoient entrer."

(*Destr.* ll. 1378-80.)

p. 21, l. 723. The *Destruction*, ll. 1384—1408, has:

"Si dirrai de Charlon, le fort roi corone.
De par totes ses terres avoit ses gens mande,
N'i remest dus ne quiens ne baron el regne,
Qu'il assemble ne soient a Paris la cite.
Quant il i furent tous venu et ajouste,
L'emperere de France en halt en ad parle:
'Seignours, or escoutes, si vous dirrai verte,
Li admirails d'Espaigne a no pais gaste
Et oue lui CM sarrazin diffaie.
Il ont ensegie Rome, m'admirable cite,
Tot le pais entour ont il pour voir robbe;
Si jeo ne les soccour tot l'auront il gaste.'
'Sire,' firent li princes, 'a vostre volonte:
Nous ne vous failliromes tant que poons durer.'
Adonc en ad li rois grant joie demene.
Quant si gent furent prest a complir son pense,
Adonc s'en est li rois eralment aprestes
Et si firent li contes de France le regne.
Quant sont appareillie si sont enchemine:
iii C mil chevaliers ad li rois el barne
Oliviers porte sa baneer que ben leu ad guie,
Rollans fu en arriere, li vassals adures.
De soccoure Guion s'en est li rois hastes.
Tant ont il nuit et jor chivalche et erre,
Qu'il sont en Romenie, n'i ont reine tire."

p. 22, l. 744. *He knewe the baner of France.* The French text has:

"Guis parceut le baniere le roi de saint Dine,
Encontre lui chevalche, la novele ont conte,
Come la forte cite li payen ont gaste :
La corone et les clous d'iloec en sont robbe
Et les altres reliques. . ."

p. 23, l. 766. *for*, "notwithstanding, in spite of." So also in l. 2904.

p. 23, l. 771. *Destr.*, l. 1425 :

"Li vens en fiert es voiles que les a ben guies."

p. 23, l. 776. *for south*, "forsooth," cf. ll. 2014, 897, 2024, 1025, 2246.

p. 23, l. 778. French : "il sont en terre entre."

p. 23, l. 779. *fonde : grounde.* *fonde* is spelt *founde* in ll. 1857, 3020, 344, 2353, 2363.

p. 23, l. 780. *stroyeth* = "destroyeth." "Compounds of Romance origin, the first part of which is a preposition, or words derived from such, often mutilate, or even entirely drop the preposition" (Zupitza's note to *Guy*, l. 576). Thus we have *sail*, l. 385, = "assail;" *longeth*, l. 3254, = "belongeth;" *skomfited*, l. 1320, = "diskomfited," ll. 336, 1464 ; *quite*, l. 520, = "requite;" *perceived*, l. 2659, = "aperceived;" *saut*, ll. 619, 2200, = "assaut," l. 615 ; *ginne*, l. 2326, = "enginne," l. 333 ; *playne*, l. 177, = "complayn ;" *skaped*, l. 2049, = "askaped," l. 2218.

p. 23, l. 787. French : "iiiC mile François."

p. 24, l. 812. *ychoon : Mahounde.* See *Introduction*, p. xlii.

p. 24, l. 820. *stroke : stoupe.* See *Introduction*, p. xliii.

p. 24, l. 820. *stenyed*, "stunned," not from O.Fr. *estaindre*, as the editor of the Roxb. Club ed. suggests, but from O.E. *stunian*, "percellere, stupefacere." See *Stratmann*, p. 540.

p. 24, l. 835. Observe the subject expressed twice ; cf. ll. 723, 1031, 1682, 1814, 2331.

p. 25, l. 836. *Neymes.* This celebrated hero has been especially famous by the advices and counsels of which even in matters of greatest difficulty he was never at a loss. "Tel conseiller n'orent onques li Franc," *i. e.* the French had never such a counsellor. This passage of the romance of *Aspremont* may be looked upon as containing the portrait of Neymes as we find him described in all poems. The story of his birth and youth is in the romance of *Aubri le Bourgoing.* He was the son of Gasselin, king of Bavaria. Cassile, an usurper, is about to seize the throne and to kill the young Neymes, when Charlemagne comes to his help and re-establishes the legitimate inheritor.

p. 25, l. 836. *Ogier Danoys* (cf. l. 1687) is one of the twelve peers in this poem. His life is contained in the French poem of the "*Chevallerie Ogier*" by Raimbert de Paris. According to that romance Ogier had been delivered in his youth to Charlemagne as a pledge to secure the discharge of the tribute which his father Geffroi, king of Denmark, was bound to pay to the emperor. The French ambassadors having once been insulted by Geffroy, Charlemagne swears to make Ogier pay with his life the offence done by his father, and Ogier is going to be executed when the emperor, following the urgent requests of messengers arrived from Rome, suddenly starts to deliver this city from the Saracens. On this expedition the French army is hard pressed by the enemy, but Ogier by his eminent prowess and valour enables Charles to enter Rome. He now is pardoned and becomes the favourite of the emperor. Several years afterwards Ogier's son Baudouinet is slain by Charlot, the son of Charlemagne, as they were quarrelling about a party of chess. Ogier, in order to revenge his son, goes as far as to attack Charlemagne himself, but on the point of being taken a prisoner, he escapes and flees to Didier, king of Lombardy. Charles makes war on Didier, and after a long struggle Ogier is taken and imprisoned at Reims, where he is going to be starved, when a sudden invasion of the Saracens obliges Charlemagne again to have recourse to the courage and valour of the Dane. Ogier delivers France by slaying the giant Bréhus. To reward him for the service done to his country, Charles gives him the county of Hainaut, where afterwards, as the poem tells us, he died in the renown of holiness.

p. 25, l. 845. *it* = "hit." Cf. note to l. 41.

p. 25, l. 847-50. These four lines seem to be incorrect. As they stand, the three first lines are rhymed together, and there is no rhyme to the fourth. The diction of the whole passage, which cannot be said to be ungrammatical, is nevertheless wanting in precision and exactness.

p. 25, l. 866. *rafe* = rave.

p. 25, l. 868. *Moun-joye* is the name of Charlemagne's sword in this poem (cf. ll. 3111, 850), whereas, according to all other romances, the emperor's sword was called *Joyeuse*. *Mounjoie* or *Montjoie* was the name of the French standard; it was likewise used as the battle-cry of the French, cf. *Fierabras*, l. 1703, and *Syr Ferumbras*, ll. 2285, 2652, 4577, 4727. The sword *Joyeuse* had been forged by the celebrated Weland or Galand, as we read in the French *Fierabras*, l. 635:

> "Et *Galans* fist Floberge à l'acier atrempé,
> Hauteclere et *Joiouse*, où moult ot dignité;
> Cele tint Karlemaines longuement en certé."

Compare Gaston Paris, *Histoire Poétique*, p. 374.

p. 26, l. 875. *Durnedale.* This renowned sword was forged by the famous Galand or Weland. The French *Fierabras* (l. 645) is the only romance which attributes it to Munifican. It had been given by Charlemagne to Roland as the best of his warriors. As to the exploits achieved with it, Roland enumerates them himself in that celebrated passage, where in his death-hour he tries to break

Durnedale to prevent it from falling into the hands of the Saracens (*Chanson de Roland*, ll. 2316-2337). The steel blade of this sword has been highly praised for its extraordinary hardness. It had been tried by Charlemagne himself on that "perron," or steel block before the emperor's palace in Aix-la-Chapelle (see *Histoire Pcëtique*, p. 370). Durnedale proved good as well as Almace, the sword of Turpin. But Courtain, Ogier's sword, was then shortened by half a foot. According to l. 1407 of the *Sowdan*, Durnedale broke; but this incident has been mentioned nowhere else. Cf. *Syr Ferumbras*, l. 997, and *Fierabras*, l. 1740.

p. 26, l. 876. *romme*, spelt also *rome*, *rowme*, *roum*, is Mod. E. *room*, O.E. *rûm*, "spatium."

p. 26, l. 880. *dinge;* read *gan dinge*. *Dinge* is the infinitive mood, but the sense requires a preterite tense. The preterite of *dinge* is *dong*, *dongen*, which occurs in l. 1263. But as *dinge* cannot be altered here, on account of the rhyme, the passage is easily corrected by adding *gan* = "he began to strike, he struck."

p. 26, l. 884. *Alloreynes of Loreynes* and *Aleroyse* (l. 1699) are probably identical. Then *Alloreynes* would be an error of the scribe, who having already the following *Loreynes* in his mind wrote *Alloreynes* instead of *Alleroyse*.

p. 26, l. 900. *in fay* = "truly," *fay* = "faith, truth." O.Fr. *fei* or *feid*, Lat. *fides*.

p. 26, l. 904-5. Cf. *Chanson de Roland*, ll. 1903-4:

> "Rollanz est proz e Oliviers est sages,
> Ambedui unt merveillus vasselage."

p. 27, l. 913. I cannot tell what *treyumple* means, or whether it be a corruption.

p. 27, l. 939. This kind of prayer or apostrophe addressed to the God of War is certainly taken from another English work, which I am unable to trace, but which must have been much known at the time of our author, as we find it referred to in different authors. That it has been taken from another poem is proved by some phrases of this prayer which are somewhat obscure or rather unintelligible here, and which we certainly should be able to explain if we knew the original context in which they occurred. Then the form *hase* (l. 940) is somewhat suspicious, as it is the only instance of the 2nd person singular present dropping the *t*, which it has always in this poem. The arrangement, too, of the following stanzas differs from that generally observed in the *Sowdan*. If we consider our poem as composed in eight-line stanzas (but see *Introduction*, p. xl) we mostly find the 1st and 3rd lines rhyming together, then the 2nd and 4th, the 5th and 7th, and finally the 6th and 8th, so that *four* different rhyme-endings are necessary to one stanza. If now we consider the stanza from l. 939 to 946, we only have two rhyme-endings, all the pair lines rhyming together, and all the odd ones together. In ll. 947 to 950 the 1st and 4th rhyme together, whilst the 2nd and 3rd are paired off together.—ll. 939-941 we find alluded to in *Chaucer*, see *Introduction*, p. xlvi, and the *Prioress's Tale*, ed. Skeat (Clarendon Press), p. xvii. Compare also Lindsay, *The Historie of Squyer Meldrum*, l. 390:

"Like Mars, the God Armipotent."

p. 27, l. 939. *rede Mars.* "Bocaccio uses the same epithet in the opening of his Teseide: 'O rubiconde Marte.' *Rede* refers to the colour of the planet." Morris, note to *Knight's Tale*, l. 889.

p. 27, l. 940. *Baye* never means "sword," as the editor of the Roxburghe Club ed. renders it, nor does this translation make any sense here at all; *baye* signifies "a wide, open room or space in a building." See Mätzner's *Wörterbuch*, p. 164. Morris, in the Glossary to the *Alliterative Poems*, has "bay = recess. The original meaning seems to be *opening of any kind.* Cf. bay, space in a building between two main beams." Halliwell, *s. v.* bay, has: "A principal compartment or division in the architectural arrangement of a building." It appears to be etymologically the same word as Ital. *baja*, French *baie*, "bay, gulf, harbour," the French *baie* being equally used for "opening of any kind." The Catalan form for *baie* is *badia*, which corresponds to the verb *badar*, meaning "to open." See Diez, *Etym. Wörterb.* I. 46. *Bay* is retained in the Mod. E. compound "*bay-window.*" Cf. also the French "*la bée d'une fenestre*," cited by Carpentier-Ducange, *s. v.* beare. With regard to the signification of *trende*, the editor of the Roxb. Club ed. wrongly guessed again in explaining it as "drawn" or "trenchant, cutting." *Trende* means "turned, bent, vaulted in the form of an arch." See *Halliwell*, p. 887, and *Stratmann*, p. 572, *s. v.* trenden (= "volvere"). But I am at a loss how to explain why Mars is said to have put up his throne in an arched recess, or compartment, of a building.

p. 28, l. 957. *some*, a clerical error for *sone*.

p. 28, l. 965. *prymsauns of grene vere* = "the earliest days of green spring" (Glossary to the Roxb. Club ed.). This may be the sense; but what is the literal meaning of *prymsauns?* If we had *prymtauns*, or *prymtaunce*, we might be inclined to take it for a corruption of French *printemps*, as we find *pastaunce* or *pastance* corrupted from *passe-temps.* (See Skeat, *Spec. of Eng. Literature*, 460/149 and 427/1096.) Cf. also the *Romaunt of the Rose*, ll. 3373-74: "*At prime temps*, Love to manace, Ful ofte I have been in this caas." Or is *prymtauns* perhaps a clerical error for *entrauns* or *entraunce?* This would then make us think of such passages as the following one:

"Che fu ou mois de mai, à l'*entree* d'esté,
Que florissent cil bos et verdissent cil pré."

Fierabras, ll. 5094-5.

p. 28, l. 966. *spryngyn*, the only instance of the 3rd person present plural ending in *-yn* (for the common *-en*). This perhaps is due to the scribe thinking already of the following *yn* in beg*ynne*. But it must be stated that the whole passage is rather obscure. Neither the meaning of *springyn and begynne* nor the connection of l. 966 with the following lines is very clear. *Floures* occurring twice looks also somewhat suspicious. Moreover, these two stanzas do not well suit the context and might easily be done without; they are evidently borrowed from some other poem. Observe besides the alliteration in *f*loures, *f*rithe, *f*reshly.

p. 28, l. 973. *lithe*, "to hear." O.Icel. *hlýða*, "auscultare." *Stratmann*, s. v. *hliþen*, p. 315.

p. 29, l. 993. *lese* miswritten for *lefe*, which sense and rhyme require, and which occurs in ll. 832, 1526.

p. 29, l. 995. *bassatours* (?) = "vavassours, vavasors."

p. 29, l. 999. *Inde Major*. The meaning of *Major* is not clear. Cf. besides *Chanson de Roland*, ed. Gautier, *Glossarial Index*, s. v. *Major*. Compare also *Destr*. l. 690: *terre Majour*.

p. 29, l. 1000. The great number of geographical names contained in these two lines is probably due to the favourite habit of mediæval romance writers, who thought that they showed their geographical knowledge by introducing long strings of names. Thus we find in *Web. Rom.* II. l. 632 *et seq.*, the names of sixteen towns mentioned in fourteen lines, all of which are said to have been visited by Richard the Lion-hearted. Again in the same poem, ll. 3679, *et seq.*, we find the names of thirteen countries occurring in ten lines. Cf. also *King Alis.*, *Web. Rom.* I. ll. 1440 and 1692. Often, too, geographical names seem to be inserted on account of the rhyme, as *Chaunder* in l. 123, and *Europe* in l. 1001.

p. 29, l. 1008. *Camalyon*, "meaning, probably, the camelopardalis. The blood of a cameleon would go a very little way towards satisfying a thirsty Saracen" (Ellis, *Metr. R.* 387). Perhaps also the poet did not know much of either of these two kinds of animals, and all he wished was to cite an animal with some outlandish name.

p. 30, l. 1025. *southe: wrothe*. The spelling *sothe* occurs in ll. 2014, 2024, 2246, 2719. There must be a lacuna of one or more lines here. The rhyme-word to *dute* (l. 1024) is wanting; the context also evidently shows that ll. 1025 and 1026, as they stand together, make no sense. It is worth while to add that the next five lines, contrary to the common usage of our poem, are all rhymed together.

p. 30, l. 1040. Observe *Paens*, i. e. "pagans," used as a proper name here; cf. the *Destr*. l. 98, and *Fierabras*, l. 5673.

p. 31, l. 1051. For a description of Ferumbras, compare *Fierabras*, ll. 578 *et seq.*, and ll. 611 *et seq.*, and *Syr Ferumbras*, l. 550.

p. 35, l. 1060. *trwes* = trues, truce.

p. 31, l. 1067. *sex*. So in the French *Fierabras*, l. 84:

"Ja n'en refuserai, par Mahom, jusqu'à vi."

In the English *Ferumbras*, l. 102, we read:

"And þoȝ þer come *twelue*, þe beste of þy fered,
I will kuþe on hem my miȝt, & dyngen hem al to douste."

p. 31, l. 1071. *in fere* = "together." *fere*, literally "one who fares with one," means "a travelling companion, a comrade, a mate; a company." O.E. *(ge-)fera.*

p. 31, l. 1074. *man* = "bondman, subject, vassal." So in ll. 1354 1466.

p. 31, l. 1077. *childe*, "young knight, young man." See Skeat's note to Sir Thopas (Clarendon Press), 162/2020.

p. 31, l. 1084. Cf. the French text:

"Sire, ce dist Rollans, chertes, tort en aves,
Car, par icel seigneur Ki Dix est appelés,
Je vauroie moult miex que fuissiés desmenbrés
Ke jou en baillasse armes ne ne fuisse adobés.
Hier quant paien nous vindrent à l'issue des gués
L. mile furent, à vers helmes jesmés,
Grans caus en soustenimes sur les escus bandés;
Oliviers mes compaigns i fu le jour navrés.
Tout fuissons desconfit, c'est fines verités,
Quant vous nous secourustes e vos riches barnés,
Et paien s'en tournerent les frains abandonnés.
Quant fumes repairié as loges et as trés,
Puis te vantas le soir, quant tu fus enivrés,
Que li viel chevalier c'avoies amené
L'avoient moult miex fait que li joule d'assés,
Assés en fui le soir laidement ramponés."

(ll. 144-161.)

Compare also *Syr Ferumbras*, ll. 144-163

p. 32, l. 1088. *of* = "on account of."

p. 32, l. 1092. According to most of the old romances Roland was invulnerable. He never lost any blood by a wound but on the occasion when he was beaten by Charlemagne

"For trois goutes sans plus, quant Charles par irour
Le feri de son gant que le virent plousour."

See *Histoire Poëtique*, p. 264.

The French text (ll. 166-170) runs as follows:

"Karles trait son gant destre, qui fu à or parés
Fiert le comte Rollant en travers sur le nés;
Après le caup en est li sans vermaus volés.
Rollans jete le main au brano qui est letrés;
Ja en ferist son oncle se il n'en fust ostés."

p. 32, l. 1094. *abye*, "to pay for, suffer for." In Mod. Eng. *abye* is corrupted into *abide.* See Morris, Gloss. to *Chaucer* (Clarend. Press), *s. v.* aboughte.

p. 32, l. 1096. Double negatives like *never none* are pretty common in mediæval writers. Cf. in the *Sowdan*, ll. 1876, 2181, 2199, 2279, 2305.

p. 32, l. 1103. *at one,* "of one mind, agreement." Cf. *King Horn*, ed. Lumby, l. 925:

"At on he was wiþ þe king."

Hence Mod. Eng. *atone,* "to set at one, to reconcile." See Zupitza's note to *Guy*, l. 5308.

p. 32, l. 1106. *to make voydaunce*, the same as to *voide*, l. 1768 = "to quit, to depart from, to get rid of."

p. 32, l. 1110. *withoute more* = "without delay, immediately." *more* is O.E. *mâra*, comparative to *micel;* it is not the Latin *more.* See Zupitza's note to *Guy*, l. 719.

p. 33, l. 1126. *renewed*, "tied." Fr. *renouer*, from *nœud* = Lat. *nodius.* It is to be distinguished from *renewed* = "renovated," which occurs in l. 2200.

p. 32, l. 1128. *hidur* is spelt *hider* in ll. 810, 833, etc.

p. 32, l. 1135. *Generyse.* In the other versions Olyver calls himself *Garin.* See *Introduction* on p. xxxiii.

p. 32, l. 1141. *lerne*, "to teach." See Zupitza's note to *Guy*, l. 6352. *scole*, O.E. *scôl*, Mod. Eng. *school*, means here "style, or manner of fighting." It must not be confounded with *schole*, O.E. *scolu*, "troop, band," Mod. Eng. *shoal.* Cf. also *The Song of Roland*, 129/786.

p. 33, l. 1145. *myghty men of honde.* So in l. 3029. The same phrase occurs in M.H.G. "ein helt *ze sînen handen*," which is explained as meaning, "a hero [or one who becomes a hero] by the strength of his hands or arms." See Jänicke's note to *Biterolf*, 5078, and Grimm's *Grammatik*, IV. 727 note. The expression seems to be originally French; cf. Méon, *Fabliaux*, III. 478: "chevaliers *de sa main*"; *Renard*, ed. Martin, l. 21409: "proedom *de sa main.*" Cf. also *Roman des Eles*, ed. Scheler, l. 433, where *main* is wrongly explained by the editor.

p. 33, l. 1151. *plete*, "plead." The rhyme leads us to suppose that the author pronounced *plede*, which indeed is the more common form.

p. 33, l. 1154. *and* makes no sense here. *thenkes* must also be incorrect, the 3rd person present singular always terminating in *-eth* in this poem, and not in *-es.* Read *as thenketh me; thenketh me* occurs in l. 465.

p. 34, l. 1158. *pight*, "pitched, fixed." The infinitive mood is *picchen;* cf. O.Dutch *picken*, O.Icel. *pikka*, "pungere, pangere."

p. 34, l. 1159. In the French *Fierabras*, l. 606 *et seq.*, Oliver also assists the Saracen to put on his gear. This point is not mentioned in the Ashmolean version, see *Introduction*, p. xxviii.

p. 34, l. 1163. *worthed up*, "became up, got up, mounted." It is the past tense of the verb *worthen*, O.E. *weorðan*, "to become." Another past tense of this verb is *worth*, l. 1204.

p 34, l. 1164. *areest*, or *arest* = "a rest, or support for the spear when couched for the attack" (Morris). Originally = "stoppage, waiting, readiness." Cf. Mätzner's *Wörterbuch*, p. 107.

p. 34, l. 1167. *as fire of thonder*, cf. *dinte of thondir* in l. 1207.

p. 34, l. 1168. *to-braste*, "burst in pieces." The prefix *to-*, answering to Germ. *zer-*, has the force of "in twain, asunder."

p. 34, l. 1170. *threste*, O.E. *þrǽstan*, "premere, trudere." The author probably pronounced *thraste*, which will improve the rhyme.

p. 34, ll. 1179-80. *upon the hede* (blank in MS) *the hede.* This is evidently a mistake of the scribe; *sore*, l. 1180, too, which does not rhyme with *crowne*, is probably miswritten for *sone.* The rhyme as well as the context shows that the true reading is.:

"Olyver him hitte again
Upon the hede than fulle sone
He carfe awaye with myght and mayne
The cercle that sate uppon his crowne."

p. 34, l. 1182. About the *cercle*, see Demay, *Le Costume de guerre*, p. 132. "Non seulement le cône du heaume (helme) est bordé par ce cercle, mais il est parfois renforcé dans toute sa hauteur par deux arêtes placées l'une devant, l'autre derrière, ou par quatre bandes de métal ornementées (de verroteries), venant aboutir et se croiser à son sommet."—*crowne* means the "tonsure of the head," then topically "the skull or head."

p. 34, l. 1185. *the botteles of bawme* are not mentioned anywhere else in the *Sowdan;* the other versions tell us that the balm contained in those vessels was the same as that with which Christ was anointed. Cf. *Syr Ferumbras*, ll. 510—517; and see *Introduction*, p. vi and xxix.

p. 34, l. 1191. *the river.* According to the oldest version of the poem the whole combat took place on the shore of the Tiber, near Rome. See *Introduction*, pp. xi and xxxii. Cf. *Fierabras*, l. 1049:

"Pres fu du far de Rome, ses a dedes jetés,"

and *Philippe Mousket*, I. 4705-6:

"Les .ii. barius qu'à Rome prist,
Si les gieta enmi le Toivre."

In the *Sowdan* as well as in the *Ashmole* MS. there is no mention of Oliver's drinking of the balm before throwing it into the water, which both the Provençal and the French versions tell us he did. Cf. *Fierabras*, ll. 1031—1048, and the Provençal version, ll. 1335, *et seq.*

p. 35, l. 1210. *fille*, "fel."

p. 35, ll. 1221. *dere* spoils the rhyme. Read "*free.*"

p. 36, l. 1250. *Cousyn to King Charles*, cf. l. 1117. In ll. 1499 and 1671 Oliver is said to be nephew to Charlemagne. He was the son of Renier de Gennes, who according to *Sir Ferumbras*, l. 652: "Y am Charlis emys sone"—was the uncle of Charlemagne. In the poem *Girar de Viane* we find Oliver among the enemies of the

Emperor and fighting with Roland in close combat; they are at length stopped by divine interposition. Then began a close friendship which lasted till their death at Roncesvaux. Oliver's sister Aude was betrothed to Roland. See, besides, *Syr Ferumbras*, ll. 422, 1297, 1305, 1354.

p. 36, l. 1258. *harde grace*, "misfortune," cf. l. 2790.

p. 36, l. 1259. *Persagyn*. This name does not occur in any other version again, except in the *Destruction*, where one Persagon appears in the list of the Saracen barons. But it is not stated there that he is uncle to Ferumbras; cf. besides *Fierabras*, ll. 2614, 2784.

p. 37, l. 1263. Observe the four consecutive feminine rhymes.

p. 37, l. 1277. The scene as related here widely differs from that described in the Ashmolean version. In the *Sowdone*, Oliver gets hold of the sword which is "trussed on Ferumbras's stede." In the Ashmolean poem it is not Oliver who is disarmed, but Ferumbras, and Oliver allows him to pick up his weapon again. This in itself furnishes us an argument for conjecturing that the author of the *Sowdon* did not follow, or even know of, the Ashmolean version. In the French poem, as well as in the Provençal, it is likewise Oliver who is disarmed. If in those poems we find mentioned besides that Ferumbras offered his enemy to take up his sword again—an incident not related in the *Sowdan*—we do not consider this to disprove our supposition that the French version was the source of the *Sowdan*, as we may consider our author in this case simply to have adhered to his favourite practice of shortening his original as much as possible, so far as no essential point is concerned. Cf. the French *Fierabras*, ll. 1289—1346.

p. 37, l. 1286. *saught* is a misprint for *raught*.

p. 37, l. 1289. *He thought he quyte*. *quyte* may be explained as standing for *quyted*, or else *he* must be changed into *to*: *He thought to quyte*, the latter reading is perhaps preferable. We find in l. 3110 a passage agreeing almost exactly with this.

p. 38, l. 1298. *Qwyntyn*. The name of this Saint does not occur in any other version of our romance.

p. 38, l. 1308. There is no mention made of this prayer in the Ashmolean version, the *Sowdan* here (ll. 1308—1340) agrees again with the French *Fierabras*, ll. 1164—1244 (and with the Provençal poem, l. 1493, *et seq.*), with the only difference, that the prayer which Charlemagne addressed to God, in order to bestow the victory upon the Christian hero, is much longer in *F*, and is stuffed with so many details of the Scripture, that in some way it may be regarded as a succinct account of the whole life of the Lord.

p. 38, l. 1320. *skomfited* = *discomfited*, l. 1464. It is formed by the same analogy as stroyeth = destroyeth. See note to l. 780. The substantive *discumfiture*, O.Fr. *desconfiture*, occurs in l. 336; the same word, without prefix, is found in M.H.G., cf. *Kudrun*, ed. Martin, 646, 2:

"dô si hêten gerne die porten zuo getân
dô muosten si daz lernen durch *schumphentiuren* verlân."

The Italian noun is *sconfitta*, and the verb *sconfiggere*.

p. 32, l. 1327. *God aboue* does not rhyme with *lord almighty*. The rhyme is easily restored if we read *of might* (cf. l. 2059) for *aboue*, and if we change *almighty* into *almighte*, so that we have:

l. 1327. "Tho Charles thanked God of myghte."
l. 1329. "And saide, 'blessed be thou, lord almyghte.'"

The adjective *almiȝt* is of frequent occurrence in Mid. Eng. writers. So in *Allit. Poems*, I. 497: "in sothful gospel of god almyȝt;" *Syr Ferumbras*, l. 3580, "God almyȝte: siȝte;" *ibid.* l. 3815, "god almyȝt: wyȝt."

p. 39, l. 1349. *cas* is an erratum for *ras*.—"Ras, shave." "Rees 1693, evening." These explanations given by the editor of the Roxb. Club ed. are wrong. *Ras* and *rees* being both derived from O.E. *rǽs*, "impetus cursus," are indiscriminately used in three meanings: (1) "onset, assault;" (2) "course, run, rush, haste, hurry;" (3) "space, time, occasion." The last signification is well shewn by the following passages:

"Hit lasteþ but a lutel rees."
(*Cl. Maydenhod*, l. 26.)

"þat ys to seye upon a rees,
Stynkyng Saxone, be on pees."
(*Arthur*, ed. Furnivall, l. 525.)

In the *Sowdan ras* or *rees* means (1) "time, instant, occasion," ll. 1349, 1693; (2) "rush, hurry, haste," ll. 645, 489. *rase*, l. 774 = "current in the sea," the same word as the preceding *ras* and *rees*, meaning properly, "a narrow rush, or violent current of water." See Morris, *Chaucer's Prologue* (Clarendon Press), s. v. *reyse*. Cf. the French expressions, "raz de mer," "raz de courent," "raz de marée."

p. 39, l. 1361. *sene: be*. Read *se* as in ll. 1124, 658, 1826.

p. 40, l. 1372. *ryden*, which does not rhyme with *foghten*, is evidently a clerical error. I suppose *soghten* to be the true reading. For examples of *soght* = "came, went, moved," see Zupitza's note to *Guy*, l. 7151, and Skeat's Glossary to *Specimens*, s. v. *socht*.—There is still another corruption in this passage, as *assembled* does not rhyme with *ordeyned*.

p. 40, l. 1380. Note the transition from the indirect to the direct speech.

p. 40, l. 1381. As it stands, the line is too long and spoils the rhythm. The words "if ye cast me downe" can be dispensed with.

p. 40, l. 1383. *thare: were* (O.E. werian). The rhyme is easily restored by reading *there* instead of *thare*, cf. ll. 2604, 2404, 2245, etc. and see *Introduction*, p. xxxv.

p. 41, ll. 1419-22. Observe the weak rhymes alternating with the strong ones.

p. 41, l. 1420. *brother* means "brother-in-law." Oliver's sister Aude was Roland's intended bride. Perhaps also *brother* may be taken here in sense of "brother in arms," as in most romances we find Roland and Oliver mentioned as a couple of true friends united by the most tender ties of comradeship. Besides, Oliver was highly indebted to Roland, who had rescued him when he had been made a prisoner after his duel with Ferragus.

p. 41, l. 1423. *cowthe* miswritten for *caughte*, which we read in ll. 1411, 1603.

p. 41, l. 1424. *Ascopartes* is the correct form. See note on l. 495.

p. 51, l. 1427. *foolde* cannot be "earth" here, for which the editor of the Roxburghe Club ed. takes it. *Foolde* is the participle past of *fealden*, "to fold, plicare." It means, "folded, bent down, fallen." This seems also to be the sense of *folde* in the following passages:

Laȝamon, 23983-4:

"Þa feol Frolle
folde to grunde."

Ibid. ll. 27054-6:

"Romanisce veollen
fiftene hundred
folden to grunden."

Ibid. ll. 20057-60:

"he þohte to quellen
Þe king on his þeode
& his folc valden
volden to grunde."

Cf. *Stratmann*, p. 194.

p. 41, l. 1433. Roland and Olyver are taken prisoners. This incident is differently related in the other poems. There Roland is not taken at all, but sent afterwards among the messengers to the Soudan's court. Together with Oliver four knights are taken, viz. Gwylmer, Berard, Geoffrey and Aubry, who all are carried away by the flying Saracens in spite of the efforts of Roland and Ogier.

p. 42, l. 1451. *what* = "who." See Koch, *Eng. Gr.* II. § 339, and Skeat's note to *Piers the Plowman* (Clarendon Press), 113/19. So in ll. 1133, 1623.

p. 42, l. 1456. *astyte* has nothing to do with the Latin *astutus* with which the editor of the Roxb. Club ed. apparently confounds it in explaining it as "cunningly devised." *Astyte* means "at once, immediately, suddenly"; see Morris, Glossary to *Allit. Poems.* It is a compound of the simple word *tyte*, "soon, quickly," which see above, l. 181.

p. 43, l. 1475. *Turpyn.* The name of the archbishop is not mentioned in the Ashmolean version. The French text, ll. 1836-40, runs as follows:

"Karles, nostre empereres, en est en piés levés,
Il apela Milon et Turpin l'alosés,
Deus rices arcevesques de moult grant sainteté:
Faites moi tost uns fons beneir et sacrer;
Je woel que cis rois soit bauptiziés et levés."

Cf. also the Provençal poem, l. 1899, *et seq.*

p. 43, l. 1483. *nought for thane* = "nevertheless," cf. Koch, *Eng. Gr.* II. p. 473.

p. 43, l. 1486. *Rome* is a corruption of *Roye*, as follows from the French *Fierabras*, l. 1851:

"C'est sains Florans de Roie, ce dist l'auctorités."

Cf. the Ashmole *Ferumbras*, l. 1087, and Grœber, *Zeitschrift für romanische Philologie*, IV. p. 167.

p. 43, l. 1495. *affrayned*, which must not be confounded with *affrayed*, as the editor of the Roxburghe Club ed. does, means "asked, inquired." It is the compound of *freynen* or *fraynen*, O.E. *frignan*, "to ask." Goth. *fraihnan*. Germ. *fragen*.

p. 43, l. 1497. *allayned*, "concealed." The simple verb *layne* (from Icel. *leyna*, cf. Zupitza's note to *Guy*, l. 2994) is still retained in the Scottish dialect, with the sense of "to hide." Cf. also Morris, *Allit. Poems*, Gloss. s. v. *layned*.

p. 43, l. 1498. In the other poems the prisoners do not tell their true names; see *Introduction*, pp. xxvii and xxix; and cf. *Syr Ferumbras*, l. 1167.

p. 43, l. 1499. Roland is nephew to Charlemagne on his mother's side. See note to l. 1888, and cf. the Ashmole *Ferumbras*, l. 2066. For Oliver, see above, note to l. 1250.

p. 44, l. 1515. In the *Sowdan* Floripas herself advises Laban not to slay his captives, but to imprison them. In the other versions it is one of the barons who gives the same advice. See *Introduction*, p. xxviii.

p. 44, l. 1538. *depe: myrke.* The rhyme will be restored by reading *dirke* or *derke* instead of *depe*. *derke* occurs in l. 2541.

p. 45, l. 1604. *maute.* "In Old French *mauté* is malice." Gloss. to Roxburghe Club ed. I do not know whether *mauté* exists in O.Fr., but even if it did, it would make no sense here. I feel sure *maute* is a corruption of *mynte* or *mente* (cf. l. 1784), the preterite of *minten* or *menten* = "to aim a blow, to strike," from O.E. *myntan*, "to intend, to purpose." See Zupitza's note to *Guy*, l. 6579, and Morris, *Allit. Poems*, s. v. *mynte*. Cf. also *Syr Ferumbras*, l. 5587:

"þan Charlis a strok till hym gan mynte;
Ac hym faylede of ys dynte,
for þat swerd hym glente . . ."

p. 47, l. 1615. *trew* instead of *free* will restore the rhyme. The same rhyme *trewe: newe* occurs in ll. 67, 588.

p. 47, l. 1619. *fele sithe*, "many a time, often." So in ll. 2740, 2815. Cf. *ofte sithe*, l. 916.

p. 47, l. 1624. *ruly*, O.E. hrêowlîc = "rueful, sorrowful, mournful, piteous."

p. 47, l. 1645. *harme skathe* makes no sense. Read *harme & skathe*, which occurs in *Gen. and Exod.* l. 2314:

"ðis sonde hem overtakeð raðe
And bicalleð of harme and scaðe."

p. 48, l. 1665. In the French *Fierabras* (as well as in the Ashmolean version) it is Roland whom Charlemagne addresses first (see above, note to l. 1433); he tells him that he must go on a mission to demand the surrender of Oliver and his companions. Upon which Naymes and the other twelve peers remonstrate, but are all sent to Laban one after the other, just as in the *Sowdan*. In the Provençal poem it is only Guy who protests. Cf. ll. 2263-2282 of the French *Fierabras*:

"Rollant regarda tost, si l'a araisonné:
Biaus nés, ce dist li rois, trop sui por vous irés;
Vous movrés le matin, à Aigremore irés;
Si dirés l'amirant, gardés ne li celés,
Rende moi la courone dont Dix fu couronés
Et les autres reliques dont je sui moult penés;
Et en après demant mes chevalier menbrés;
Et se il ne le fait si que deviserés,
Dites jel ferai pendre par la goule à un trefs,
En destre le menrai com .i. larron prové,
Ne troverai putel où il ne soit passé." etc.

p. 48, l. 1668. Cf. *Fierabras*, ll. 2309-2321, and *Syr Ferumbras*, l. 1486-1493.

p. 49, l. 1683. *lese*, "lose." So in l. 2655 and 1696, where it rhymes with *chese*, which occurs again in ll. 2748, 2934.

p. 49, l. 1687. French text gives (ll. 2297, *et seq.*):

"Ogiers li boins Danois s'en est levés en piés:
Sire drois emperere, pour amour Dieu. oiés:
Bien sai se il i vont ja n'en revenra piés.
Avoec irés, dist Karles, par les ex de mon cief:
Or i serés vous .v. qui porterés mes briés."

p. 49, l. 1691. *Bery* must be miswritten for *Terry*, as we find Terris d'Ardane in the French *Fierabras*, l. 2290, and Terry of Ardane in *Syr Ferumbras*, l. 1469. According to l. 3187 of *Sir Ferumbras*, Thierry is the father of Berard (Bryer) of Mountdidier. Cf. the French text, ll. 2290-96 and *Syr Ferumbras*, ll. 1468-1473.

p. 49, l. 1693. *rees*, "time, occasion." See note to l. 1349.

p. 49, l. 1695. Folk Baliant is not mentioned in any other poem of our romance. See *Introduction*, p. xxvii.

p. 49, l. 1698. *chese*, O.E. *cêosan*, Mod. E. *choose*. It here means "to be free to choose":—"You shall not be free to choose," "you shall have no choice," "you shall do what you are ordered." See Mätzner's remark [in his *Wörterb.*, p. 562, s. v. *cheosen*] to Halliwell, *Dict.* p. 250.

p. 49, l. 1699. *Aleroyse.* See note to l. 884.

p. 49, l. 1711. *Turpyn.* There was a real bishop of this name, who, according to the *Gallia Christiana*, held the see of Reims from A.D. 753 to 794. As we find him described in the romances, Turpin was the very type of a knight-bishop. In the poem of *Aspremont*, he bears before the Christian army the wood of the true cross which in his hands beams with brightness like the sun. In the romance of the *Enfances Ogier* it was he, into whose custody Ogier was given, when he had been made a prisoner after his revolt, in company with the king of Lombardy, against Charlemagne (see above, note to l. 856), and who, notwithstanding the order of Charles to have Ogier starved to death, kept the Dane alive, who afterwards, when the Saracens invaded France, proved a great help to the Christian arms. As we read in the *Chanson de Roland*, ll. 2242ss, Turpin met his death at Roncesvaux, but according to the *Chronicle of Turpin*, he survived the disaster of Roncesvaux, and was saying mass for the dead, when he saw the angels carrying the soul of Roland up to heaven. But from Gaston Paris's Essay *De Pseudo-Turpino* we know this chronicle to be an apocryphical book written by two monks of the eleventh and twelfth century.

p. 49, l. 1717. *set not of youre barons so light* = "do not count, consider them so little." Cf. "to take one so lighte," in *Syr Ferumbras*, ll. 114, 156.

p. 50, l. 1721. *gyfe no coost* has the same meaning as *give no tale* = "make no account, do not mind." See Zupitza's note to *Guy*, 8143. Cf. also *Sowdan*, l. 2793, and *Syr Ferumbras*, l. 5847, 101, 4975; and also ll. 173, 1578.

p. 50, l. 1723. Bryer of Mounteȝ or Berard de Montdidier was celebrated for his gallantries and attentions to the ladies:

"D'ardimen vail Rotlan et Olivier
E de domnei Berart de Mondesdier."

i. e.—"In prowess I am equal to Rolland and to Oliver, in matters of love to Berart of M." says the troubadour Peire Vidal in his poem *Dragoman seiner*; cf. also *Fierabras*, ll. 2125-7:

"Je ne sai cui vous estes, car ne vous puis viser,
Mais je cuit c'as pucieles sivés moult bien juer,
En cambre sous cortine baisier et acoler."

See, besides, *Syr Ferumbras*, ll. 422, 1297, 1305, 1354. This Bryer of Mountes must be the same as the one slain in a sally of the twelve peers, ll. 2604, 2622, because, according to l. 1723, it was he who was among the peers sent on a mission to the Soudan. There is one Bryer of Brytaine occurring in l. 886, whom one might be inclined to think identical with Bryer of Mountes, as in l. 886 he is cited together with the other peers. But since we find him again as the treasurer of Charlemagne (l. 3205), this is impossible, unless we suppose the mention of Bryer in l. 3205 to be owing to the absentmindedness of the author, who may be accused of a similar inadvertency with regard to Rychard of Normandy; cf. note to l. 2797, and Index of Names, *s. v.* Flagot.

p. 50, l. 1743. *Bronland.* The true reading is *Brouland*, as shewn by *Fierabras*, ll. 1549, 5174, &c.; *Destruction*, ll. 1240-159, 441, and *Sowdan*, ll. 1759, 2456. The Ashmole MS. has *Bruyllant.*

p. 51, l. 1751. *thane* = "thane that." See Zupitza's note to *Guy*, 992, p. 363.

p. 51, l. 1778. *charke* hardly makes sense here. It is perhaps a clerical error for *charge*, "to command, to order." The sense would then be, "and to tell him the Soudan's strict orders which by peril of death (= *upon life and lithe*) Laban recommended him to obey."

p. 51, l. 1779. *þen* instead of *þan* would improve the rhyme.

p. 52, l. 1788. *lorde of Spayne.* Cf. the French expression, "amirans d'Espaigne," which we find so often used in the *Destruction.*

p. 52, l. 1802. *trappe* is Mod. Eng. *trape*, which is used in the sense of "to traipse, to walk sluttishly." Halliwell has "trapes = to wander about."

p. 52, l. 1816. *byleved.* Rhyme and sense will be improved by reading *byleven.*

p. 53, l. 1854. *tyme* makes no sense here. Perhaps we ought to read *I dyne;* cf. ll. 1508, 1114, 1837, and *Syr Ferumbras*, l. 5621:

> "Oþer elles þoo shalt þyn hefd forgon,
> To morwen, or y wil dyne."

Fierabras, l. 1914:

> "Ja mais ne mengerai si sera desmembrés.'

See also *Guy*, l. 3695.

p. 54, l. 1888. *Syr Gy, nevew unto the king Charles.* Cf. *Fierabras*, ll. 3406-8:

> "On m'apele Guion, de Borgoigne fui nés,
> Et fils d'une des filles au duc Millon d'Aingler,
> Cousin germain Rollant, qui tant fait à douter."

Duke Milon d'Anglers was brother-in-law to Charlemagne, whose sister Berte was Milon's wife and mother to Roland. Cf. Philippe Mouskett, l. 2706-8:

> "S'ot Charles une autre sereur,
> Bertain: cele prist à seigneur
> Milon d'Anglers, s'en ot Rollant."

If, therefore, in the passage quoted above from *Fierabras*, Guy is said to be the grandson of Milon, he must have been the grand-nephew of Charlemagne, and nephew to Rollant. As we learn from the French poem of *Guy de Bourgoyne*, Guy's father was Samson of Burgundy. Cf. besides, *Histoire Poëtique*, p. 407, and *Syr Ferumbras*, ll. 1922, 2091, 1410, etc.

p. 55, l. 1892. *And yet knowe I him noght.* Floripas has already once seen Guy when he was defeating Lukafer before Rome; cf. *Fierabras*, ll. 2237-2245:

".i. chevalier de France ai lontans enamé
Guis a nom de Borgoigne, moult i a bel armé;
Parens est Karlemaine et Rollant l'aduré.
Dès que je fui à Romme, m'a tout mon cuer emblé·
Quant l'amirans mes peres fist gaster la cité,
Lucafer de Baudas abati ens ou pré,
Et lui et le ceval, d'un fort espiel quarré.
Se cis n'est mes maris, je n'arai homme né;
Pour lui voel je croire ou roi de sainte maïsté."

See also *Syr Ferumbras*, ll. 2073-2087. Our line does not necessarily imply a contradiction to the French text, as on the former occasion she probably saw the duel from a great distance, when the latter's features were hidden by his helmet. That she really did not recognize him follows from the following passage of *Fierabras*, l. 2800, *et seq.*

"Je aim en douce France .i. leger baceler."
—"Dame, comment a nom?" ce dist Rollans li her
Et respont la puciele: "ja le m'orrés nommer;
Guis a nom de Borgoigne, moult i a bel armé."
—"Par mon clef" dist Rollans "à vos ex le véés
N'a pas entre vous deus iiii piés mesurés."

Besides there are numerous instances to be met with in mediæval poetry of persons enamoured of some one they had never seen:

"Ans no la vi et am la fort"

says Guilhelm de Poitiers in speaking of his lady (Mahn, *Werke der Troubadours*, p. 3). Cf. also *Rits. Rom.* II. 19, and *Web. Rom.* II. 131.

p. 55, l. 1927. *myghty* seems to mean "excellent, delicious," rather than "heavy."

p. 57, l. 1974. *amonge*, "every now and then, from time to time, occasionally." See Zupitza's note to *Guy*, 2301. It is often used as a kind of expletive.

p. 57, l. 1995. *foulis*, "fools, foolish." Cf. the French text:

"Par Mahoun, dist li rois, trestout sont *fol* prové."

p. 57, l. 1996. There is no mention made of this game in the Provençal poem. It is described here even more explicitly than in the French *Fierabras*, ll. 2907—2932. Cf. also *Syr Ferumbras*, ll. 2230—2251.

p. 57, l. 1997. *assorte* = "assembly, company;" by one assorte = "in one company" (Halliwell). It seems to be connected with *sort* = "set, assemblage," see Skeat, *Specimens of E. E.*, 425/999

p. 58, l. 2000. *i-fest: blast.* Perhaps we ought to read *i-fast.*

p. 59, l. 2036. *maden orders.* I do not know the exact meaning of this expression. Perhaps it may be taken with the same sense as the Mod. H. Germ. phrase = "ordnung schaffen," which literally means "to set in order, to put matters straight," but is often used in the sense of "to clear away," or, "to remove or despatch."

p. 59, l. 2045. *that he wente awaye with lym* = "that he had escaped with (his limbs, or having) his limbs safe and sound. *lyme*, O.E. *lim.*, Mod. Eng. *limb.*

p. 59, l. 2052. *tho* = O.E. *þâ*, "those, them," it is used as a definite article in l. 2063.

p. 59, l. 2057. *amapide*, miswritten for *awapide* (Herrtage), "astounded, bewildered." Cf. Stratmann, p. 10.—Mätzner, *Wörterbuch*, p. 150, connects it with Goth. *afhvapjan*, "to suffocate." We find *m* written for *w* several times in our poem; thus we read *gamylokes* for *gawylokes* in l. 2650, and *romme* for *rowme* in l. 876.

p. 60, l. 2085. *Assyne.* The rhyme shows that *Assye* is the true reading. *Assye* occurs in ll. 102, 123.

p. 60, l. 2093. *wone*, "heap, plenty." O.Icel. *wân.* See Zupitza's note to *Guy*, p. 444.

p. 61, l. 2119. *Brenlande.* It ought to be *Breuland* or *Brouland*; see above note to l. 1743.

p. 61, l. 2120. The first foot in the line consists of the single word *what.* Thus in ll. 2288, 2374, 2394, etc.

p. 62, l. 2145. *Espyarde.* This name only occurs in this poem. In *Syr Ferumbras*, l. 3824, the messenger sent to the bridge-keeper is called Malyngryas. There is no name mentioned in the French *Fierabras*, l. 4265.

p. 62, l. 2156. *That no man by the brigge.* There is no verb in the sentence. Perhaps we ought to read *that no man passe by the brigge*, or, *that no man passe the brigge.*

p. 63, l. 2191. Cf. the description of the giant in *Fierabras*, ll. 4740—4755, and *Syr Ferumbras*, ll. 4435—4441.

p. 63, l. 2199. *nolde not.* See note to l. 1096.

p. 64, l. 2225. The line is too long. *Wilde* can be dispensed with, and instead of *horses* we may read *hors*; cf. Skeat, Gloss. to *Prioress's Tale* (Clarendon Press), *s. v.* hors.

p. 64, l. 2233. *a magnelle*, "a mangonel," an ancient military engine used for battering down walls (Halliwell). *Magnelle* is the O.Fr. *Mangonel*, or *Mangoneau*, the Italian *manganello* (= "arbalist, cross-bow"). The latter is the diminutive form of *mangano*, "a sling;" Greek, *μαγγανον*. See Diez, *Etym. Wörterb.*, I. 261.

p. 64, l. 2238. *Cornel* or *carnel*, Fr. *carnel*, Mod.Fr. *créneau*, "battlement, pinnacle." Literally it means, "a piece carved out," *i. e.* of the wall on the top of a building; the French verb *carneler* or *creneler* signifying, "to carve out, to jag, to notch." *Carnel* is derived from Latin *crena* (See Diez, *Gramm.*, I. 14), which means "a notch, a cut, an incision" (Diez, *Etym. Wörterb.*, II. 266). Thus *carnel* came to denote a battlement or indented parapet; or more exactly it was applied to those parts of the wall projecting upwards between the openings or embrasures. It was one of these projecting portions that was here knocked down. Cf. also *Syr Ferumbras*, l. 3314.

p. 65, l. 2245. The line is too long. Perhaps *or he hit* may be dispensed with.

p. 65, l. 2247. The episode of Marsedag being slain by Guy is not found in any other poem of this romance.

p. 65, l. 2271. *Alkaron*, "the Koran," *al* is the Arabic article. There is a god named Alcaron occurring in l. 2762.

p. 66, l. 2282. *dye: waye.* See l. 441. *forfamelid* = "famished, starved to death." I am not aware of any other instance of this word. Halliwell has "famele = to be famished." The prefix *for-* has intensive or augmentative power; it is particularly used in past participles. See Mätzner's *Grammatik*, I^2. 542.

p. 66, l. 2290. *faile* is the infinitive mood = "to be wanting, to become deficient." "Roland seeing the ladies white and pale (with hunger) and (seeing) the bread wanting on their table spoke some words of lamentation," etc.

p. 66, l. 2303. *forcere*, "chest, coffer." For the etymology see Diez, *Wörterb.*, II. 31, *s. v.* forziere.

p. 66, l. 2309. As it stands the line is too long. As *you* and *that* may be dispensed with, we ought perhaps to read, *I pray ye wole us alle it shewe.*

p. 66, l. 2310. *saule*, "fill, hunger satisfied to repletion." The rhyme shows that the last syllable is accentuated. Therefore it cannot be derived from the French *soûl* (Gloss. to Roxb. Club ed.), but from *soûlée.*

p. 66, l. 2311. *yede* = "went." Not from O.E. *eode*, but from *ge-eode.* See Zupitza's note to *Guy*, l. 60, and Skeat, *Piers the Plowman* (Clarendon Press), 94/40.

p. 66, l. 2312. *vertue : fewe ;* the rhyme is perfect, see the Abstract of Mr. Nicol's paper in the *Academy* of June 23, 1877 (vol. xi. p. 564, col. 1).

p. 66, l. 2313. We must scan this line thus:

And díden it aboúte hem éverychón.

-en in *diden* is mute; see *Introduction*, p. xxxix.

p. 67, l. 2326. *ginne* = "engin, contrivance, trick." See note to l. 780.

p. 67, l. 2337. *lefte.* The rhyme shows that the author pronounced *lafte*, which we find in l. 426.

p 68, l. 2351. Cf. *Fierabras*, ll. 3046—3097. In the Provençal poem Maubyn or Malpi, as he is called in Provençal, enters the room by means of a charm which makes the door open itself:

"Vengutz es al fossat, pres de la tor cayrada.
Tantost intret dedins cuendamens a celada,
Venc a l'us de la cambra: si la trobet tancada.
Et *a dit son conjur:* tota s'es desfermada."
ll. 2757-60.

p. 68, l. 2365. The rhyme is restored if we read *ledde* instead of *ladde*. See l. 1651.

p. 69, l. 2390. *By God and seynte Mary, myn avour.* I think the words *myn avoure* are due to the scribe, not to the author, as they spoil the rhythm. So we get *Mary : we.* This rhyme, although not perfect, is of no rare occurrence in Mid. Eng. works, see *Introduction*, p. xliv. As to the spelling of *avour* I am not aware of any other instance of this form of the word. There is a form *avyowre* cited by Halliwell. Besides, *avoury* and *avowery*, which he quotes under different heads, are perhaps only different spellings of the same word.

p. 69, l. 2399. *slepinge* must be altered into *slepande* in order to restore the rhyme. The author employed *-and* and *-ynge* as terminations of the present participle. See *Introduction,* p. xxxviii.

p. 69, l. 2421. *also* belongs to l. 2422.

p. 70, l. 2433. *so mete I spede,* "as I may succeed." See Zupitza's note to *Guy*, l. 615.

p. 71, l. 2477. *and now* is perhaps miswritten for *inow;* cf. the French text, l. 3803:

"*Tant* y a plates d'or, nus nes porroit nombrer."

p. 71, l. 2482. *wast* gives no sense. Perhaps we ought to read *went.*

p. 72, ll. 2491—2502. The arrangement of the stanzas seems, as regards the rhymes, to be incorrect.

p. 72, l. 2507. In the Ashmole *Ferumbras* this episode of the Soudan breaking the image of Mahound is omitted. In the French text he only threatens to make him cry, as soon as he gets hold of him, but he is rebuked by Sorbrance telling him that Mahomet being overtired with guarding the treasure has only fallen asleep. Cf. *Fierabras*, ll. 3820—3829.

p. 72, l. 2512. *ore,* O.E. *âr*, "mercy, favour." *Thyn ore* = "grant us thy favour," "have mercy upon us," or, "with thy favour."

p. 73, l. 2535. Richard of Normandy appearing here as in the French *Fierabras*, among the twelve peers besieged by the Soudan, without having been mentioned before in the number of the knights sent on a mission by Charles, furnishes us with an argument in support of our supposition that the French *Fierabras* was the source of our poem. See *Introduction*, p. xxx, and of *Fierabras*, ll. 3957—3994, and *Syr Ferumbras*, l. 4921.

p. 73, l. 2538. *wynde: hende; wende* which occurs in l. 2328 would improve the rhyme.

p. 73, l. 2549. *paramour* = "object of chivalrous affection and devotion."

p. 73, l. 2557. *wronge*, preterite of *wringe*, "to press well out, force one's way."

p. 73, l. 2558. Does *thile* stand for *while*, as *then*, l. 2527, seems to be miswritten for *when?* Or is *thile* = the while?

p. 74, l. 2564. *sloughe : drowe.* Read *slowe*, as in ll. 2401, 2683, 304, 2208, etc.

p. 75, l. 2597. *itolde*, "in number," see Zupitza's note to *Guy*, 1770.

p. 75, l. 2614. *quell* = "*kill*," which occurs in l. 3006.

p. 75, l. 2616. *bistadde*, "hard bestead, greatly imperilled."

p. 75, l. 2617. *japed*, "mocked, tricked, laughed at." Connected with Icel. *gabba*, "to mock."

p. 76, l. 2639. *tha*. See *Introduction*, p. xxxvii.

p. 76, l. 2651. *lurdeyn*, Mod. Eng. *lurdan*, which is said to be the Fr. *lourdin* (diminutive of *lourd*). Regarding it as a corruption of "lord Dane" is a mere joke:

> "In every house lord Dane did then rule all,
> Whence laysie lozels lurdanes now we call."
>
> *Mirrour for Magistrates*, p. 588.

p. 76, l. 2654. *sewes*. See Skeat, *Prioress's Tale*, p. 286.

p. 76, l. 2660. *let armes* makes no sense. Read *as armes*—*As armes* = Fr. *aux armes*, "to arms," is of pretty frequent occurrence in Mid. Eng. poems; see Mätzner's *Wörterb.*, p. 112. Cf. also *Syr Ferumbras*, l. 2933:

> "As armes," þanne cride Rolond,
> "As armes everychone!"

Cf. *ibidem*, l. 4125. So we read in the *Destruction*, l. 1460.

> "Ore as armes, seignours, franc chevalier membré."

Perhaps we ought to read *as armes* also in l. 491, where the reading *and armes* is somewhat suspicious, since *armes*, if we regard *and armes* to be the true reading, would be the only instance of the imperative plural ending in *-es* (instead of *-eth*) in the *Sowdan*.

p. 77 l. 2689. *Thay thanked God that thay him hadde Gyfe thaye suche grace to spede.* These lines are corrupt. I propose to read:

> "Thay thanked God that hem hadde
> Gyfen suche grace to spede."

p. 77, l. 2694. *alaye*, written as one word in the MS., must be divided into two, *a* being the indefinite article, and *laye* meaning "unploughed ground, field, pasture, meadow." Mod. Eng. *ley, lea, lay* See *Stratmann*, s. v. *leȝe*, p. 356.

p. 77, l. 2698. *he*, "they." This is the only instance of *he* instead of the common *thay*. But *he*, which is further confirmed by the rhyme, must certainly be attributed to the author; *thay* occurs only once,

(l. 3021) as a rhyme, but the rhyme is not a good one, and there also it would be preferable to read *he*.

p. 78, l. 2706. *by my thrifte*, the same as "so mote y thryve," or, "so mote y spede" = "as (verily as) I may thrive," "in truth."

p. 78, l. 2707. *see;* cf. Zupitza's note to *Guy*, 163.

p. 78, l. 2719. *wole: skille*. The rhyme shows that *wole* cannot be due to the author; we must read *wille* (or *welle* which occurs l. 2633).

p. 78, l. 2732. *bikure* or *bykeringe*, l. 2559 = "fight, battle, skirmish." *Er durste bikure abide*. The subject is wanting, see note to l. 67. Or is there any corruption in this line? Perhaps we ought to read: "Lenger durste [thay] no bikure abyde." Cf. ll. 3117, 2610, 2947.

p. 79, l. 2748. *love*. The rhyme requires *leef* or *leeve*. *leef*, O.E. *leof*, means "dear, beloved." For examples of *leef* being used as a substantive, see Stratmann, p. 359.

p. 80, l. 2793. *eye*, "egg." See Koch, *Eng. Gr.* II. § 582, and compare the French phrase "valoir un œuf pelé."

p. 80, l. 2797. *and his meyne*. This must be a mistake of the author himself. According to l. 2557, Richard had ventured alone on a mission to Charlemagne. There is no mention whatever made afterwards that he was joined by any one; the other poems likewise state that Richard was without any companion.

p. 80, l. 2805. *lete: gate*. The rhyme requires *late*.

p. 81, l. 2810. *cliffe*. Here the author of the *Sowdan* goes so far in shortening his original as to be wholly unintelligible. Indeed, any reader, not comparing these lines with corresponding passages in the French poem, will be left without any clue to what *cliff* is here intended to mean. From the French *Fierabras* we know that the water of the river was very deep and broad, and that the banks were exceedingly steep and almost inaccessible. Cf. *Fierabras*, ll. 4349:

"Et voit l'augue bruiant, le flot parfont et lé."

l. 4358: "La rive en est moult haute, bien fait à redouter." Cf. also the Provençal poem, ll. 3733, *et seq.:*

"Richart regarda l'aygua, que fe mot a duptar,
E fo grans e preonda, que no y auza intrar,
E la riba fou *auta de C pes* ses gaber."

Now it was by means of a twofold myracle that the Christian knight was enabled to cross the river:

(1) The waters suddenly increased and rose so as to reach the very top of the banks; cf. *Fierabras*, ll. 4365-69:

"Or oiés quel vertu Diex i vaut demonstrer
Por le roi Karlemaine, qui tant fait à douter.
Ançois que on ëust une liuée alé,
Veïssiés si Flagot engroissier et enfler,
Que par *desous la rive commence à seronder*."

Provençal, ll. 3741-45:

"Ara podetz auzir, si m voletz escoutar:
Tan bela meravilha li volc dieus demostrar
Per lo bon rey de Fransa que el volc tant amar;
Ans un trag de balesta pogues lunhs hom anar,
Pogratz vezer Flagot *sus la riba montar.*"

(2) A deer appears and shows Richard the way across the river to the top of the opposite bank.

"Atant es vous .i. cerf, que Diex i fist aler,
Et fu blans comme nois, biaus fu à resgarder.
Devant le ber Richart se prent à demostrer,
Devant lui est tantost ens en Flagot entrés.
Li dus voit Sarrazins après lui aroutés,
S'il ot paour de mort ne fait à demander.
Après le blance bisse commencha à crrer
Tout ainsi com ele vait, lait le ceval aler;
Et li ciers vait devant, qui bien s' i sot garder,
D'autre part à la rive se prent à ariver."

Cf. also the Provençal version, ll. 3751-54:

"Apres la blanca bestia laycha 'l destrier anar.
E lo cer vay denan, que l saup mot ben guizar,
De l'autra part de l'aygua l'a fayt ben aribar,
E dieus a fayt Flagot en son estat tornar."

This bank which formerly was steep and inaccessible, but is now covered with water, is called *cliff* by our poet. In the Ashmolean poem the first miracle is not mentioned; cf. *Syr Ferumbras*, ll. 3943, *et seq.*

p. 81, l. 2811. *he blessed him in Godis name.* The phrase occurs also in *Syr Ferumbras*, l. 3961, but is not to be found in the French text. Mr. John Shelley (in his paper printed in the *Annual Report and Transactions* of the Plymouth Institution, IV. i. 71) took this phrase as a proof that the original of the *Sowdan* could not have been the French poem. But it must be stated that as in the *Sowdan*, l. 2807, so in the French version Richard is said to have addressed a prayer to God:

"Escortrement commence Jhesu à reclamer:
Glorieus sire pere, qui te laissas pener
En la crois beneoite pour ton pule sauver,
Garisiés hui mon cors de mort et d'afoler,
Que je puisse Karlon mon message conter."
Fierabras, ll. 4360-64.

If now we consider that some lines back (l. 4093) the French poem expressively states that Richard seeing himself hard pressed by the Saracens, signed himself with the sign of the cross—

"Lors a levé sa main, de Jhesu s'est signiés"

an incident which at that moment is omitted in the *Sowdan*—we think ourselves entitled to regard this proof as not very convincing.

p. 81, l. 2820. *Ganelon*, one of Charlemagne's officers, who by his treachery was the cause of the defeat of Roncesvaux, the death of Roland, etc., for which he was torn to death by horses. For several centuries his name was a synonymous word with traitor. *Ganelo* = Germ. *Wenhilo*.

p. 81, l. 2845. *Fremounde* cannot be the true reading, as it does not rhyme with *kinge*. Besides *Fremounde* does not occur again in the poem. Perhaps we ought to read *Qwyntyne*, as in l. 1298. In the corresponding passage of the French *Fierabras* (l. 4625) it is to St. Denis that Charles swears; cf. also *Syr Ferumbras*, l. 4289.

p. 82, l. 2850. *And* makes no sense. Read "*God.*"

p. 83, l. 2887. *gryse: assaye.* We get a perfect rhyme if we read *gray* instead of *gryse*. Halliwell, *s. v.* "gray," has: "the skin or fur of a badger."

p. 83, l. 2891. As it stands, the line does not rhyme with l. 2893. The rhyme will be restored if we read:

"*Lycence gete ye noone nere,*" or perhaps
"*Lycence gete ye of me nere,*"

nere meaning *ne'er, never*, as in *Guy*, 10550 and 10716.

p. 84, l. 2939. The name of the giantess is *Amiette* or *Amiote* in the other poems.

p. 84, l. 2941. This line is too long; *as þikke* may be omitted.

p. 84, l. 2942. *bydene*, "immediately, all at once." On the etymology see Zupitza's note to *Guy*, 2408.

p. 85, l. 2981. *ayene* means "back." So in *Genesis and Exodus*, l. 1097:

"And bodem hem and tagten wel
ðat here non wente agen."

Again, l. 3267: "ðo quoðen he 'wende agen,
An israel folc lete we ben.'"

p. 86, l. 3020. As it stands, this line does not scan well. Perhaps we may read *month* instead of *monthes*, and *childre* instead of *children*, and scan the line thus:

Foúnd two chíldre of séven month oólde.

p. 87, l. 3021. *thay: Normandy.* The rhyme, though imperfect, cannot be objected to; but as the rhyme *e: y* (*i*) is frequently employed by our author (see *Introduction*, p. xliv), and was of rather common use about that period (see Ellis, *Pronunciation*, I. 271), we might incline to the supposition that *he* is the true reading. Cf. besides l. 2698.

p. 87, l. 3034. *mene* makes no sense. Perhaps we ought to read: *mete*, "food."

p. 87, l. 3044. In the French poem, l. 5108, Hoel and Riol are appointed governors of Mantrible, whereas Richard goes on with Charles and commands one of the divisions of his army (l. 5577). Cf. *Syr Ferumbras*, l. 5643.

p. 88, l. 3062. *coost*, "country, region." See Mätzner's *Wörterb.*, 487.

p. 88, l. 3084. In the *Fierabras*, l. 5374, it is Naymes who first recognizes the banner of France; cf. *Syr Ferumbras*, l. 5209.

p. 89, l. 3098. *of the Ethiopes* = "some of the Ethiopians." This may be regarded as an example of the partitive use of *of*. Cf. Zupitza's note to *Guy*, 1961.

p. 89, l. 3103. *alto hewe* must be more correctly written *al to-hewe*;—*to-*, as a mere prefix (signifying "in twain, asunder, apart" = Germ. *zer*) belongs essentially to the verb; the intensive adverb *al* (= "utterly, omnino,") used before verbs beginning not only with *to-*, but also before other prefixes, still further strengthens, and belongs to, the whole expression. So *al to-treden*, l. 1382, *to-braste*, l. 1168.

p. 89, l. 3122. *Belmore.* Perhaps identical with Belmarine.

p. 90, l. 3130. *wode-wroth*, "madly angry." Cf. Skeat, *Specimens of Early Eng. Lit.*, 80/37.

p. 90, l. 3141. *game*, "sport, joke, affair."

p. 90, l. 3154. *hat*, "be called." See note, l. 613.

p. 91, l. 3164. *bronde*, "sword." In the next line *bronte* means "blow, stroke."

p. 91, l. 3189. *lande: commaunde.* See note, l. 59.

p. 91, l. 3191. The rhyme is spoiled. Perhaps *than* must be transposed so that we get the rhyme *baptysed: imaryed.*

p. 92, l. 3210. *there to abide in store* = "to be kept in store"; cf. Skelton, ed. Dyce, I. 162, 221.

p. 92, l. 3227. *victory* = "booty, spoils of victory, trophy."

p. 92, l. 3232. *the hyer honde to have* = "to have conquered or vanquished." The same phrase is found in M. H. G.; cf. Hartmann's *Iwein*, ed. Lachmann, l. 1537-8:

"Vrou Minne nam die obern hant,
daz sî in vienc unde bant."

p 93, l. 3236. In the French *Fierabras*, l. 6082, *et seq.*, and in the Provençal poem, l. 5067, *et seq.*, the relics are distributed as follows: Part of the crown and one nail to St. Denis, and "*li signes*," the winding-sheet of the Lord, to Compiègne. There is no mention made of the cross in the French poem (see note to l. 665); cf. Introd. pp. l and liv.

p. 93, l. 3253. According to the *Chanson de Roland*, Ganelon has been drawn and quartered in a field near Aix-la-Chapelle.

p. 94, l. 3254. *By lawe*, cf. *Syr Ferumbras*, l. 307: "As for traytours ȝaf þe lawe." On this law compare Léon Gautier's note to l. 3736 of the *Chanson de Roland.*

p. 95, l. 3274. The French poem ends with the assertion of the poet (or the scribe) that whoever has well listened to this romance will find every part of it good and excellent, the opening, the middle, and the end:

"De cest roumant est boine et la fin et l'entree,
Et enmi et partout, qui bien l'a escoutée."

GLOSSARY.

O.E. = Old English or Anglo Saxon. O.Fr. = Old French.
32/1094 = page 32, line 1094.

ABYE, 32/1094, *vb.* to pay for, expiate. O.E. âbycgan.
adaunte, 28/957, *vb.* to subdue. Fr. danter, donter, dompter.
aferde, 39/1337, *pp.* afraid. O.E. âfæ̂rde.
affrayned, 43/1495, *pt. s.* asked. O.E. frignan.
afraye, 26/896, *sb.* disturbance, fight.
agreved, 29/992, *pp.* aggrieved. Fr. aggrever.
alayned, 43/1497, *pt. s.* concealed, dissembled. Icel. leyna.
alle and some, 22/749, altogether, every one.
almiht, 38/1329, *adj.* *See note.*
ameved, 29/994, *pp.* moved.
amonge, 57/1994, *adv.* in the mean time, now and then, sometimes. *See note to* l. 1974.
aplight, 17/573, *adv.* certainly, indeed. *See note.*
areeste, 34/1166, *sb.* rest, support. O.Fr. arrest.
arson, 41/1410, *sb.* pommel. Fr. arçon.
aspied, 10/314, *pp.* espied. Fr. espier.
assaye, 83/2889, *sb.* value. Fr. essai.
assorte, 57/1997, *sb.* assembly, company. *See note.*
assoyled, 70/2455, *pt. pl.* absolved.
astraye, 16/532, *adv.* out of the right way, roving about without guidance.
astyte, 42/1456, *adv.* immediately.
asure, 5/134, *sb.* azure.
atame, 27/935, *vb.* to tame, subdue. O.E. âtamian.
atone, 32/1103, agree.
attones, 31/1067, at once.
avente, 36/1237, *vb.* to take breath. Fr. venter.
avoure, 69/2390, *sb.* protection, protectress.
avyse, 49/1716, *vb.* to consider, advise with one's self. Fr. aviser.
awapide, 59/2057, *pp.* astounded, bewildered. *See note.*
ayene, 85/2981, *adv.* back.

Bandon, 19/636, *sb.* disposal.
bassatours (?), 29/995, *sb.* vavassors.
bawson, 2/52, *sb.* badger.
baye, 27/940, *sb.* recess, niche. *See note.*
beckyn, 3/64, *vb.* beckon. O.E. bêacnian.
bedight, 88/3070, *vb.* to dispose, to surrender, to send forth.
behight, 25/859, *pt. s.* promised. O.E. heht.
bende, 13/420, *vb.* to direct.
bente, 20/665, *adj.* bent, crooked.

benysone, 9/289, *sb.* blessing. Fr. benoison.

bette, 49/1716, *adv.* better.

bikure, 78/2732, *sb.* skirmish.

bispake, 5/165, *pt. s.* spoke with.

bistadde, 75/2616, *pp.* placed in peril, hardly bestead. Cf. O.E. stæððan. Dan. bestede.

biwry, 46/1580, *vb.* betray. O.E. biwrêgan.

bloo, 29/1005, *adj.* blue. Icel. blâr.

blynne, 70/2442, *vb.* to cease, stop. O.E. belinnan.

bobaunce, 7/211, *sb.* boasting.

boure, 54/1870, *sb.* a lady's apartment, boudoir. O.E. bûr.

bowe, 53/1853, *sb.* bough, branch. O.E. bôg.

braide, 32/1098, *pt. s.* drew. O.E. brægd.

brayde, 8/247, *sb.* craft, deceit, artifice. *See note.*

breddes, 5/131, *sb.* birds. O.E. bridas.

broke, 57/1965, *vb.* to break.

bronte, 91/3166, *sb.* blow.

buskede, 31/1055, *pt. s.* prepared, arrayed. Icel. bûask.

by, 3/87, *vb.* buy, pay. O.E. bycgan.

bydene, 84/2942, immediately. *Originally* mid one. *See note.*

bygone, 3/79, *pp.* afflicted. *See note.*

bykeringe, 74/2595, *sb.* skirmish.

by than, 10/344. *See note.*

Camalyon, 29/1008, *sb.* camelleopard. *See note.*

carrikes, 4/118, a kind of large ship. *See note.*

caste, 12/394, *sb.* plan, stratagem; 60/2091, the throwing; 71/2471, missile. *See note to* l. 394.

ceased, 89/3109, *pt. s.* seized.

chaffer, 83/2885, *sb.* merchandise. O.E. cêap, faru.

charke, 51/1778, *vb.* to creak, crack. *See note.*

chek, 8/189, *sb.* a checkered cloth.

chere, 6/201, *sb.* demeanour, behaviour, humour.

chere, 80/2781, *sb.* friendliness, willingness.

chere, 87/3030, *adj.* pleased, merry.

chese, 49/1698, *vb.* to be free to choose. O.E. cêosan.

clepeth, 24/809, *pr. s.* calls.

clipped, 56/1935, *pt. pl.* embraced, hugged. O.E. clyppan.

clog, 46/1603, *sb.* "truncus," block.

cloute, 58/2014, *sb.* blow.

combrest, 83/2909, *pr. s.* encumberest. Fr. combrer.

coost, 50/1721, *sb.* regard, account. *See note.*

cornell, 64/2238, *sb.* shaft of a pinnacle or battlement. O.Fr. carnell. *See note to* l. 2238, and compare Du Cange, *s. v.* quarnellus: "pinna muri per quam milites jaculantur."

coude, 16/541, *pt. s.* knew.

counsail, 46/1590, secret.

Defouled, 7/233, *pp.* polluted. Cf. O.E. fŷlan, fûlian.

delte, 16/526, *pp.* dealt.

dere, 92/3202, *vb.* to harm, injure. O.E. derian.

derke, 73/2541, *adj.* dark.

dewe, 70/2452, *adj.* due.

dight, 79/2763, *pp.* dressed, prepared. O.E. dihtan.

dinge, 26/880, *vb.* to dash, beat. Cf. Icel. dengja.

dirke, 44/1539. *See note.*

dobbet, 33/1136, *pp.* dubbed. O.E. dubban. Fr. dober.

dome, 14/478, *sb.* glory.

don, 88/3078, *vb.* cause, order O.E. dôn.

donne, 11/347, *adj.* dun.

dowte, 9/297, *sb.* fear.

dradde, 36/1232, *pt. s.* feared. Cf. O.E. on-drǽdan.

dresse, 49/1702, *vb.* to direct one's self, go, start. Fr. dresser.

dromonde, 3/63, *sb.* vessel of war.

dute, 30/1024, *sb.* duty. Deriv. of due, dewe. Fr. deu.

Egre, 29/1009, *vb.* to excite, to urge.

eke, 20/662, *adv.* also. O.E. êac.

engyn, 28/948, *sb.* a skilful contrivance. Fr. engin.

ensample, 27/931, *sb.* example.

ententc, 16/550, *vb.* to turn one's attention to, to try to get, to attempt.

entente, 28/945, *sb.* meaning, will, mind.

erille, 11/368, *sb.* earl.

erraunte, 5/139, quick, immediately.

eye, 80/2793, *sb.* egg. O.E. æg.

Fade, 20/678, *vb.* to dispose, to arrange, to set up (?).

fade, 30/1033, *adj.* weak, faint.

faste, 32/1086, *adv.* much, greatly.

fat, 90/3152, *sb.* vat, tub. O.E. fæt.

fauchon, 76/2650, *sb.* a sword or falchion.

faye, 26/900, *vb.* truth, faith.

fele, 47/1619, *adj.* many

felle, 29/1004, *adj.* fierce, furious.

felte, 41/1405, *pt. s.* made fall, killed.

fende, 92/3231, *pp.* defended, protected, granted.

fere, 36/1248, *sb.* fear. O.E. fǽr.

fere, 44/1505, *sb.* companion. In fere, 31/1071, together.

fere, 2/59, *vb.* to terrify.

ferre, 4/103, *adv.* far.

fet, 91/3188, *pp.* fetched.

fille, 35/1210, *pt. s.* fell.

fleen, 88/3065, to flay. O.E. flêan.

folde, 71/1427, *pp.* felled, knocked down.

forcere, 66/2303, *sb.* chest, coffer. O.Fr. forcier.

for-famelid, 66/2282, *pp.* entirely famished.

foule, 77/2686, *vb.* foul luck, mischance.

fowarde, 15/502, 22/732, *sb.* vanguard.

frankensense, 20/679, *sb.* an odorous resin, pure incense.

fraye, 15/514, *vb.* to frighten, attack.

frike, 4/104, *adj.* quick, bold, active.

frith, 2/43, *sb.* enclosed wood.

froo, 79/760, *prep.* from.

fyne, 9/306, *sb.* end.

Game, 90/3141, *sb.* affair; 92/3199, pleasure. O.E. gamen.

gan, 16/549, *pt. s.* began.

gavylok, 41/1426, *sb.* a spear or javelin. O.E. gafoluc.

geaunesse, 84/2943 (?), *sb.* giantess.

geder, 45/1553, *vb.* to gather. O.E. gædrian.

glased, 35/1208, *pt. s.* glided. O.Fr. glacier. See Zupitza's note to *Guy*, l. 5067.

glede, 7/205, *sb.* a glowing coal, ember. O.E. glêd.

god, 3/67, *adj.* versed in, master of.

gome, 5/144, *sb.* man. O.E. guma.

gonge, 84/2934, *vb.* to go. O.E. gongan.

goulis, 6/189, *sb.* gules, a red colour. Fr. geules.

gray, 83/2887, *sb.* the fur of a gray, or badger. O.E. grǽg.

gree, 82/2850, *sb.* grace, favour. Fr. gré. Lat. gratum.

grenned, 84/2948, *pt. s.* grinned, roared. O.E. grennian.

grevaunce, 29/993, *sb.* grievance.

greved, 45/1543, *pt. s.* grieved, molested, troubled.

grith, 82/2850, *sb.* peace, agreement. O.E. grið.

grysе, 83/2887, *sb.* a kind of fur. Fr. gris.

guttis, 39/1351, *sb.* guts. O.E. gut.

gydoure, 5/163, *sb.* leader, guide.

gynne, 67/2326, *sb.* enginne, contrivance.

Harde, 59/2056, *pt. s.* heard.

hat, 90/3154, *vb.* to be called. O.E. hâtan.

he, 77/2698, *pron. nominat.* thay. O.E. hí.

heede, 62/2158, *sb.* head. O.E. hêafod.

hende, 73/2536, *adj.* gentle, polite. O.E. hendig.

hennys, 55/1922, *adv.* hence. O.E. heonan.

hente, 40/1370, *vb.* hold, take. O.E. hentan.

hie, 14/455, *sb.* haste.

hight, 18/613, *pt. s.* promised; 36/1242, art called. O.E. heht.

honde of honde, 12/394, in close fight.

hoole, 32/1119, *adj.* whole, sound. O.E. hâl.

hurle, 27/929, *vb.* to jostle, to strike. A contraction of *hurtle.*

hurteled, 24/831, *pt. pl.* clashed against, jostled. Frequentative of *hurt.* Fr. hurter, heurter.

hye, 32/1092, *sb.* haste.

I-fast, 58/2000, fixed.

ilkadele, 58/2016, every part. O.E. ǣlc, dǣl.

ilke, 9/281, *adj.* same. O.E. ylca.

inowe, 25/854, *adv.* enough. O.E. genôh.

ishente, 66/2286, *pp.* destroyed. O.E. ge-scended.

istoke, 56/1963, *pp.* shut up, fastened. From steken. O.L.G. stecan.

istonge, 16/533, *pp.* stung, pierced. O.E. stungen.

it, 25/845, *vb.* to hit. Icel. hitta.

iwis, 3/71, *adv.* certainly, indeed. O.E. gewiss.

iwone, 11/358, *adj.* accustomed.

Japed, 75/2617, *pp.* mocked, laughed at. O.Icel. gabba.

jouste, 57/1991, *vb.* to joust, fight. Fr. jouster.

Kele, 93/3258, *vb.* to keel, cool. O.E. cêlan.

kind, 63/2196, *sb.* race, family.

kithe, 28/971, *vb.* to show, manifest. O.E. cýðan.

kon, 66/2297, *prs. pl.* can.

kynde, 28/968, *sb.* nature, temper.

kynde, 2/42, *adj.* natural, inborn.

Lan, 15/516, *pt. s.* ceased, stopped. O.E. lan.

late, 71/2460, *pt. pl.* let, caused, ordered. O.E. lêt, lǣton.

launde, 2/59, *sb.* park, lawn.

laye, 77/2694, *sb.* lea, field. O.E. lêah. Cf. Water-*loo.*

laye, 28/951, *sb.* law. O.E. lagu.

layne, 16/538, *pt. pl.* lay. O.E. lǣgon.

lefe, 23/763, *vb.* leave, abandon, forsake. O.E. lǣfan.

lefe-long, 24/832, *adj.* long, tedious.

logeeȝ, 23/775, leagues. Fr. lieue. O.Fr. legue. Lat. leuca.

leke, 50/1726, *sb.* leek. O.E. lêac.

lele, 33/1129, *adj.* leal, loyal. Fr. leal.

lenger, 72/2500, *compar.* longer.

lere, 66/2289, *sb.* countenance, complexion. O.E. hlêor.

lere, 74/2569, *vb.* to teach.

lered, 58/2005, *pp.* learned.

lerne, 33/1141, *vb.* to teach.

lese, 49/1683, *vb.* to loose. O.E. lêosan.

lette, 17/585, *vb.* leave off; 74/2610, to put a stop to, hinder, tarry. O.E. lettan.

leve, 23/794, *vb.* leave. O.E. lǣfan; 30/1045, omit, neglect.

leve, 19/651, *vb.* live, remain. O.E. gelýfan.

leven, 31/1050, *vb.* believe. O.E. lêfan.

lewde, 75/2601, *sb.* laymen, unlearned. O.E. lǽwed.

light, 26/905, *adj.* active, nimble.

light, 33/1125, *pp.* alighted. O.E. lihtan.

lithe, 81/1778, *sb.* limb, member. O.E. lið.

logges, 69/2399, *sb.* huts. Fr. loge.

longith, 28/951, *prs. s.* belongeth, becomes.

loute, 72/2513, *vb.* to stoop, bow down. O.E. lûtan.

lowly, 70/2454, *adv.* low, not loud.

lurdeynes, 76/2651, *sb.* lurdan, lout. Fr. lourdin.

lym, 59/2045, *sb.* limb.

lyued, 66/1261, *pt. pl.* lived.

Magre, 42/1442, *prep.* in spite of.

maistryes, 89/3117, *sb. pl.* mastery, proof of skill, combat.

manly, 29/989, *adj.* brave.

mayne, 16/528, *sb.* main, strength.

me, 9/287, *sb.* men, people, one.

meche, 6/179, *adj.* much. O.E. mycel.

mede, 31/1054, *sb.* meadow. O.E. mǽd.

mede, 37/1289. *sb.* meed, pay. O.E. mêd.

medel, 73/2540, *vb.* meddle. O.Fr. mesler, mestler.

men, 4/115, *sb.* men, people, one.

menske, 28/972, *sb.* manliness, honour. O.E. mennisc.

mente, 51/1784, *vb.* to aim at, to intend to go. O.E. myntan. *See note to* l. 1604.

mervaylyth, 88/3066, *prs. s.* marvels, wonders. Cf. Fr. merveille.

mete, 47/1633, *sb.* food, repast.

meyne, 7/219, *sb.* host, company, retinue. O.Fr. maisniee.

mikille, 30/1016, *adj.* many. O.E. mycel.

moche, 15/505, *adj.* much.

mode, 29/1009, *sb.* mind, temper, courage. O.E. môd.

moolde, 5/136, *sb.* earth, worth. O.E. molde.

moone, 28/944, *sb.* moan, complaint. Cf. O.E. mǽnan.

more, 23/777, delay. *See note to* l. 1110.

more, 29/1005, *sb.* moor, Maurian.

mot, 19/650, *vb.* may.

myghty, 56/1927, *adj.* *See the note.*

myrke, 45/1541, *adj.* dark. O.E. myrce.

Natheless, 15/506, *adv.* nevertheless.

nather, 36/1232, *adj.* nother.

ner, 13/416, *conj.* nor.

nere, 22/756, *adv.* near.

nerehond, 86/2998, *adv.* almost.

noght, 43/1497, *adv.* not.

noght, 78/2712, *sb.* nothing.

none, 32/1114, *sb.* noon.

nones, 3/74, *sb.* nonce, occasion.

nothinge, 6/175, not at all.

nothir, 8/267, *conj.* neither.

nought for than, 43/1483, nevertheless.

nyl, 17/585, *prs. s.* will not. O.E. nyle.

Of, 32/1088, *prp.* on account of.

oght, 78/2713, *sb.* aught.

onarmede, 14/464, unarmed.

onneþe, 89/3105, *adv.* scarcely.

onworthily, 49/1634, *adv.* unusefully.

orders, 59/2036. *See the note.*

ore, 72/2512, *sb.* mercy, favour. O.E. âr.

orfrays, 83/2888, *sb.* gold embroidery. Lat. Aurifrisum.

overlede, 72/2502, *vb.* to domineer over, to oppress.

Parelles, 55/1917, *sb. pl.* perils. Fr. péril.

paynym, 16/539, *sb.* pagan.

pellure, 83/2887, *sb.* fur. O.Fr. pelure.

pight, 34/1158, *pp.* pitched, fixed.
pinne, 88/3077, *vb.* to torment. O.E. pînan.
playn, 6/177, *vb.* to complain.
plete, 33/1151, *vb.* plead, prattle. From Fr. plet, plaid.
plight, 26/889, *prs. s.* promise, assure.
poleyne, 6/176, *sb.* pully-pieces, knee-armour.
praye, 16/550, *sb.* press, crowd.
prees, 40/1399, *sb.* crowd, struggle. Fr. presse.
preest, 34/1169, *adj.* ready. Fr. prest.
prik, 81/2831, *vb.* to spur a horse, to ride.
prikke, 65/2260, *sb.* a piece of wood in the centre of the target. See Halliwell's *Diction. s. v.* proke.
prove, 6/183, *vb.* to try.
prowe, 51/1766, *sb.* profit, advantage, honour. Fr. prou.
prymsauns, 28/965 (?). *See the note.*

Quod, 32/1095, *prt. s.* quoth.
qwelle, 75/2614, *vb.* to kill. O.E. cwellan.
qwere, 17/566, *sb.* quire, choir-service.
qweynte, 3/74, *adj.* excellent, elegant. O.Fr. coint. Lat. cognitus.
qwike, 58/2001, *adj.* alive, burning. O.E. cwic.
qwite, 16/520, *vb.* to requite, to reward.

Racches, 2/56, *sb.* setting dogs, pointers.
rafe, 25/866, *vb.* to rave. O.Fr. raver. Span. rabiar. Lat. rabiare.
ras, 39/1349, *sb.* instant, occasion. *See the note.* 19/645, hurry, haste.
rase, 23/774, *sb.* rush, channel of the sea.
raught, 46/1605, *prt. s.* reached, aimed at, struck. O.E. rǣhte.
rede, 85/2980, *sb.* counsel, advice. O.E. rǣd.
rees, 49/1693, *sb.* time, occasion.
rehete, 59/2035, *vb.* to cheer.
rekyneth, 57/1982, *prs. s.* reckons, deduces.
releve, 7/219, *vb.* to rally.
renew, 33/1126, *vb.* to tie? Fr. renouer.
renew, 63/2200, *vb.* to renovate, to recommence. Renew.
resyn, 16/534, *prs. pl.* rise.
rew, 89/3105, *sb.* row, order. O.E. rǣw.
roght, 54/1878, *pt. pl.* recked, cared. O.E. rôhton.
roial, 20/686, 51/1765, *adj.* exquisite, distinguished; 71/2483, delightful. Cf. l. 2247.
rome, 14/484, *vb.* to walk about. See Stratmann, *s. v.* râmen, p. 452.
romme, 26/876, *sb.* room, space. O.E. rûm.
rowte, 2/54, *sb.* company, host.
rowte, 60/2073, *vb.* to assemble in a company, to throng, to rally.
ruly, 47/1624, *adj.* rueful. O.E. hrêowlîc.
ryme, 10/339, *vb.* to cry out, to moan.

Saile, 12/385, *vb.* to assail.
same, all in s., 56/1938, altogether.
sare, 21/706, *adv.* sorely, sadly.
saule, 66/2310. *See the note.*
saute, 18/619, *sb.* assault.
saye, 58/1998, *pt. pl.* saw. O.E. sǣgon.
scole, 33/1141, *vb.* style, manner.
sede, 7/235, *sb.* seed.
seke, 32/1116, *adj.* sick.
semely, 2/39, *adj.* seemly, comely, beautiful.
sendelle, 4/129, *sb.* a kind of rich thin silk.

sot, 49/1717, *vb.* to consider, estimate.

sote, 3/62, *sb.* a seat.

sowes, 76/2654, *sb.* juices, delicacies. O.E. seaw.

seyne, 14/472, *vb.* to speak.

shente, 1/23, *pp.* destroyed.

shifte, 78/2704, *vb.* to divide, to share. O.E. sciftan.

shonde, 64/2222, *sb.* disgrace, ignominy. O.E. sceand.

shoon, 40/1381, *sb.* shoes. O.E. scêon, scêos.

shope him, 2/50, *pt. s.* got himself ready to, arrayed himself.

shoure, 15/509, *sb.* fight.

shrew, 72/2518, *vb.* to curse.

shrewes, 76/2652, *sb.* wicked beings.

sikerlye, 62/2172, *adv.* surely.

sith, 47/1632, *conj.* since.

sithe, 47/1619, *sb. pl.* times. O.E. sîð.

skaped, 59/2043, *pt. s.* escaped.

skath, 47/1645, *sb.* loss, damage, ruin. Cf. O.E. sceaðan.

skomfited, 38/1320, *pp.* discomfited. O.Fr. desconfire.

skulkyng, 76/2651, *prs. p.* lurking, breaking forth from a hiding place.

smerte, 38/1309, *adj.* smart, pungent.

smertly, 41/1419, *adv.* smartly, at once.

socoure, 15/507, *sb.* succour, assistant.

soghten, 40/1372, *pt. pl.* moved on, rode. *See the note.*

solas, 20/675, *sb.* relief, recreation, pleasure. O.Fr. solaz. Lat. solatium.

somer, 77/2702, *sb.* a sumpter horse. Fr. sommier. Cf. Diez, *Etym. Dict.* I., p. 364, *s. v.* salma.

sonde, 61/2134, *sb.* message, order.

sore, 2/47, *adv.* very much, eagerly.

sore, 33/1138, *adv.* sadly.

sowdeoures, 21/727, *sb.* soldiers, hirelings. Lat. solidarius. Cf. Fr. soudard, soudoyé.

spede, 70/2433, *vb.* thrive.

spille, 36/1226, *vb.* to destroy. O.E. spillan.

stonyed, 24/825, *pt. s.* shook, astounded.

steven, 65/2258, *sb.* voice. O.E. stefn.

stondart, 78/2717, *sb.* standard-bearer. Fr. étendard.

store, 23/768, *sb.* provision.

store, 92/3210, *sb.* stock, preservation, keeping.

stoure, 7/212, *sb.* battle, tumult.

stoute, 53/1825, *adj.* proud, boasting.

stronde, 2/53, *sb.* strand, shore.

stroyeth, 5/159, *prs. s.* destroyeth.

stynte, 52/1804, *pt. pl.* stopped.

sue, 46/1601, *vb.* to follow. Fr. suivre.

sware, 13/428, *adj.* heavy.

swyth, 47/1621, *adv.* quick, fast. O.E. swîðe.

Tan, 74/2581, *pp.* taken.

tene, 30/1032, *sb.* grief, anger, insult, injury. O.E. têona.

tene, 83/2902, *vb.* to vex, to wax wroth. O.E. tŷnan.

teyde, 48/1648, *pp.* tied.

tha, 76/2639. *See the note.*

thane, 51/1756, than that.

then, 46/1593, *vb.* to prosper. O.E. þêon.

thikke, 30/1027, *adj.* numerous, plentiful, plenty.

threste, 34/1170, *vb.* to thrust, shake, totter.

thrifte, 78/2706, *sb.* thriving, prosperity, success. O.Icel. þrift.

tho, 59/2052, *pron.* those, them.

tho, 59/2063, *art.* the, those.

tho, 2/53, *adv.* then. O.E. ðâ.

thronge, 41/1401, *sb.* thrusts, throwing of arrows.

tobraste, 34/1168, *pt. pl.* burst, or broke in pieces. O.E. (tôbærst) tôburston.

tohowe, 89/3103, *pp.* hewn to pieces. O.E. tô-hêawen.

tokenyng, 8/242, *sb.* news, intelligence.

totreden, 40/1382, *pp.* crushed, trodden down.

trappe, 52/1802, *vb.* to go. Cf. Ger. trippeln, E. trip, O.Fr. troper.

tredde, 58/1999, *sb.* thread. O.E. þræd.

trende, 27/940, *pp.* turned, vaulted.

treted, 55/1923, *pt. pl.* treated, pressed. Fr. traiter.

trewe, 3/67, *adj.* a thorough master of, a trustworthy interpreter of.

troyumple, 27/913 (?)

trowe, 8/246, *vb.* to believe.

trusse, 49/1707, *vb.* to pack off, to be off.

trwes, 31/1060, *sb.* truce.

tyte, 6/181, *adj.* soon, quickly, fast.

Unneth, 5/160, *adv.* scarcely.

Vere, 28/965, *sb.* spring.

vertue, 66/2312, *sb.* magic, power.

viage, 82/2846, *sb.* voyage, journey.

victory, 92/3227, *sb.* booty.

voydance, 32/1106, *sb.* relinquishment, deliverance.

voyde, 51/1768, *vb.* to give up, abandon, leave.

Wage, 18/590, *vb.* to hire, pay.

ware, 7/204, *adj.* aware.

waste, 8/246, in = in vain.

wende, 92/3214, *vb.* to turn, go. O.E. wendan.

wende, 85/2958, *pt. s.* thought, O.E. wênde.

wene, 31/1061, *vb.* to think.

were, 7/210, *vb.* to defend, to protect, to fight. O.E. werian.

werre, 16/541, *sb.* war.

wery, 3/60, *adj.* weary, fatigued.

wessh, 54/1871, *pt. pl.* washed.

wete, 94/3270, *vb.* to know.

what, 47/1623, *pron.* = who.

wifle, 76/2650, *sb.* a kind of axe. O.E. wifel, "bipennis."

wight, 27/933, *adj.* nimble, active. Sw. *vig*, active.

wirch, 5/148, *vb.* to work, to do. O.E. wyrcan.

wiste, 48/1662, *pt. s.* knew.

wode, 9/276, *adj.* mad, furious.

wode-wroth, 90/3130, *adj.* madly angry. O.E. wôd and wrâð.

wone, 60/2093, *sb.* lot, quantity. Icel. wân.

worche, 59/2046, *vb.* to work, to do. O.E. wyrcan.

worthed up, 34/1163, *pt. s.* got up, mounted.

wote, 2/36, *prs. s.* know. O.E. wât.

wotist, 61/2123, *prs. s.* knowest. O.E. wâst.

wrake, 70/2446, *sb.* persecution, mischief, destruction. O.E. wracu.

wreke, 88/3058, *pp.* wreaked, revenged.

wrong, 73/2557, *pt. s.* pressed, forced his way, hurried off. O.E. wringan.

wyne, 9/275, *vb.* get, attain. O.E. winnan.

Yare, 19/639, *adj.* ready. O.E. gearu.

yates, 66/2285, *sb.* gates. O.E. gatu.

yede, 66/2311, *pt. s.* went. O.E. ge-eode.

yolde, 12/403, *vb.* yield. O.E. gieldan, *pp.* golden

yolowe, 29/1005, *adj.* yellow. O.E. geolo.

Þilke, 76/2644, *pron.* such, yon. O.E. þylc.

þon, 4/108, *art.* the. O.E. þone.

INDEX OF NAMES.

AGREMARE, Agremour or Egromour, a town in Spain situated on the river Flagot. The soudan is holding his court there (l. 33), when he hears of the injuries done to his subjects by the Romans. Having destroyed Rome, he returns to Agremor (l. 672) [not to Morimonde, as in the *Destruction*, l. 1351, and in *Fierabras*, l. 27]. At Agremor the twelve peers are imprisoned and besieged. *Syr Ferumbras* reads *Egremoygne*, *Egremoun*, *Agremoun*.

ALAGOLOFUR, a Saracen giant, warden of the bridge of Mantrible; ll. 2135, 2881, 2149, 2175, 2801, 3053. In *Syr Ferumbras*, l. 3831, etc., he is called Agolafre. In the French poem of *Fierabras* we find Agolafre and Golafre.

ALCARON, l. 2762, a Saracen deity; cf. note to l. 2271.

ALEROYSE, l. 1699, one of the twelve peers; cf. note to l. 884.

ALISAUNDRE. Ferumbras is called King of Alisaundre, ll. 510, 984. Cf. *Destr.* 71, 1237, 1315. *Fierabras*, 50, 66, 538, etc. Ashmole *Ferumbras*, 53, 88, etc.

APPOLYN, one of the Mahometan deities. See note to l. 86.

ARABYE, l. 3097. Cf. *Destr.* 75; *Fierabras*, 3160, 4096.

ASCALON. Laban's birthplace, l. 100, and subject to him. This name does not occur in any other version.

ASCAROT, l. 2762, a Mahometan god. Occurring in none of the other versions.

ASCOPARS, see note to l. 495.

ASKALOUS, l. 497.

ASSAYNES, l. 497.

ASSIENS, ll. 1039, 2085. In this poem only the last three nations are mentioned as being included among Laban's subjects.

ASSYE, l. 102, 123, 1000. See note to l. 1000.

ASTRAGOT, *or* ESTRAGOT, a Saracen giant who kills Sabaris, ll. 346, 352. He is slain by the portcullis let down by the Romans, l. 432. He was husband to Barrock, the giantess of the bridge of Mantriblo, ll. 3944, 4902. Cf. *Destr.* 1090. Not in *Fierabras* nor in the Ashmolean version. See note to l. 346.

AUFRIKE, ll. 102, 114. Aufricanes, l. 257, part of the soudan's dominions. Cf. *Syr Ferumbras*, l. 5465, *Destr.* 76, *Fierabras*, 4913.

BABILON, see note to l. 69; cf. *Destr.* 78, 204, 85; *Fierabras*, 51; *Syr Fer.* 53.

BALDESEYNES, 501, 871. Occurring in no other version; cf. besides Martin's note to Kudrun, 161, 2, and perhaps *Fierabras*, 2873, 4721 Balegué = Baluguer (Ballegarium, Valaguaria) near Lerida in Spain.

BARBARYE, l. 1001, mentioned only in this poem.

BARROK, ll. 2939, 2950, 3022, a giantess, wife to Astragot, slain by Charles. See note to l. 2939.

BELMORE, does not occur in the other versions; see note to l. 3122.

BELSABUB, l. 357, occurs only in this poem.

BERNARD OF SPRUWSE (? Prussia); 1715, one of the twelve knights. See *Introduction*, p. xxvii.

BOLOYNE, 3238. Charles presents

the nails to that place. · See note to l. 3236, and cf. *Fierabras*, l. 6199.

BRETOMAYN, Laban's gaoler at Agremor, ll. 1533, 1591, slain by Floripas, l. 1606. This name is spelt 'Brutamont' in *Fierabras*, 'Brytamoun' in *Syr Ferumbras*. It is not to be met with in the *Destruction*.

BROULAND, chief counsellor to Laban. See note on l. 1743.

BRYER OF BRYTAYN,—of Mountez; see note to l. 1723.

BRYER OF POYLE, a Roman knight, slain by Ferumbras; see note to l. 514.

BULGARE, l. 1002. Occurring in no other poem.

CASSAUNDRE, ll. 986, 512, town belonging to Lukafer. This name is not found in the other versions.

CHARLES, Charlemayne, the French king.

CHAUNDER, l. 123, a town in Asia; only mentioned here. See note to l. 1000.

COSDROYE escorts a convoy destined for the soudan; he is slain by Roland; cf. note to l. 2695.

CRAMADAS, a Saracen bishop, ll. 2775, 2788. Not found in the other versions.

CURRAUNTES, the bridge near Mantrible, l. 2866. This name occurs only in this poem.

DASABERDE, l. 1707, (?) mentioned only here.

DENYS, ll. 27, 61, etc. Occurring in all versions.

DURNEDALE, Roland's sword; see note to l. 875.

ESPIARD, l. 111, Laban's messenger; cf. note to l. 2145.

ETHIOPES, subject to Laban. See note to l. 257.

EUROPE, l. 1002. Mentioned only in this poem.

FERUMBRAS, see note to l. 93.

FLAGOT, the river on which the city of Mantrible with its famous bridge is situated, cf. ll. 2559, 2798, 2855, etc., and *Fierabras*, ll. 7348, 4886, etc. When the twelve peers besieged in Agremar send Richard of Normandy to Charlemagne to ask his aid, Richard is said to have started in the direction of Mantrible, l. 2559; but finding the bridge blocked up and guarded, l. 2799, he is obliged to swim across the water, 'Flagot the flode,' l. 2804. Charlemagne being informed of the distress of his peers, starts towards Mantrible, l. 2849, and having first taken it and left Richard there with two hundred knights, l. 3044, he continues his march against the soudan at Agremar, l. 3047. Whence it is clear that Agremar cannot be situated on the river Flagot, as is stated in l. 34; a mistake evidently owing to an oversight on the part of the poet. Cf. besides, note to l. 1723.

FLOREYN OF ROME, name given to Ferumbras after his baptism; see note to l. 1486.

FLORIP, Florypas; see note to l. 614. In the Ashmolean versions we find *Floryppe*, a spelling which does not occur in any of the French poems. But once we find *Floripes* in *Fierabras*, l. 2035.

FOCARD, l. 2900, one of the Christian knights who struck at the bridge-keeper of Mantrible when he refused to let them pass. The name occurs only in this poem.

FOLK BALIANT, l. 1695, one of the twelve peers. Only found in this poem.

FORTIBRAUNCE, l. 422, one of the soudan's engineers. Only occurring in this poem.

FRAUNCE. Charles is called king of dowse Fraunce, cf. *Fierabras*, 2103; *Syr Ferumbras*, 1269. This phrase does not occur in the *Destruction*.

FREMOUNDE, a saint; see note to l. 2845.
FRIGE, l. 1000; Frigys, l. 1040. Part of the soudan's dominions, not mentioned in the other versions.

GALLOPES, l. 251, mentioned only in this poem.
GAȜE, a town in Spain, where Charlemagne lands his troops. The name is found only in this poem (in rhyme), l. 772.
GENELYN, a French knight, notorious for his treachery. He advised Charles to leave Spain and to return home, urging that the twelve peers must be dead at Agremor, since no news arrived from them, l. 2820. When in assaulting Mantrible he saw Charles shut in in the city, he treacherously proclaimed the king to be dead, and ordered the French to return to France, where he hoped to be crowned king. But he was rebuked by Ferumbras (ll. 2970-2991). For his treason he is hanged and drawn at Montfaucon in Paris (ll. 3244-3254).
GENERYSE, ll. 1139, 1239, is the name Oliver gives himself when asked by Ferumbras. The French *Fierabras* and the Ashmole *Ferumbras* have Garin instead.
GY OF BOURGOYNE, see note to ll. 1888, 1892.
GYNDARD, l. 543, a Roman senator who kills ten Saracens. He is slain by Lukafer. Occurring only in this poem.

HUBERT, l. 518, a Roman knight, slain by Ferumbras. Not mentioned in the other versions.

IFFREZ, a Roman senator who advises to send to Charles for help. See note to l. 165.
INDE, l. 999. Not mentioned in the other poems. Cf. note to l. 999.
ISRES, 625, 641, the chief porter of Rome, who treacherously delivers the keys to the Saracens. See note to l. 625.

JUBYTER, ll. 2254, 2762, a Saracen god, mentioned only in this poem.

LABAN, see note to l. 29.
LOWES, occurring in the *Sowdan* and the *Destruction*, but not mentioned in the other versions. See note to l. 24.
LUKAFER OF BALDAS, see note to l. 113. Once, l. 236, this name is spelt Lukefere.

MACEDOYNE, l. 1002. Occurring only in this poem.
MAHOUND, see note to l. 86.
MAPYN, l. 2326, introduces himself into the bed-chamber of Floripas to steal the fatal girdle. In the French poem, l. 3046, he is called Maubrun d' Agremolée; in the Ashmolean version Maubyn of Egremolee, l. 2385. Cf. *Introduction*, pp. xx, xxx, xxxi.
MARAGONDE, the name of Floripas's governess, l. 1563. Spelt Morabunde in the French poem. See *Introduction*, pp. xxx, xxxi.
MARIE, ll. 917, 2390; cf. *Destr.* ll. 374, 564; *Fierabras*, ll. 285, 815; *Syr Ferumbras*, ll. 5177, 5451.
MARSEDAG, king of Barbarye, occurs only in this poem. See note to l. 2247.
MAUNTRIBLE, a town in Spain on the river Flagot (see above) with a bridge; cf. also *Destr.* 211, and *Fierabras*, 1867, etc.
MAVON, ll. 278, 422, 2230, Laban's engineer; spelt Mabon in the *Destr.* ll. 908, 941, and in *Fierabras*, l. 3735. The name does not occur in the Ashmole MS.
MIRON OF BRABANE, one of the twelve peers, occurring only in this poem, l. 1703.
MONTFAWCON, l. 3253. Not found in the other versions.

MOUNPELERS, after having conquered the soudan, Charlemagne sails from Spain to Mounpeler, l. 3228. The name does not occur in the *Fierabras*, where the king returns to France in an eight days' journey (ll. 6164—6187). Cf. *Destr.* ll. 250, 286.
MOWNJOYE, see note to l. 868, and cf. the *Song of Roland*, 128/746.

NEYMES OF BAVERE, one of the twelve peers, see note to l. 836.
NUBENS, l. 873, NUBYE, l. 1001, a people subject to the soudan.

OGER DANOYS, one of the twelve peers, see note to l. 836.
OLIBORN, l. 99, the soudan's chancellor; only found in this poem.
OLYVER, one of the twelve peers; see note to l. 1250.

PARIS, l. 917; see note to l. 3254.
PERSAGYN, a king of Italy, and uncle to Ferumbras, slain by Oliver, l. 1259. In the *Destr.* l. 162, we find one Parsagon mentioned among the peers of the soudan's empire. See note to l. 1259.
PERSE, l. 2888, cf. *Destr.* ll. 77, 421. *Fierabras*, 1640, 1713.
SEINT PETER, ll. 161, 480, etc., the saint; cf. *Fierabras*, l. 1261; *Syr Ferumbras*, l. 3756; *Destr.* l. 501.
CEINT PETER, l. 453, the cathedral; cf. *Fierabras*, l. 57; *Destr.* l. 1109.
SEINT POUL, ll. 163, 3269, the saint; cf. *Syr Ferumbras*, l. 3756; not mentioned in the other poems.
POYLE, l. 514, ? Apulia; found only in this poem; cf. note to l. 1000.

QWYNTYN, l. 1298, a saint by whom Ferumbras swears; see note to l. 2845.

RICHARD OF NORMANDY, see notes to ll. 2535, 2795, 3044.
ROMAYNE, l. 77, inhabitant of Rome.
ROME, l. 17.
ROULAND, see note to ll. 1499, 1888.

SATHANAS, l. 2777, a Saracen god.
SAVARIS, l. 171, a duke of Rome who leads the Roman troops against the Saracens. He is slain by Estragot (l. 346). He also occurs in the *Destr. de Rome*. In the French *Fierabras* appears a French knight Savaris, l. 1699.
SORTYBRAUNCE, the chief councillor of the soudan.
SPAYN, l. 717, belonging to the soudan's dominions. It is the scene of the principal action narrated in this poem, as indeed the only part where the scene is laid elsewhere is that describing the destruction of Rome.
SYMON, a saint by whom Charles swears, l. 1713.

TAMPER, a name peculiar to this poem. He erects a gallows before Agremore castle to hang Guy, l. 2641.
TERMAGANT, l. 137, a Saracen deity; cf. note to l. 86. Spelt Ternagant in *Syr Ferumbras*, Tervagant in the French *Fierabras*.
TERY LARDENEYS, one of the twelve peers; see note to l. 1691.
TURKES, l. 874, cf. *Fierabras*, 128, 1641, 3767. *Syr Ferumbras*, 5433, 5677.
TURPYN, the French bishop who baptizes Ferumbras, l. 1475. This name does not occur in the Ashmole MS.

VENYS, subject to Laban; see note to l. 1000. Mentioned only in this poem.

RICHARD CLAY & SONS, LIMITED, LONDON & BUNGAY.

www.ingramcontent.com/pod-product-compliance
Lightning Source LLC
Chambersburg PA
CBHW020826230426
43666CB00007B/1124
* 9 7 8 3 3 3 7 2 4 6 1 2 9 *